LEADERSHIP AND MANAGEMENT IN EDUCATION

Leadership and Management in Education

Developing Essential Skills and Competencies

David Thenuwara Gamage

and

Nicholas Sun-keung Pang

The ⁣ss

Leadership and Management in Education:
Developing Essential Skills and Competencies
  By David Thenuwara Gamage and
  Nicholas Sun-keung Pang

ISBN 962–996–054–0

First edition 2003
Second printing 2003

THE CHINESE UNIVERSITY PRESS
The Chinese University of Hong Kong
SHA TIN, N.T., HONG KONG
Fax: +852 2603 6692
    +852 2603 7355
E-mail: cup@cuhk.edu.hk
Web-site: www.chineseupress.com

Printed in Hong Kong

Contents

PART II: Structures and Processes of Educational Administration

Foreword

If we subscribe to the general notion that teaching is more an art than a science, then there are infinite ways that knowledge can be shared and information delivered. Teaching becomes a uniquely personalized endeavour, with the course organization being, primarily, a reflection of personal selection and interpretation of massive information available in relevant literature. In this context, one of the persistent problems facing faculty members in teaching meaningfully, innovatively, and passionately, is the availability of information that can be conveniently tailored for classes. Too often, they have to go through the cumbersome task of collecting bits and pieces of information from diverse sources (prepared by different authors and designed for different purposes) before sufficient sensible contents can be woven into a logical theme for delivery. The alternative is to condense one's thoughts into a single text, so that all critical topics can be congregated for deliberation. Such an undertaking is more wishful thinking than reality. Yet this is precisely the momentum driving Gamage and Pang in preparing this book.

As the title of the text suggests, it is intended to develop essential skills and competencies for leadership and management in educational contexts. To achieve such an objective, the text covers three inter-related components: history and foundation of educational administration, structures and processes, leadership and management skills in running educational organizations. Each component contains five chapters covering a comprehensive list of information that helps readers zero in on essential skills of modern educational leadership. To the delight of those who would use the book, each chapter has clear learning objectives and focus. The materials in each chapter are systematically and thoroughly prepared so that both pioneer works and the most recent thrusts in each domain are fused into themes that tend to reinforce each other. Given such a nature, both practitioners and graduate students of educational administration would find the text both useful and practical for classes or for reference in action.

Jack Yee-lay Lam
Chair Professor
Department of Educational Administration and Policy
The Chinese University of Hong Kong

Preface and Acknowledgements

This publication is the result of extensive research and a long period of experience in offering graduate courses in Leadership and Management in the field of education. The work included, an extensive review of theoretical and applied literature and research in some of the Australian, American, British, Canadian, Japanese, Chinese and Hong Kong universities and school systems. These were supplemented by discussions with both academics and practitioners. There are currently a number of introductory books in educational leadership and management, however, hardly any of these provide a comprehensive coverage of the field of theory and practice. This book is an attempt to bridge this gap.

We would like to emphasize that leadership is a concept that is of paramount importance to the success of any organization, whether large or small, including that of a country. Similarly, management is a process applicable to all forms of organized activities, whether it is business, charitable, religious, governmental, hospital, military or educational organizations. It is leadership and management that make organizations efficient and effective. Historically, books on management and administration tended to draw pictures of some ideal organizations, managed by some ideal leaders or managers. This book is a deviation, which blends the theoretical concepts with practice, enabling the leaders and managers to refine and improve their practice.

Training is the process of learning a sequence of programmed behaviours. Thus, we train bricklayers, word-processors, photographers etc. The activities of these jobs can be precisely defined, broken down and analysed to find the best approaches and methods to perform the job effectively. In contrast, education instils sound reasoning processes, rather than imparting a series of facts. Education is the understanding and interpretation of knowledge. It does not provide definitive answers, but rather develops a logical and rational mind that can determine relationships amongst pertinent variables and thereby understand phenomena. In this context, we suggest that leaders and managers must be educated, rather than merely trained. It is true that there are specific managerial abilities that can be taught, but little of what leaders and managers do lends itself to training. Management is a discipline that is situational, having few laws and principles, and hence, the need for education of leaders and managers. We know that many, who are exposed to a short course in leadership or management, return to their positions unaffected by the experience. Such "instant leaders/managers" are doomed to fail, as there are no instant solutions to organizational problems.

Successful leaders and managers have analytical, human, conceptual and specialized skills. They are able to think and understand. However, training can fine-tune specific skills, and all leaders and managers need to develop specialized functional expertise. Leaders and Managers must have particular expertise in the area within which they lead and manage. They must possess an awareness of leadership and managerial concepts so that they are able to conceptualize, to question and to understand the leadership and managerial processes. By merging specialized skills with knowledge of leadership and managerial processes, people prepare themselves for successful leadership and managerial careers.

Baltzell and Dentler have pointed out that the need to hold a master's degree in educational administration is one of the key criteria for a position of principal in almost every state in the United States. Research by Baron reveals that the US Superintendents believe that in the process of selection of school principals, high ratings should be given to the standard of administrative certification, followed by teaching experience and the possession of a master's degree. Albright and Nottingham and Kirkpatrick have pointed out the need to place strong emphasis on the leadership and management skills of the candidates. The research has revealed that while innate characteristics influence the capacity to lead and manage, most leadership qualities and managerial concepts and practices can be learned or acquired, adding credibility to the study of leadership and management as distinct professions. In the circumstances, *we recommend this book to graduate students, as well as, current and prospective leaders and managers, as a means to developing their leadership and managerial skills and competencies.*

We would like to acknowledge, with gratitude, the assistance provided by Mr Diosdado San Antonio, a secondary principal from the Philippines, in updating some of the material and designing the figures, while on study leave at the University of Newcastle. Our sincere thanks are also extended to the school principals, teachers, and system administrators in Australia, America, Britain, Canada, Japan, China and Hong Kong, for spending their valuable time in providing necessary clarifications and information. We also greatly appreciate the valuable support extended by Dushani Gamage in editing the final draft.

A special word of thanks is extended to Professor Jack Y. L. Lam, the Chair Professor of the Department of Educational Administration and Policy, at The Chinese University of Hong Kong, for his valuable time in reading the manuscript and contributing a foreword. The research projects were made possible by the research and travel grants provided by the University of Newcastle, Australia, and The Chinese University of Hong Kong. We extend our sincere thanks to the university authorities.

To all those referred to above, those who were interviewed by one or both of us, to those with whom we had discussions and to others who knowingly or unknowingly contributed to this study, we offer our heartfelt thanks and the usual absolution from responsibility.

Last but not least, special thanks are extended to Mrs Sriya Gamage and Mrs Rowena Pang, for their patience and support, without which we would not have been able to complete this difficult task.

David Thenuwara Gamage

Nicholas Sun-keung Pang

PART I

Foundations in Educational Administration and Management

CHAPTER 1

Historical Evolution of Educational Administration

1.0 Learning Outcomes

Based on a systematic study of this chapter, the readers will:

- Gain a better knowledge and understanding as to how the administration has evolved, including the practices in ancient civilizations;
- Improve knowledge and understanding of the development of public and business administration and the beginning of educational administration; and
- Gain a better understanding of how educational administration developed as a separate professional field of study and how at times history repeats itself.

1.1 Focus

This chapter focuses on the historical evolution of administration as a generic field, including practices in ancient civilizations; the development of public, business and educational administration as separate fields of study. The topic discusses the development of theoretical concepts by the pioneers of the cult of efficiency, such as Frederick Taylor, Henry Fayol, Luther Gulick and Lyndall Urwick followed by a new beginning with contributions by Mary Parker Follett, Elton Mayo and Fred Roethlisberger, Chester Barnard, Herbert Simon and Max Weber. Attention is also focused on the development of educational administration as a separate field of study in the universities of the United States, later to be embraced by Australia, Canada, Britain and other parts of the world. It also examines the renewed interest in educational administration and management in the 1990s.

1.2 Evolution of Administration

In an historical evaluation, administration appears to be one of the most ancient of all human endeavours. It is clear from archaeological excavations that Egyptians organized and administered vast complex organizations, strong leadership and well-coordinated efforts at least 2000 years before the Birth of Christ. To build, the Giza Pyramid consisting of 2.5 million stone blocks weighing 2.5 tons each, would have taken 20 long years for 100,000 men. This is equivalent to three times the size of the Shell Oil Company in the modern world (Owens, 2001).

Similarly, Chinese are known to have had highly systematic, large-scale administrative systems for thousands of years. Similar archaeological evidence has been discovered in Sri Lanka, where a British engineer turned scholar has compared the three pyramids in Cairo with three Stupas found in the ancient City of Anuradhapura. According to him, the smallest one, which was built in the First Century BC, consists of millions of tons of bricks and would have taken 14 years for 500 bricklayers (working British trade union time), only to lay the bricks. This archaeological evidence confirms the existence of leadership, planning, organization, direction, coordination and control systems, thousands of years before the modern concepts of leadership and management emerged (Williams, cited in Gamage, 1996a, p. 55).

We also have evidence that approximately 1100 BC, the Chinese recognized the need for planning, organizing, leading and controlling. By the time of Christ, we find evidence that unity of command, management by exception, and delegation of authority to subordinate administrators were practiced. Alexander the Great practiced both decentralization and devolution in the governance of his vast empire.

Two other institutions that contributed significantly to the development of organizational design and administrative theory were the Church and the military. The organizational design is best exemplified by the Roman Catholic Church, which has endured for 2000 years with a simple five level hierarchy (i.e. Pope, Cardinals, Archbishops, Bishops and the Parish Priests).

George, Jr. (1972) noted that the English industrial revolution (1700–1785) brought changes in the basic organization of production from the domestic, to the factory system. Early managerial practices and concepts included production control — giving a piece rate, is likely to encourage a worker to out-produce his counterparts on a daily wage; and financial control — double entry bookkeeping justified by Thomas Watt as anti-theft, anti-inaccuracy, and anti-ineptitude. The Soho Foundry in Great Britain, founded by Matthew Boutton and James Watt, used detailed operating plans, separating problems into elements, used statistical data as the bases for inferences, and organized production processes based on the machine and the worker. Robert Owens of Scotland adopted paternalistic labour policies to show that productivity is enhanced when workers are given a favourable environment.

Belisle and Sargent (1957) attributed the popularization of the concept of administration to the Cameralists in Germany and Austria. Having flourished in the 1700s, the Cameralists organized the knowledge and practice associated with the various functions of the civil state. Similarly, they developed special terminology for these activities.

In the 19th Century USA, the term "administration" was used in the context of government, and the ideas it represented gave rise to the growth of public administration. British civil service is another good example of an organized administrative system. In 1887, Woodrow Wilson, a young American University lecturer, advanced early thinking about the professionalization of administration, with the publication of his essay "The Study of Administration" in the *Political Science Quarterly*. He pointed out that the improvement of administrative techniques depended on scholarly study in the specialized field of administration.

However, in the modern world, if we are required, specifically to pinpoint the time when the field of modern management or administrative theory was born, the date that most scholars agree on is 1911, when Frederick Taylor's *Principles of Scientific Management* was published. However, Wrege and Stotka (1978) have claimed that Taylor has borrowed substantially from Cooke's unpublished manuscript *Industrial Management*. But, along with the studies conducted prior to and after the publication of his book, Taylor came to be known as the father of scientific management. Towards the end of the 19th and early 20th Centuries, Taylor's ideas developed out of his engineering work at Midvale and Bethlehem Steel companies. He spent nearly two decades employing scientific method on the shop floor in investigating "one best way" for each job.

Initially, public administration and industrial management were isolated fields. Disciples of public administration included historians, political scientists and philosophers, while management specialists included physical scientists, technologists, and engineers. What triggered the integration of the basic concepts and language from these fields is the conceptualization of the formal structure of an organization.

1.3 The Pioneers of the Gospel of Efficiency

Two clearly defined streams of thought developed during the first half of the 20th Century. The first of these can be called administrative efficiency. Although there were many who wrote on improving efficiency, the sense of the movement can be gained by a study of the findings of four men: Taylor, Fayol, Gulick and Urwick.

Frederick Taylor (1858–1915)	USA, engineering, private business, middle management
Henry Fayol (1841–1925)	France, engineering, private business, top management
Luther Gulick (1892–?)	USA, political scientist, public service, Research & Consultant
Lyndall Urwick (1891–1983)	USA, engineering, military service, middle management.

These men shared the common characteristics of being personally involved in the management process, as well as being predominantly from engineering backgrounds.

1.3.1   Taylor: More from Workers

His approach was how to get more work out of workers, who were assumed to be naturally lazy and engage in systematic "soldiering". This was the dilemma, which concerned Taylor during the mid-19th Century, when he became the Foreman of Midvale Steel Works in Philadelphia. Taylor proposed that managers use scientific research methods in discovering the best way of performing every piece of work. There would also be changes in the specifications for tools and materials, the selection and training of workers, and the supervision of work. With all of this done, it would then be possible to make proper use of bonuses and premiums for higher individual outputs. He maintained and demonstrated that the combination of these methods would lead to a dramatic increase in productivity or output (Time and Motion Studies).

Taylor divided the task of a foreman or a forelady into eight separate functions. Four, on shop floor: inspector, repair foreman, speed boss, and gang boss; and four in the planning room, dealing with routine, preparation of instruction cards, time and cost cards and discipline. From this, he started the analysis of work methods. With the use of experiments from 3.5 years, he concluded that 140 men were doing the work of 400–600 men. Taylor insisted that each worker should be given the job of which he was best suited and in addition be trained to use prescribed motions with standardized tools and materials.

Taylor's methods were deeply resented by both management and workers. Managers were unhappy as Taylor insisted that they were unqualified unless assisted by highly trained experts. Workers resisted being asked to behave like machines and move mechanically in accordance with predetermined patterns.

The Scientific Management Movement — In the early period, Taylor referred to his bundle of administrative techniques as "the task system" or "task management". In 1910, a new and more popular label was provided by Louis Brandeis (a lawyer who represented Eastern Shipping concerns against railroad rates) by referring to "the task system" as "scientific management". Taylor's closest associates and innumerable followers served as advisors to hundreds of companies thus developing the profession of "efficiency expert", or "management consultant". Engineering and business schools started providing courses in "shop management" and "industrial management", based on "scientific management".

1.3.2 Fayol: More from Managers

Like Taylor, he concentrated on industrial administration but maintained that the basic principles of administration were applicable to all forms of organizations. But here the similarity ends and differences between the approaches of the two men began. He focused more and more on what is to be expected from a manager.

Fayol was the first writer to develop what might be called a "general approach", to administration. As a top executive himself, he looked at administration from the top down. Fayol in his *General and Industrial Management*, in 1949 (originally published in French in 1916), defined administration as "to plan, to organize, to command, to co-ordinate and to control".

Fayol contended that administration was not the exclusive privilege or responsibility of a few people, but was spread throughout the organization.

Everyone participates to some extent in administration, but the degree of responsibility and participation increases as one moves up the hierarchy. For this purpose he called for smooth operation of six essential functions:

- Technical activities,
- Commercial activities,
- Financial activities,
- Security activities,
- Accounting activities; and
- Administration.

Fayol was a strong advocate of teaching administration from primary school through to university, and the task should then be taken up by all employing institutions and be developed as a theory of administration for this purpose.

Fayol listed 14 principles in his *General and Industrial Management*. These were:

(1) Division of work,	(9) Order,
(2) Authority,	(10) Equity,
(3) Discipline,	(11) Stability of tenure of personnel,
(4) Unity of command,	(12) Initiative,
(5) Unity of direction,	(13) Esprit de corps, and interests to
(6) Remuneration,	the general interest,
(7) Centralization,	(14) Subordination of individual.
(8) Scalar chain (line of authority),	

(Adapted from Fayol, 1949, pp. 19–20)

He believed that all the principles of administration were flexible, and that their proper adaptation to specific circumstances was a difficult art requiring intelligence, experience, decision-making and communication.

1.3.3   Gulick and Urwick: The Architects of Organization

The First World War gave a tremendous impetus to the gospel of efficiency. At a technical level the followers of Taylor developed more mature techniques of work-study and production management, of testing and selection of workers, and of cost accounting. At a more general level, the principles of management advocated by Fayol were developed into more precisely articulated principles of formal organization. Gulick and Urwick formulated organizational principles to a far superior level than those formulated by others, leading to the publication of the *Papers on the Science of Administration*, in 1937.

Urwick expanded Fayol's categories to make them more inclusive. In order to answer the questions, "what is the work of the chief executive?" Urwick coined the easy to remember acronym "POSDCORB" by combining the initial letters of seven types of administrative activities, which are the responsibilities of the chief executive.

- Planning — is working broad outline of the things that need to be done and the methods for doing them including the time lines to accomplish the purpose of achieving organizational goals.
- Organizing — is the establishment of the formal structures of authority through which work sub-divisions are arranged, defined and coordinated for the defined objective[s].
- Staffing — is the whole function of bringing in and training the staff and maintaining favourable conditions of work.
- Directing — is the continuous task of making decisions and embodying them in specific and general orders and instructions and serving as the leader of the enterprise.
- Coordinating — is the all-important task of interrelating the various parts of work.
- Reporting — is keeping those to whom the executive is responsible informed as to what is going on, which includes keeping himself and his subordinates informed through records, research and inspection.
- Budgeting — is all aspects of budgeting in the form of fiscal planning, accounting and control (Adapted from Gulick & Urwick, 1937, p. 13).

Gulick reiterated Fayol's maxim that "A man cannot serve two masters". Although, rigid adherence to this principle may have its absurdities, according to Urwick, no supervisor can supervise directly the work of more than five, or at the most, six subordinates whose work interlocks.

1.4 The Pioneers of New Beginnings

Although the gospel of efficiency obtained a wide following, it never achieved a monopoly. The new pioneers did not dispute the importance of efficiency as a goal, but they held that other goals must also be considered.

Perhaps the best way to illustrate the richness of these new beginnings is to summarize the work of the following people: Mary Parker Follett (1942), Elton Mayo (1933), Fritz Roethlisberger (1939), Chester Barnard (1938), Herbert Simon (1957) and Max Weber (1947).

1.4.1   Follett: Dynamics of Human Integration

Although less known to the public than Florence Nightingale and Madame Curie, Parker Follett's achievements in Administration, are significant. She was one of the first to recognize the psychological aspects of administration, and to deal with them on the basis of modern psychological thought, instead of just reference to the mysteries of human nature. After the Great Depression of the early 1930s, her ideas helped to modify the trend towards rigidity. She was the first to insert the word "power" into the vocabulary of administration. She was one of the first to indicate how business management might develop into a profession.

1.4.2   Mayo-Roethlisberger: Research on Workers' Behaviour

In Chicago at the Western Electric Company's Hawthorn Plant, research was conducted under the guidance of Elton Mayo and Fritz Roethlisberger of the Harvard Graduate School of Business. The most significant effect of the Hawthorne studies was the discovery of the significance of "human relations" and "informal organization" by Mayo and Roethlisberger, which significantly affected administrative thought and practice (Robbins, 1976).

1.4.3   Barnard: Leadership in Cooperative Systems

In the preface to the *Functions of the Executive*, published in 1938, Barnard detailed the lack of attention to the informal organization. Barnard's discussion of formal and informal organizations was the most definitive to his time and still basic to the work of theorists. In analysing informal organization Barnard went beyond the conclusions drawn by Mayo and Roethlisberger from the bank wiring observation room. He was also careful to distinguish between "leadership", as referring to prominence or excellence in some special field of activity, and "leadership" in the sense of the guidance of people in organizations. Barnard recognized decision-making as a fundamental part of the administrative process. In so doing he looked at an organization not only as a system of communication, but as a system of logical decision-making.

1.4.4 Simon: Behaviour of Administrative Mass

Herbert Simon's work, *Administrative Behavior*, published in 1945, can be regarded as a significant extension to the work of his immediate pre-decessors. Simon's central goal was to develop a value-free science of administrative behaviour, if not indeed a "science of man". For Simon, the people in organizations are not passive instruments or neutral means; they are decision-making organisms or mechanisms. Simon defined com-munication as "any process whereby decision premises are transmitted from one member of an organization to another". He has probably gone further than anyone else in applying advanced mathematical analysis to the social sciences (Robbins, 1976).

1.4.5 Weber: Bureaucratic Model

Max Weber, who was a German sociologist, identified and developed the bureaucratic model, which has made a long-lasting contribution to the development of organizations. It is often used to refer to characteristics, which are generic to formal organizations. It is also suggested that bureaucracy is an inevitable consequence of increasing size and complexity of organizations. When we refer to smaller organizations with one or two people in full-time positions, most aspects of the operations are taken care of by informal understandings, with no written rules and regulations, but, when it grows in size then gradually bureaucratic rules and formal hierarchical structures have to be introduced. For example, in developing the hierarchical structure in the Australian context, one can reflect on the development of a level six, one-teacher school to that of a level one school, with a non-teaching principal, supported by a fairly large bureaucracy. Most formal organizations seek maximum efficiency through rational approaches to management. The key features of a bureaucracy are the following:

- Hierarchical authority structure with formal chains of command between the different positions in the hierarchy. The organizational chart takes a pyramidal shape.
- It seeks goal orientation from the members of the organization. Usually, the hierarchy determines the goals, and staff is directed towards the accomplishment of goals, as directed by appointed leaders.
- It adheres to division of labour. The bureaucratic rules ensure a degree of uniformity of operations and are coordinated by the hierarchical structure.

- The rules and regulations govern bureaucratic decisions and behaviour. Personal initiative is not encouraged.
- Bureaucratic model emphasizes impersonal relationships between staff and clients. This is designed to minimize the impact of individuality on decision-making.
- In bureaucracies, the technical competence and merit determine the staff recruitment and career progression (Adapted from Weber, 1947).

Of course, there are merits as well as de-merits in the bureaucratic model. But, with all the advances in technology and modern approaches, so far no organization has been successful in getting rid of all the features of the bureaucratic model. In the contemporary world, it is true that the organizations are being flattened, yet the bureaucratic model is not being eliminated, a modified form is adopted.

1.5 Developments in Educational Administration

At the turn of the 20th Century, the United States had reason to be proud of its development of the education system. All white Americans enjoyed free education from the kindergarten through to university.

However, the story of the next quarter century of American Education was a story of opportunity lost and of the acceptance by educational administrators of an inappropriate philosophy. It must be seen within the larger context of the forces and events, which were shaping American society. Schools everywhere reflected, to some extent the culture of which they were a part and responded to forces within that culture. Because of the nature of their pattern of organization, support, and control, the American public schools were especially vulnerable and responded quickly to the strongest social forces. In this period, as in the decades immediately preceding it, the most powerful force was industrialization. The application of the mechanical power to the production of goods (and along with the economic philosophy of free enterprise, capitalistic system under which industrialism developed) affected educational administration.

The rise of businessmen such as Andrew Carnegie, John D. Rockefeller and J. P. Morgan as pillars of leadership in the American community, led to the acceptance of the business philosophy as one of the basic characteristics of the American society, in this period. Calvin Coolidge referred to this prevalent situation in the 1920s as "The business of America is — Business" (Cited in Callahan, 1962, p. 2).

Hence the business influence was exerted upon education in several ways: through newspapers, popular magazines and books; through speeches at educational meetings; and more directly through actions of school boards. It was exerted by laymen, by professional journalists, by businessmen or industrialists either individually or in-groups and finally by educators themselves. Whatever the source, influence was exerted in the form of suggestions or demands that the schools be organized and operated in a more businesslike manner and that more emphasis be placed upon a practical and immediately useful education.

The procedure for bringing about more business like organizations and operations were fairly well standardized from 1900 to 1925. It consisted of making unfavourable comparisons between the schools and business enterprises, by applying business and industrial criteria (e.g. economy and efficiency) to education and suggesting that business, and industrial practices be adopted by educators. The commercial and industrial influence was not limited to the elementary and secondary schools but was felt in higher education as well.

Efforts were made to gear the curriculum to be more practical, on the basis of business concepts. Americans, who generally trace their ancestry to the underprivileged Europe, had little tradition in learning or scholarship. In the industrial age, the richly endowed new land afforded them an economic opportunity, i.e. the acquisition of material wealth.

Carnegie was right in stating that there was a new idea of education being introduced upon America. At the National Education Association (NEA) Convention held in Detroit, in 1892, the Governor of Michigan welcomed the delegates by stating that "the demand of the age is ... for a practical education." Further, the Governor emphasized that he was glad to note that Michigan Educators were "herding all their energies in that direction" (Cited in Callahan, 1962). Drost (1971) noted that Samuel Dutton and David Snedden published the first textbook on school administration, *The Administration of Public Education in the United States* in 1908. This book delved into education from the point of view of social efficiency.

In 1909 the drive for vocational education reached its peak, and it was discussed in almost every session of the annual meeting of the NEA. Successful businessmen dominated all walks of life in America. Business values (especially the concern for economy and efficiency) were accepted by the society. The predominant feature of the society was a critical, cost-conscious, reform-minded public, led by profit-seeking journals. They alleged that there was mismanagement in all-American institutions, leading to increases in the cost of living, creating a situation of readiness for the great preacher of the gospel of efficiency, Fredrick W. Taylor and his disciples. The school administrators, who were already under constant pressure to make education more practical in order to serve a business society better, were brought under even stronger criticism and forced to demonstrate that they were operating the schools efficiently.

The great influence of business on schools via the school administrators sprang from twin factors that were like the two sides of a coin. These were the vulnerability of schools and staff to the great strength of the business community and the business philosophy in an age of efficiency. These factors were largely responsible for the new developments in the schools and for the changes in the professional behaviour of school superintendent, on the job.

The men who were leaders in the Educational Administration in the period from 1910–1918 included Spaulding, Bobbitt, Ayres, Elliott, Strayer and Cubberly. Of the six, Strayer, Cubberly, Bobbitt and Elliott were professors of Education and taught courses in Educational Administration at the Universities of Columbia, Stanford, Chicago and Wisconsin respectively. Ayres and Spaulding contributed a lot with their work to the development of the field. Later in 1920, Spaulding joined the University of Yale.

These educational leaders were active in introducing and using business and industrial procedures and technology in education and they centred their attention almost exclusively upon the financial, organizational and mechanical problems. The situation in American education, after 1911, demanded leaders who were oriented towards the business side of education. The social or philosophical side of these men was not considered important in meeting the needs of the times.

Of the six, it was Strayer and Cubberly who had the greatest influence upon the development of educational administration. The reason for this was primarily because they had a greater number of publications on the subject, taught more students, directed more research in administration and stayed longer in the job. Cubberly promoted the efficiency movement in education as a change from intuitive trade or a common-sense–based job, into a specialized profession, whose principles are grounded upon the discoveries of science. However, Callahan regarded this era as an "American Tragedy", as he felt that the education issues were subordinated to business considerations. The so-called educational administrators were not, in any true sense, educators. A scientific label was placed on some of the very unscientific methods and practices. An anti-intellectual climate, already prevalent, was strengthened (Callahan, 1962).

1.6 Study of Educational Administration in Universities

The development of specialized training in education was a natural outgrowth of the increasing specialization of American life. With specialization came the need for specialized training, which was being provided by the increasing numbers of technical and professional schools.

This situation resulted in a rapid expansion of the study of educational administration. In the colleges and universities, the diversity of courses offered and the number of students enrolled increased. The records show that the ideas of Spaulding and Elliott prevailed. This ideological success was partly due to the strength of leadership and those fellow supporters at the Universities of Chicago and Stanford. But it was also a result of efficiency mania, and the subsequent demands made upon educators and educational administrators to demonstrate efficiency and economy. The courses which were developed in administration provided training in activities such as: records and reports, cost accounting, child-accounting and general business management, with which superintendents on the job were preoccupied. This of course, was in keeping with what Spaulding and Strayer advocated in sorting out practical problems.

1.7 Education of the School Executive

In 1899/1900, Teachers College of the University of Columbia offered only two courses in administration. The following year, administration was listed for the first time as a separate section, but the offerings again consisted of only one basic course and one seminar. By the fall of 1907, the administration offerings had increased to eight courses, two sessions of practice and one seminar. By the academic year 1924/25, twenty-nine courses were offered to administrators under three main divisions. These included:

- Courses for college administration and instructors in education.
- Courses in educational administration for school superintendents.
- Courses for teacher supervisors and administrators in normal schools and teachers colleges.

The University of Chicago (which was second in importance only to the Teachers College of the University of Columbia), in training administrators, followed the same trend through the years. Harvard moved more slowly but eventually followed much the same pattern as the other two schools.

In April 1920, Harvard established its graduate school of education. By 1922, it offered a number of narrowly specialized administration courses, including Administration of Vocational Education, Management of an Elementary School, Administration of Secondary Education, Organization and Administration of Play and Recreation, as well as, Administration of Physical Education. For some years the catalogue was describing the work in city school administration in phrases similar, to but somewhat shorter and less heroic than, those used by Cubberly in 1916. Thus, by 1927, the superintendent of schools was referred to as the professional general manager of the entire school system. Other universities followed the leadership of Columbia, Chicago and Harvard, in introducing courses in Educational Administration.

1.8 The Fear of Insecurity by the School Administrators

While the professors of Education were busy in developing courses in Administration, superintendents of schools were seeking ways and means of meeting the criticisms directed at them and maintaining their positions. They did this by applying to education their individual interpretations of various industrial and business procedures, including scientific management. Undoubtedly, the increasing complexity of American Education would have brought an increase in the number of individuals enrolled in graduate courses in educational administration. But, such increases were accelerated by the insecurity of school administrators, who were keen to improve their performance to match public expectations.

The combination of the development of specialized graduate work in school administration, and the growing influence of business in education made a big impact on educational administration. Thus, the concept of education as a business, led to the idea of school administration as a profession distinct from teaching.

1.9 Development of Educational Administration as a Specialist Field

Halpin (1958) noted three important influences during the post-war period that contributed to the interest in developing a theory of educational administration. First, is the National Conference for Professors of

Educational Administration (NCPEA), which was established in 1947. This group provided a forum for a closer exchange of ideas among the professors who educated and trained administrators.

The support of the Kellogg Foundation to the Co-operative Program in Educational Administration (CPEA) was another influence that enabled professors of educational administration and the social scientists to exchange views about the field. The grants from the Foundation for research and development enabled them to pursue their research interests and offer deeper knowledge and understanding of educational administration.

The third major influence in the birth of the applied science of educational administration was the University Council for Educational Administration (UCEA) seminar in 1957, which focused on the role of theory in educational administration. Culbertson (1983) summarized the core ideas presented in this seminar as follows:

- Statements about what administrators and organizations ought to do cannot be encompassed in science or theory;
- Scientific theories treat phenomena as they are;
- Effective research has its origins in theory and is guided by theory;
- Hypothetical-deductive systems are the best exemplars of theory;
- The use of the social sciences is essential in theory development and training; and
- Administration is best viewed as a generic concept applicable to all types of organizations.

One of the most significant features of educational thinking, at the time, was that administration is an integral part of the learning situation and not extrinsic to it. In an age of rapid change, it is necessarily dynamic and innovative. Most important of all, administration can be studied and overall performance improved, with the help of social and managerial sciences developed during the 20th Century.

The development is, of course, in line with the expanding role of education in a technological society. It was clear that more and more activities could be brought within the realms of study, training and research. In taking account of the wider context of the study of educational administration, we can structure our thinking in terms of four main approaches:

(1) The behavioural,   (3) The managerial, and
(2) The economic,   (4) The political.

However, any behavioural approach must necessarily be concerned with political attitudes and action. Any economic approach has to be concerned with managerial techniques for resource allocation and control. Similarly managerial techniques are likely to have highly political overtones. The behavioural sciences of sociology and social psychology are being used in organizational theory and analysis.

In the 1950s and 1960s, the new movement stressed purely pragmatic approaches, and the search began for theories, which would sustain programmes of empirical research, modelled on the methods of the natural sciences. This new movement spread to Canada and Australia and more recently to Britain and its general influence has been felt in all English-speaking countries in which study and research in educational administration have taken root.

Perhaps the most dominant and influential development in Britain and Australia, at present is the management approach. It embraces the concern for the efficient use of resources, for specified ends advocated by the planner and the economist. Above all, it emphasizes the need for a clearer statement of objectives, for a rational sequence of operations, for the measurement of "inputs" and "outputs" and for built-in feedback mechanisms. In its conduct, it works on the assumption that operational theories developed in industry and public services can be generalized and applied to educational systems and institutions. It is also possible to identify a political approach to educational administration. The approach is focused on the power relationships within educational systems and also their relationships with the social environments.

1.10 Conclusion

In an examination of the evolution of the field of administration, existence of fairly advanced systems of administration in the ancient world is evident from the archaeological ruins of huge structures of the ancient civilizations. Some of the good examples are: the Pyramids of Egypt, the Great Wall of China and the Stupas of Sri Lanka, as well as, the huge structures in Rome, Italy and Athens, Greece, even though written documentation is not available. Systematic development of administration, in the modern period, commenced with the time and motion studies relating to workers undertaken by Frederick Taylor and his associates relating to workers, as well as, Henry Fayol's studies to train the managers to get the best out of workers. The contributions of these studies were refined and systematized by Gulick and Urwick, leading to the development of principles of scientific management.

These developments were further enhanced by the contributions of Mary Parker Follett, Elton Mayo and Fritz Roethlisberger, Chester Barnard, Herbert Simon and Max Weber. Attention needs to be focused on Peter Drucker, who is one of the foremost contributors to the development of management. It is true that most scholars have classified the principles of scientific management and bureaucracy as classical theories, but, even in the 21st Century, it is rare to find an organization does not incorporate some of these so-called classical theories.

1.11 Review Questions

1. Trace the evolution of educational administration as a separate field of study.
2. Discuss the different types of contributions made by the theoreticians and scholars, Frederick Taylor, Henry Fayol, Gulick and Urwick, Elton Mayo, Chester Bernard, Herbert Simon and Max Weber to the development of administration as a generic field of study.

CHAPTER 2

The Nature and Importance of Educational Administration

2.0 Learning Outcomes

Based on a systematic study of this chapter, the readers will:

- Gain an improved knowledge and understanding of what is meant by educational administration and management;
- Gain a better understanding as to how educational administration and management developed as an applied field based on other disciplines, similar to that of medicine and engineering;
- Develop skills based on a sound knowledge and understanding of how the profession of educational administrators has been shaped to be pro-active and competent professionals.

2.1 Focus

This chapter focuses on the meaning of the concept of educational administration and the distinction between business administration and educational administration. Attention is also drawn to how educational administration was developed as an applied field based on the disciplines of sociology, anthropology, psychology, economics and politics, similar to that of medicine and engineering. Discussions also centre on the development of the profession of educational administrators, including desirable backgrounds and how the current and prospective educational administrators need to be trained, in order to perform their functions effectively. Further,

it shows how an appropriate understanding helps educational administrators
to be efficient and effective leaders and managers.

2.2 What Do We Mean by Educational Administration?

In trying to understand Educational Administration we have to make certain
assumptions that:

- Organizations are essential in the present day world;
- Administration can perform useful functions in organizations;
- Knowledge and understanding of organizational behaviour, both
  internal and external could permit an administrator to act more
  effectively; and
- Educational organizations and their administrations have some
  unique characteristics that deserve distinctive treatment.

In an examination of the terms "administration" and "management", it
is clear that, currently, the two terms are being used to convey more or less
the same meaning. In USA, Canada and Australia, where the education
systems are based mainly on the American models, the term "administration"
is more commonly used. In Britain and systems mainly influenced by the
British system, the term "management" is preferred. Then, in the context
of business and industry, the term "management" is commonly used.
However, even in the case of business management, when it comes to
choosing a degree title the term "administration" is being preferred; i.e.
Master of Business Administration (MBA). Similarly, even in the British
context, the degree title of, Master of Business Administration (MBA) in
Educational Management is being used. Again, both in Australia and Britain,
there is a trend to use both terms in combination to convey more or less an
identical meaning. Some examples are the title of the British journal —
Educational Management and Administration and the journal of the
Australian Council of Educational Administration — *Leading and
Managing*. In keeping with these practices, in this book, the terms
"administration", and "management" are being employed to convey the
same meaning, without a distinction.

Educational Administration is the administration and/or management
of institutions designed to foster teaching and learning. These institutions
include — public and private schools, technical and further education
(TAFE) colleges, public and private universities, two-year and three-year
colleges, other private educational institutions and industry sponsored

educational institutions. Further, educational resource centres, school district offices, regional directorates, and central executives of the state ministries of education and Federal/Central/State/Provincial/Regional Government Departments of Education, and all other institutions fostering teaching and learning, can be included in this category.

The management or administration of this broad range of institutions supports the notion that Educational Administration is a field of practice. Therefore, it has certain aspects common to other fields of management, such as, public administration, hospital administration and business management. Yet, there are certain unique aspects specific to Educational Administration, as the aims and objectives as well as the goals that are to be achieved are quite different from those of business and industrial organizations.

Educational Administration is not only a field of practice but is also a field of study. It was only in the early part of the 20th Century that Educational Administration emerged as a separate field of study. First at the Teachers College of the University of Columbia, followed by Stanford and Chicago universities and other institutions. It is only since the 1950s that it has become a primary field of study. In Australia the first institution to commence teaching in Educational Administration was the University of New England, and the foundation professor was William G. Walker. In fact, the first author had the privilege of being one of his students, while reading for the Master's in Educational Administration at the University of New England.

On the other hand, we must understand that Educational Administration is an applied field and not a discipline like chemistry or history. As an applied field it has much in common with other applied fields, such as, engineering and medicine. Just as engineering has to build on disciplines such as mathematics and physics, and medicine upon anatomy and biology, Educational Administration has to build upon basic disciplines such as psychology, sociology, political science and economics. However, it must be understood that the concepts of those disciplines cannot be borrowed indiscriminately but have to be adapted and tested in educational settings.

Educational Administration is a field of study, mainly, for those who are aspiring to be administrators or currently engaged as teachers and lecturers in schools and colleges/universities. It is true that the teachers are aware of such problems and issues as decision-making, leadership and communication from the perspective of the classroom teacher and not as an administrator. The task of administration is to view these problems and issues from a new perspective, that of the administrator who must see the organization as a whole, and not just as one teacher/lecturer in a classroom situation. Much of what we discuss about schools, school districts and educational regions has some application to the administration of other educational organizations.

2.3 Functions Performed by Educational Administrators

On many occasions, parents, teachers, and parents and citizen's association members and the school administrators themselves raise the question, "what are the functions performed by educational administrators?" The basic purpose of administration is to enhance teaching and learning. In short, administration serves an instrumental or supportive role and not a primary role. Since many administrative activities do not deal directly with students, the relationships of these activities to teaching and learning are not always apparent.

When one considers the range of activities that a school principal is involved in, s/he can be viewed as a generalist needing and relying on the expertise of others. Indeed the expertise that is needed in principals is to know how to fit the pieces together. Because the total programme of teaching and learning, whether in the more formal arena of the classroom or in the school as a whole, could be performed better and more effectively when it is co-ordinated by the principal. In short, principals must help shape a safe and positive environment, so that teaching and learning is fostered more effectively.

The distinctive functions that administrators should perform to enhance teaching and learning are:

- The administrator should discern and influence the development of a shared vision for the educational institution or organization that s/he leads.
- The administrator should articulate the shared vision and involve others in setting the goals and developing the strategies, to achieve the realization of the shared vision of the organization. The goals may reside in the culture of the community and of the school or the other organization and, if so, they should be identified and perhaps made explicit.
- The administrator should stimulate and direct the development of programmes to achieve the goals and purposes.

- The administrator should establish the structures and processes to co-ordinate and organize the implementation of the programmes. Central to this function is the determination of staff requirements, identification of potential and the employment or empowerment of competent persons to fill the positions and the establishment of necessary relationships amongst staff members. The empowerment of "yes" men and women, or loyalists, should not be preferred to competency.

- The administrator should procure and manage the resources needed to support the organization and its programmes. In times of decreasing public funds, the administrators need to be more entrepreneurial and innovative in their approaches in supplementing the available resources.

- The administrator should represent the organization to groups in the local or larger community, and whenever a necessity arises, mediate amongst the groups. This is perhaps the most forthright function that an administrator is called upon to perform.

- The administrator should evaluate and monitor the efficiency and effectiveness of these operations. In this context, the term effectiveness is used to mean the achievement of the set goals, and the term efficiency to mean the lowest possible unit cost (Adapted from Campbell, Corbally, & Nystrand, 1983, pp. 6–7).

Starratt (1996) argues that the work of an educational administrator is different from other fields of administration and management, because it is shaped and directed by the core business of teaching and learning. It is pointed out that educational administration has three fundamental functions, namely: administering meaning, administering community, and administering excellence. Administrators are expected to ensure that the schools are able to provide opportunities for the students to discover meaning in their world — the meaning of nature, of human affairs, of human relationships — so that they can learn beyond memorizing superficial knowledge to succeed at examinations. Administering meaning demands that learning in the schools is grounded upon human concerns, is connected to the major cultural activities of the society, and is attuned to the realities of everyday life.

Administering community demands that the administrators endeavour to transform the traditional separation of the individual from the community into their essential union. Creating more opportunities for cooperative learning and teamwork could encourage this. Further, he introduces the concept of organic management in administering community, which is defined as management by commitment rather than control. Administering excellence demands that the administrator promotes and encourages high quality performance in schools not only in terms of productivity, invention or technical virtuosity but more so in terms of the students' character courage and honour (Pang, 1999a, b).

Another way to view the functions of an organizational leader/manager, whether it is in a department, school, college, university, and an education authority or in an education system as a whole, is through the following categories:

- Integrating the organizational resources in the most efficient and effective pursuit of its goals;
- Acting as the agent of introducing and institutionalizing desirable change; and
- Maintaining, supplementing and developing its resources.

2.3.1   *Integration of Resources*

The administrative or managerial role as opposed to the teaching role is to be the glue in the organization, in the sense of holding the organization together (Pang, 1998a). When a teacher is appointed or promoted to an administrative or managerial position, s/he is required to plan, organize, direct and control the work of other staff. This involves a fundamental change in the criteria for job success. As a leader and/or manager, success depends on using the ideas and talents of a team, on arriving at decisions to which the team members feel comfortable and committed, to ensure that the decisions are put into effect.

In many instances, an administrator is less concerned with being a resource than with using resources. At most levels of school management, teachers are fulfilling classroom and managerial roles, and the danger is that one forgets that the behaviour, which succeeds in the classroom, is different from the type of behaviour required to motivate a team of colleagues or adults. In the capacity of an administrator, a teacher needs to change his attitudes, approaches and the mindset, as getting the best out of adults is different from getting the kids to learn (Sergiovanni & Carver, 1980).

2.3.2 Effecting Change

Effecting change is an essential function of an administrative role. It may be initiated from within the school or imposed from outside. Schools have to adapt to the changes in politics, educational philosophies, government policies and community needs. The success of a school, or any other educational institution, will depend on the educational administrators' ability to adapt the contents, methods, and ethos of education to the new needs.

By definition, strategic decisions involve change. Managers will have to involve others in the formulation of such changes and in that process; s/he has to observe the reactions of others. When a change is proposed it is interesting to note the comments "yes", and "but", which should be interpreted as negative. The natural tendency in people is to resist and even resent ideas which are not their own. The tendency is even stronger if a change is forced upon them. It is also natural to say, "I haven't time", as it is much easier to go on repeating what was being done. It is also not unusual to consider that "A bird in the hand is worth two in the bush", because of the risks and unforeseen problems in effecting changes. Jealousy, vested interests, and expediency, are some of the other factors that come into play. Problems of reorganization, loss of status and power, demarcation of authority and shortage of money, could be the other issues requiring change and these could be considered as "threats" on one's position (Gamage, 1992).

2.3.3 Maintaining and Developing Resources

The tangible resources of an organization can be classified as:

- Human (the staff employed by the organization);
- Material (buildings and equipment); and
- Financial (the funds available to the organization).

If these resources are not properly maintained, we simply do not have an organization to integrate or change. Consider the cases of some state corporations, which incur losses for a number of years, forcing the government to close down or sell it for private management. Mismanagement leads business ventures to incur losses, thus failing in their core-function of earning a profit, forcing them to declare bankruptcies and closure of business (Gamage, 1973).

Besides, there are a number of "intangible" resources, of which "image", or "reputation", is the most generally recognized. Without a good business reputation, survival of any business organization is doubtful. Without the right image, even the very existence of an independent school could be in doubt. Even with the state system, image is very important, wherever choice come into play — e.g. recruitment of staff, placement of high school graduates for jobs, and parental or student choice of school or college. These factors are adversely affected if an institution has not projected a good image. In case of a school, ethical standards, disciplinary standards, external relationships and support could also be considered as intangible resources.

The process of change demands that managers should focus a great deal of their attention on developing resources to meet new challenges and needs. If the education system is to progress and be relevant to society, it must be "needs driven" and not "resources driven", i.e. resources must be adapted to meet needs. These needs will be derived from the interplay of the school's core-values, beliefs and the trends within the environment.

Every manager should constantly reflect on the ethics of his or her conduct. As a leader of a group of staff, a person is likely to have a potential "power base", which can be used to influence decisions. The unscrupulous leader/manager can make life hell for those of his department/ faculty who do not support him at staff meetings. Words like "loyalty" can be corrupted to mean slavish adherence to the partisan lines or to expect support for his or her views. His colleagues could in fact regard an administrator, who fondly imagines himself/herself to be seen as a "very smart leader", or as a shrewd and sympathetic handler of people, as an unprincipled rogue.

2.4 Organizational Attributes

An organization may be defined as a group of people who work towards achieving a given set of common goals. Organizations vary substantially in their complexity and organizational structure. The major attributes of an organization could be the following:

- Goal or Goals
- Technology
- Division of Labour
- Power Centres, and
- Environment.

2.4.1 Goals

Provide meaning and direction for an organization. More importantly goals provide the reasons for the existence of an organization. An industrial firm is formed to produce a certain product at a profit for the owners or shareholders, and in this context schools are established to provide education for the children. The general goals of an organization suggest the activities in which, the respective organization should be engaged and also indicate the criteria by which the organization should be evaluated for effectiveness. Even though goals provide identity and direction for an organization, they usually permit considerable latitude in organizational behaviour. One reason for this is that organizational goals are so general that they are ambiguous and a school is not an exception.

Individuals join organizations because they support the goals of the organization. For instance, a person who joins a school as a teacher supports the concept of educating children. However, he or she may have his/her own interpretation of the goals, which may influence his/her teaching. Besides that a person may have certain other individual goals, which s/he hopes to achieve in the process of his or her teaching career.

An important distinction could be made between expected outcomes and the set goals of an organization. If we consider the case of a school, teachers assume that they'll be paid regularly if they perform their duties as set out in the official timetable. However, if by any chance, the regular pay packets are unexpectedly delayed, it is likely that the entire system will be disrupted. An organization designed to achieve certain set goals, is often structured into a number of sub-units. Each of which has its own goals, which are subordinate to the general organizational goals. For instance, a secondary school or a university is usually divided into faculties and these sub-units compete with each other in the pursuit of their own goals, but it is important to see that such competition should not displace the overall goals of the whole organization. In theory, each of these sub-units should pursue its goals to the best of its ability. This of course, could lead to conflicts between them. Allocation of organizational resources is one of the main areas, which leads to conflicting claims by the sub-units. Another area of conflict could be the emphasis placed by each sub-unit on the importance of its own particular programmes. When individuals place high emphasis on the sub-unit's goals, and lose sight of the main goals of the organization as a whole, it could be referred to as goal displacement (Everard & Morris, 1996; Campbell et al. 1983).

2.4.2 Technology

Parsons (1967) has pointed out that the organizations function at three levels — technical, managerial and institutional. Technical level refers to those activities through which the organization achieves its purposes. The managerial level is engaged in supporting the technical level, by providing it with resources, coordinating its activities, mediating between it and the environment. The institutional level provides legitimacy and overall direction to the organization and links it to the broader environment. It is the support of the managerial and institutional levels that enables organizations to develop and implement technologies too complex for individuals to carry out.

The technology of educational organizations is teaching. It involves bringing students, teachers and materials together to achieve curriculum objectives. Very often, this is done by dividing students into classes and dividing curriculum into segments called grades or subjects and arranging for interaction between them.

2.4.3 Division of Labour

The work of an organization is shared among its participants. The manner in which this sharing is done is through the division of labour. In smaller organizations, the division of labour is informal. As organizations become larger and more complex, the division of labour within them is likely to become formalized at several hierarchical levels and across various departments and divisions. The jobs of individuals within these departments and divisions become specialized. The division of labour in schools involves teachers, administrators, and classified personnel such as clerks, canteen workers, cleaners, etc. Different responsibilities are associated with each of these positions. These responsibilities and expectations are stated in documents, such as policy manuals, position or job descriptions and teacher contracts. In the regional/provincial or district and central administrative offices, there are many that play supportive roles but are not involved in teaching directly.

The division of labour in an organization is of special concern to administrators. Indeed, it is this division that results in the need for co-ordination that creates the need for administrators. Their function is to assume that the efforts of those who report to them are contributing towards the realization of organizational goals, as was expected. By coordinating the efforts of others, administrators can help them find satisfaction as individuals as well as achieve expected goals.

2.4.4 Structure and Power Centres

Organizations include one or more power centres, which establish goals, allocate resources, and monitor progress. They make the decisions that guide the efforts of others in the organization. Power centres, are often defined by organizational charters or by laws. In case of schools, position status, authority structures and rules and regulations prescribe the power centres. These could be central executive, regional office, district office, principal, head teachers, class co-ordinators and classroom teachers. Each of these individuals makes decisions that guide the decisions of others. Moreover, because of the positions they hold, others accept the fact that they have a right to do so. For example, teachers expect the principals to assign them to classrooms, and students expect teachers to make the best out of classroom time, rather than giving homework assignments. When individuals act in such ways and their directions are followed, we can say they are exercising authority. Authority relationships are essential guides to behaviour in schools as they are in other organizations. The concept of authority involves not only giving orders or directions but also the acceptance of such orders, by those within the organization as legitimate and binding.

There are various sources of legitimacy to authority — i.e. power is consistent with the values of those over whom it is exercised. The authority includes, tradition, personality, knowledge and rational bases. The rational legal authority structure is the crux of what is generally referred to as the formal organization of a school system. It includes statements of goals and policies, contractual relationships, and a specified hierarchy of authority. An important element of rational legal authority is a body of universal and impersonal rules that spell out required behaviour, at different levels of the organization.

Another kind of authority that is important in schools is professional authority. Similar to how doctors and lawyers make decisions about their patients and clients, teachers apply what is known about the best educational practices to the identified needs of individual students. However, problems arise in determining which of the decisions should be made according to rules and regulations, and which ones should be left for professional discretion. For example, to what extent should the teachers be involved in decisions relating to class sizes, the student disciplinary rules, or the use of professionals in classrooms? These and other questions lead to conflicts between the administrators and/or authorities and teachers. On the other hand, it is important to recognize the informal power structure maintained by informal groups within the organization, as such groups can shape and influence others towards authority and formal centres of power (Campbell et al., 1983).

2.4.5   *Environment*

Every organization exists in an environment with which it is interdependent. In case of a school, the local community, the school district, region, state and the national system can be considered as its environment. It is important to think of schools in the context of their environments, requiring the heads of schools to spend more time managing transactions between their schools and environments. Especially, when the authority is devolved on to the schools, and all relevant stakeholders in the school community are given opportunities to participate. Such schools become more open than closed. The school councillors, school managers, school governors, parents, local community, as well as, the industrial and business community could be given significant roles to play. In the circumstances, it could become very necessary for a head of the school to shape community expectations, to solicit cooperation and support for school activities and build a good public image. For some heads, dealing with these outsiders is among the least enjoyable aspects of their jobs, whereas, for some others it is quite the opposite (Gamage, 1993).

Some may argue that outsiders interfere, disrupt and consume time and energy. But, we should not forget that a coin has two sides. They also offer support, contribute both in finances and with voluntary labour (whenever a need arises), and go to the extent of arguing the case for and on behalf of the school. It is important for the heads to know how to engender helpful behaviour and discourage disruptive behaviour and to manage any resultant conflicts constructively. Negligence and/or ignorance often leads to conflicts and misunderstandings, as it is usual for the parents, teachers and employers to harbour suspicions and/or misconceptions about each other and the internal operations of schools. If we retreat behind our boundaries, we may not be able to understand the other person's point of view and build a genuine partnership. In this context, school leaders have a responsibility to build bridges between different categories of stakeholders enabling them to build trust and place confidence in each other. Similar to that of business and industry, schools have to project their public image and actively manage their public relations, without leaving room for outsiders to form their own mistaken impressions regarding the internal operations of schools. School-based Management is one of the best approaches to building mutual understanding and improving the public image of a school. Naturally, participation leads to ownership and commitment, whereby, school councillors and school managers as well as the parents will project a good image of the school (Gamage, 1998a). In fact, some American schools in California have put up boards inviting the community to visit their schools.

2.5 Main Features of a School

A school is a social organization with an important role to play in the society. As in other organizations, the schools prescribe many of the activities of its individual members. If we consider the case of a primary school teacher, s/he comes to the school at a particular time and works with a specific group of students in an assigned room. S/he teaches a variety of subjects, most of which are prescribed by the Department of Education or the authority in charge of the schools system. From time to time s/he consults with the Assistant/Vice Principal, Principal, Counsellor and other specialists or parents about pupils' progress. S/he takes attendance, keeps other records and submits required reports. Her/his pattern of activity will be similar each day. Similarly, school administrators, other teachers, pupils and canteen managers also will have routine types of work, all contributing to the central aspect in the life of an organization.

As we know, schools began as very simple organizations, often with a single teacher, a group of children, and parents, with similar expectations. Similar to many other social organizations, schools have become larger and more complex organizations. Now, most schools are comprised of many classrooms, and involve large numbers of teachers, students, non-teaching staff and administrators. We also refer to school systems to denote a cluster, region, state or the national system of schools, which connect a multitude of relationships between the schools, other schools, and educational authorities (Handy, 1986).

Even though schools are bureaucratic organizations, because of the fact that teachers are highly educated and consider themselves professionals, schools differ from other organizations. In this context, schools become professional bureaucracies. Therefore, there should be more participatory decision-making in schools than in other organizations. On the other hand, schools belong to the category of organized anarchies, as described by Cohen and March (1974). The provisional characteristics of such organizations are unclear goals, uncertain technology, and fluid participation. Decision-making is also marked by ambiguity (Cohen, March & Oslen, 1972). In these circumstances, administrative success could also become ambiguous.

Another perspective is that when public schools are subject to an area rule and the admission of children has to be done on the basis of school district or government rules, the schools do not have control over who enters the school. The parents also do not have a choice. On the other hand, the private schools have a better control over who enters their schools. When area rules are in operation, schools need not compete for their students. Richard Carlson (1998) has branded schools into this category of domesticated organizations. But, it is important to note that times are changing, as many school systems are allowing the schools to compete for their students.

The fourth perspective is that schools are loosely coupled systems (Weick, 1976; Orton & Weick, 1990). Loose coupling permits disparate elements of an organization to persist in the face of environmental change, allows for localized adaptations, and encourages novel solutions, and permit, breakdowns in one part without affecting other parts. In an attempt to meet changing societal demands, many universities are veering away from arts, sciences and education, and are now placing greater emphasis on business and commerce, as well as, information technology. Loose coupling has enabled these changes to occur, without major disruptions to a university's main aims.

2.6   Development of Theoretical Concepts and Their Relevance

Tradition is an important factor in school organization. Because of the tradition of schools being supported by public funds, what is taught and who the local community influences works in schools in particular, with the public opinion taken into consideration. Grading of children on age and ability levels, schools operating from Monday through to Friday and home-work as the children progress in their grades are some examples. Similarly, the length of the school day depends on the contexts and cultural traditions. One senior teacher, functioning as the head or principal, is another aspect of school organizations developed and accepted by tradition.

The view that teaching is a profession has had substantial impact on the way schools are organized. The relationship between teachers and their pupils is considered a professional one, for which teachers are especially educated and certified by the relevant authorities. Certification requirements, assure that teachers are selected on the basis of technical competence, rather than patronage or personal relationships to employing officials (Holmes & Wynne, 1989). However, the situation could be different in certain other systems where, the local and national politicians have taken control of the education system, going to the extent of determining who gets what and who does what and when?

In the contemporary world, many different innovations and experimentations are being undertaken to find the best way to successfully educate all children. In one particular experimental school in Shun De in Southern China (visited on the 14th December 2000 by the two authors), had an enrolment of 1,429 primary children with an approved cadre of 58 teachers. But officially, teachers were assigned 11 periods of 40 minutes each of teaching per week, leaving the rest of the school day for lesson preparation as well as for visiting children's homes to establish a rapport with the parents. Another unusual feature was, that the school starts at 7.30 a.m. and continues until 4.20 p.m., with a break of three hours from 10.40 a.m. to 1.40 p.m. for the children to go home and have lunch and a nap. For those parents who want to keep the children at the school during lunch break, the school offers lunch and sleeping facilities for an additional payment.

Similarly, in the evening, those who want to keep their children in the school for an extra hour could do so on a fixed payment. Another surprise was that even though on an average, teacher-pupil ratio was 1: 25; for years 1–3, officially sanctioned class size was 45 and for years 4–6, 50. However, because of its popularity, the school had enrolled up to 55 and 66 per class at the two levels respectively, on the basis of extra payments. The income generated from extra services, were used to pay the teachers and the principal, incentive allowances amounting to around 80% and 100% of their approved salaries. Another special feature was that with the extra income, the school was in a position to possess a fleet of 3–4 vehicles with drivers to be used by the staff, at the discretion of the principal. This type of new roles is affecting the role of the educational leaders/managers in a significant way.

The development of the current management theory has occurred primarily in the 20th century. Two of the early and most influential schools of thought involved job analysis and human relations. The structuralist emphasis upon bureaucracy has also been influential.

Frederick Taylor's *Principles of Scientific Management* published in 1911 and Henry Fayol's book on *Administration Industrielle General* in

1886 (translated into English in 1929), adopted the job analysis approach. Taylor developed the approaches and principles on how to get the best out of workers while Fayol developed the approaches and principles on how to get the best out of managers. But both were concerned with industrial management.

Mary Parker Follett was the first proponent of the *human behaviour approach*. Her book *Creative Experience* published in 1924 stated that the fundamental problem of any enterprise is the building and maintenance of dynamic, yet harmonious, human relationships and she placed great emphasis on coordination. Elton Mayo, who conducted the Hawthorn experiments at Western Electric Company in Chicago, pointed out that what goes on inside the worker is even more significant for productivity, than what goes on outside.

Max Weber's major contribution to managerial thought was in defining and elaborating on *bureaucracy* as an ideal organizational type. Our image of a bureaucracy is as an organization that is rule-bound, impersonal and inefficient. However, it is a fact that bureaucracy provides a structure, which facilitates the work of complex organizations. School systems too have taken the bureaucratic characteristics in order to organize the work of their employees and provide services to large numbers of students. Yet, some of the weaknesses of a bureaucracy are the tendency for goal displacement, unanticipated consequences of rules and stifling of creativity and individual initiatives. However, even in the modern world, no organization has been completely successful in eliminating or rejecting the bureaucratic model in its organizational structure.

The final perspective is that of public expectations. Past and present experiences of citizens within organizations influence public opinion, and such opinions are often translated into legislation. Standards of good business practices continue to influence the organization and administration of schools. Standards of rationality, efficiency, productivity, flexibility and accountability have crept into the schools system, through business.

Owens (2001) refers to the bureaucratic and human resources development views as the two major perspectives on educational organizations. Believers of the bureaucratic model stress that the authorities to control the organizational members adopt the following five mechanisms:

- Hierarchical control of authority and close supervision;
- Establish and maintain adequate vertical communication;
- Develop bureaucratic rules and procedures to guide actions;

- Promulgate clear plans and guidelines to be observed; and
- Addition of administrative positions to the hierarchy whenever the need arises.

The *human resources development* advocates emphasize the importance of being conscious of what the organizational members are doing to commit their capabilities and energies towards the accomplishment of organizational goals. Organizational leadership by following good human relations can coordinate the procedures and processes to encourage the participants to subscribe to the values and goals of the organization. A socialization process could be introduced to provide opportunities for organizational members to identify themselves with the values and purposes of the organization (Owens, 2001). They could also be motivated to have some congruency between the individual and organizational goals. Thus, the resulting organizational culture could be more harmonious with the organizational values and the personal aspirations of the employees.

Douglas McGregor in formulating his Theories X and Y has assumed the following about the nature of people at work:

Theory X
- People inherently dislike work and avoid it if possible.
- People must be coerced, controlled, directed or threatened to work towards achieving organizational goals.
- People prefer to be directed, avoid responsibility and seek security.

Theory Y
- People inherently like work and work can be a source of satisfaction.
- People will exercise self-direction and control if they are committed to the organizational goals.
- People are willing to seek and accept responsibility. Avoidance of responsibility is not natural; it is a consequence of experience. (Adapted from McGregor, 1960).

In an analysis of McGregor's Theory Y and Argyris' (1957) Behaviour Patterns B, are comparable to the System 4 Management advocated by Likert (1967). In terms of Likert's System 4 Management, a leader/manager has complete trust and confidence in the abilities of subordinates through a process of widely dispersed decision-making. There is an open flow of upward, downward and horizontal communication. The staff is motivated through the opportunities for participation, underpinned by a reward structure. The superior-subordinate interaction, existent in organizational controls is replaced by an extensive friendly interaction, enhanced by widespread distribution of responsibility in a collegial atmosphere. The systems theory provides valuable insights into organizational behaviour. This Social Systems view of education suggests that an organization exists in a wider environment and has subsystems.

The role advocated by Erving Goffman (1959) offers another avenue for understanding the behaviour of people within organizations. Accordingly, each person in an organization has a specific role to play, and many factors interact to determine the precise manner in which such a role needs to be performed. The other players and the audience or employer who controls the situation with multiple expectations are likely to influence the interpretation of the role. When the role expectations and role perceptions are vague, it leads to conflict. When role prescription is unclear and contradictory, and when different expectations exist among different stakeholders, it gives rise to role ambiguity.

2.7 Personal Characteristics and Administrative Roles

Organizational imperatives and personal dispositions are important dimensions in understanding organizational behaviour. Getzels and Guba (1957) have developed a model depicting the school as a social system, in which these two dimensions are central (Figure 2.1). Organizational imperatives are referred to as normative dimension and the personal disposition as personal dimension. The normative dimension consists of the roles of personnel in the school and the expectations held for each role. The personal (individual) dimension consists of the personality characteristics of the personnel and their need dispositions.

One needs not become an administrator to determine the compatibility of the role. Every teacher could be given an opportunity to chair a committee, a department, or a grade level, or some group effort, where the goals of the institution (normative dimension) will assume added importance.

2.8 Desirable Prerequisites for Prospective Administrators

We have argued that the work of the school administrator should enhance teaching and learning. To have an appropriate understanding of the role and to perform well in such a role, it is desirable for a prospective administrator to have a strong background in liberal education. Then, it needs to

Figure 2.1   Social Systems' Model

SOCIAL SYSTEM

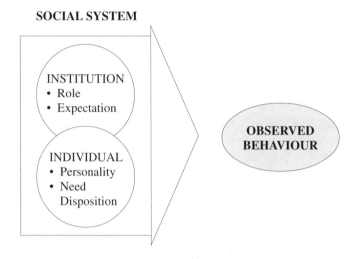

be supplemented with training in education as a broad field of study and finally training in educational administration itself. A liberal educational background has been stressed, because school is an important institution within society and is the training ground for its members. This implies that the administrator of such an organization should understand both the culture of the society and the role of the school in it.

It is also necessary that an administrator needs some knowledge and understanding about the particular system of education, whether it is Australian, American, British, Hong Kong or a Philippine system of education. The understanding needs to encompass each system's purposes, procedures, organization, historical evolution and current problems. With such understanding, the school administrators will be in a better position to comprehend more fully the organization for which they are responsible and to determine which practices should be sustained and supported, and which should be improved or eliminated.

The third important component of the background of a prospective administrator is training in educational administration itself. The teachers who appear to have the necessary personal qualities and professional interests, and commitment are badly needed to join administration. It is important to seek out and encourage such people to enter programmes in educational administration. Training in administration should be built on strengths already acquired and demonstrated. Background training in psychology, sociology, economics and political science could be relevant and useful for an educational administrator (Campbell et al., 1983).

2.9 Getting into the Field of Educational Administration: Current Trends

In Australia, the traditional route to administration has placed much emphasis on experience. First, the candidates should have experience in teaching, and sometimes, quasi-administrative positions. Later, on the basis of assessment of applicants for promotions by school inspectors, they were placed on seniority lists. But, since the mid-1970s, with the implementation of school-based management in the Australian Capital Territory (ACT) and Victoria, the seniority list system was replaced by merit selections by the school boards and school councils. With the introduction of Scott reforms in 1989, New South Wales (NSW) also moved to implement merit selections for principals and deputy principals (Gamage, 1996b). Now more emphasis is being placed on graduate study and the incentives provided and the type of programmes and prerequisites could see less on long-term administrative experience as introduced by systems of education (Pang, 1999c). In fact, in the year 2000, three vacancies for principals, which occurred in the high schools in the Hunter region of New South Wales, were filled with three of the school executives who were graduates in Master of Leadership and Management in Education (MLMEd) from the University of Newcastle.

In most American systems, middle and high school principals, as well as system administrators, are expected to have doctoral degrees, preferably in educational administration. The desire for doctoral degrees by prospective administrators was such in 1994 that when the first author visited the University of San Franciso (a fairly small university), he was made to understand that there were 450 doctoral enrolments in the areas of leadership and educational administration. For most senior teaching and administrative positions, the candidates are expected to have their masters' degrees. In 2000, this position was revealed in a comparative study of the profile characteristics of school leaders in the United States and Australia. The data indicated that 90% of the American principals have masters' degrees while 9% hold doctoral degrees whereas amongst the Australian principals, 17% have less than a bachelor's degree, 45% hold bachelor's degrees, 34% master's degrees with only 2% doctoral degrees (Su, Gamage & Mininberg, 2001).

The Canadian system also has adopted practices similar to those of USA. Even in the British system, which was a late-comer to the field of educational administration and where the discipline is referred to as educational management, applicants for administrative positions are expected to have at least a master's degree in educational management. This trend was evident at the University of Leicester in England (where in 1999 the first author spent part of his sabbatical leave), had recorded over 1,100 enrolments for MBA in Educational Management and 230 enrolments for EdD in Educational Management. In 1996, the Faculty of Education of The Chinese University of Hong Kong was the first Asian University to introduce EdD programme in Educational Administration and Policy. In 2001, two principals and a system administrator became the first EdD graduates of the University. As the Faculty is planning to increase its enrolments of doctoral students, it is likely that this option will become popular in Hong Kong.

2.10 Conclusion

This topic examined the meaning of educational administration, as it is understood today, including the wide range of organizations coming under the concept, the purpose and specific objectives of the profession of educational administrators. The development of educational administration as an applied field based on other disciplines, as well as, an applied discipline similar to medicine and engineering was also examined. It also discussed the functions of educational administrators and how the profession was taking shape. The desirable prerequisites for prospective educational administrators, such as, a background in liberal arts education and training in the specific field of leadership and management were also examined. Finally, it focused on the current trends in placing more emphasis on merit and specific training in educational administration and management, in effecting promotions and senior appointments in preference to seniority, which was the criterion in the past.

2.11 Review Questions

1. Explain in detail what you understand by educational administration. Your response should be supported by theoretical concepts drawn from the literature.
2. Examine the development of educational administration as an applied field of study.

CHAPTER 3

Responsibilities and Tasks of Educational Administrators

3.0 Learning Outcomes

On the basis of a systematic study of this chapter, the readers will:

- Have a better knowledge and understanding of the responsibilities and tasks of educational administrators;
- Be better prepared to cope with managing time, stress and organizational conflict;
- Be able to develop better strategies and techniques enabling them to provide more effective leadership and management.

3.1 Focus

First, the topic focuses on the profession of educational administrators and the nature of the job. Secondly, it examines the key responsibilities and tasks of educational administrators and how to take charge of the issues and problems confronting them. Then, the participants are reminded of the importance of time management, by focusing attention on the need to minimize time wastage, through the development of effective time control strategies. Then, it focuses on the avoidance of stress, and draws similarities between the factors contributing to stress and time management. These discussions are followed by an examination of the inevitable nature of organizational conflict. This section also discusses the stages of development of such conflict, and how to successfully manage conflict, so as to promote the positive development and/or self-renewal of the organization. Finally, effective administrators are encouraged to gain satisfaction from their own accomplishments and those of others, whom they have encouraged, motivated and supported.

3.2   Nature of the Profession of Administrators

Traditionally, in the military there are line officers and staff officers. Even though we do not equate school organizations with military organizations, the distinction between line and staff is a useful one and, with some adaptation, we can use the term in the context of educational organizations. The line officers are those in charge of operating units of an organization, in this case a cluster director or a school principal. Thus, we can classify principals and teachers as line officers, while Directors, Deputy/Assistant Directors and regional education officers, as staff officers.

In 1995, New South Wales (NSW) dismantled 10 regional offices, headed by Assistant Director Generals, and established 40 school districts, headed by District Superintendents. In keeping with the American model, Western Australia (WA) is divided into 30 Educational Districts and a School Superintendent heads each district. Similarly, South Australia also has a system of school districts headed by District Superintendents. In NSW, WA and South Australia, all these officers are appointed by the Department of School Education, currently known as the Department of Education and Training. But, in USA, in certain states, the school superintendents are appointed, while in others they are elected and function as the chief executive officers of the school districts.

In 2000, New South Wales had 2,200 state schools with over 87,000 employees including 70,702 teachers. The student population was 762,000, covering an area of eight million square kilometres. The annual budget of the Department of School Education, which was responsible for this vast system, was A\$5.45 billion supplemented by Federal Government project based funding. A principal heads each state school whether primary or secondary. In smaller primary schools, the principal was also a part time teacher, whereas in larger schools, the principal was a full time administrator (NSW, DET, 2000). In any case, the principal was the executive officer of the school, and thus, a line officer. In larger primary schools, other than the principal, there were other school executives, such as deputy principals, assistant principals and executive teachers. In high or secondary schools, other than the principal, there were deputy principals, leading teachers (same status as deputy), head-teachers, year coordinators and school executives, who were called upon to perform various administrative functions.

In 2001, Hong Kong covering an area of 1,100 square kilometres had 816 primary schools and 486 secondary schools, with 49,600 teachers and a student population of 960,000. The schools system comprised of 5% government, 85% aided and 10% private schools (Pang, 2002). These figures exclude kindergartens, as it is totally owned and managed by the private sector.

Based on recommendations arising from a consultation paper issued by the Education and Manpower Bureau in 1998, the Education Department restructured Hong Kong's schools system to be effective from 2001. Accordingly, four regional education offices, that is, Hong Kong (HK), Kowloon (KLN), New Territories East (NTE) and New Territories West (NTW) were established in place of the 19 district offices. Principal Education Officers were appointed to head each of the regions, while two Assistant Directors supervised regions (HK-NTW and KLN-NTE). Within each education region, satellite offices were also established to provide specialized services to the schools while pre-2001 District Education Officers (DEOs) were renamed as School Development Officers (SDOs) to emphasize their new role in supporting schools.

3.3 Nature of the Job of an Administrator

Accomplished administrators know how to manage their time wisely, cope with stress, and resolve conflicts within their work settings. They are also aware that these areas of work interrelate. A problem in one area inevitably affects others. Lack of time to perform all the functions that they are expected to do, is a major source of stress for many administrators. In turn, stress reduces the administrator's ability to make better decisions, while minimizing ability to manage time intelligently. What could be more stressful and time consuming, could be to confront complex organizational conflicts. On the other hand, being under stress can make leaders more vulnerable to conflicts.

The basic purpose of administration is to enhance teaching and learning. These educational administrators are expected to perform some or all of the following functions:

- Promote and influence the development of a shared vision and set appropriate goals for the school.

- Stimulate and direct the development strategies and programmes to achieve the goals and purposes.
- Establish and coordinate the organizational structures to implement the programmes.
- Procure and manage the resources to support the organization and its programmes.
- Represent the organization to groups in the local and larger community.
- Appraise the effectiveness and efficiency of these operations.

It is the responsibility of the Director General (DG), District Super-intendents (DS) and Heads of Schools to implement these functions. The efforts required to implement each of the six functions vary according to the position held by the officer concerned. For instance, the DG has a system wide interest, and the DS, a district wide interest, whereas, the principal is concerned with a single school. Similarly, the other school executives have to perform these functions relating to their area of responsibility, which could often be less than that of the whole organization. The DS have to devote more time and energy to ascertain the needs of the district and procure and manage the resources, than the principals do. On the other hand, principals will have to spend more time and energy on programme development, than a DS.

Even though it is not correct to define a principal merely as the instructional leader, it is important to stress the primary responsibility of the development and supervision of instructional programmes. These programmes are of two kinds:

- Those that concern direct and formal instruction or the core business, whether in reading or mathematics or one of the other content areas; and
- Those that could be called aspects of the school climate and culture of school regimen.

School regimen is influenced by the relationships between students and faculty; between the principal and students; between the school and parents and other adults in the community, as well as, the values and beliefs. Also included are the relationships between students, and the relationships between individual members of the faculty. In all relationships, the underlying principles need to be concerned with the values, norms and attitudes that are exemplified, i.e. courtesy, openness, fairness and equity, in short, making the school a decent place in which to live and learn. The type of celebrations, rituals, stories and heroes will reinforce these values, norms and attitudes further.

No other person can do as much as a school administrator to establish the quality of the school regimen. By the very nature of the job they have responsibility for the school. To exercise that responsibility they must be in communication with the faculty, students, parents and other adults in the community. They need help from all of these groups, but it is the principal who must give the leadership necessary to help them coalesce around some working principles. Implementation of common objectives can determine the regimen or atmosphere of the school as a social system. Let us now move from what administrators should do to a consideration of what they actually do.

3.4 Research on an Administrator's Working Day

Researchers describe a typical day in the life of a school administrator as hectic, fragmented and varied (Bezzina, 1998; O'Dempsey, 1982; Sergiovanni, Burlingame, Coombs, & Thurston, 1999; Willis, 1982).

In 1979, the National Association of Elementary School Principals, in USA published *The Elementary School Principal in 1978: A Research Study*. The report contained much information about the principals' responsibilities, but much less on what principals actually do. The principals reported serious problems they were confronting in dismissing incompetent teachers, with 54% of the principals considering it as a serious problem. According to the responding principals, the key areas in which they spent most time were, managing student behaviour, declining enrolments, staff reductions, vandalism and pupil disregard for authority.

In 1978, the National Association of Secondary School Principals completed a three-volume study of the Senior High School Principalship. Volume 2 referred to The Effective Principal. From a total survey population of 1,600 principals, 60 effective ones were identified and interviewed. Among other things, principals were asked to indicate how they planned to spend their time and how they actually spent the last fortnight.

The research outcomes produced in Figure 3.1 shows the importance of time management. It is interesting to note that even though the principals planned to spend most of their time in programme development, which is the core-business of the school, because of certain deficiencies in time management, in reality they spent most of their time on personnel.

Figure 3.1   Time Management by Principals

Areas of activity	Time planned (biweekly)	Time spent (biweekly)
Programme Development (curriculum, instructional leadership)	1	3
Personnel (evaluation, advising, conference, recruiting)	2	1
School Management (weekly calendar, office, budget, correspondence, memos, etc.)	3	2
Student Activities (meetings, supervision, planning) / District Office (meetings, task forces, reports, etc.)	4	4
Community (PTA, advisory groups, parent conferences)	5	5
Planning (annual, long-range)	6	6
Professional Development (reading, conferences, etc.)	7	7
Student Behaviour (discipline, attendance, meetings)	8	8

(Source: Adapted from Gorton & McIntyre, 1978 cited in Campbell, Corbally, & Nystrand, 1983)

In his study, Wolcott (1973) divided what the principals did into formal encounters and informal encounters. In terms of formal encounters, an "average" school day was broken down into: prearranged meetings and conferences, 26%; deliberate but not prearranged meetings and conferences, 25%; casual or chance encounters, 15%; telephoning, 9%; talking on intercom, 1%; alone in office, 15%; alone and en route, 9%.

Almost half the principals' time was devoted to meetings some scheduled and even more unscheduled. In terms of the purposes of the activities, over one third of the time was devoted to organizational operational tasks and about one sixth to the academic programmes. Pupil control task demanded about one quarter of the principals' time.

In 1982, O'Dempsey's observation of school heads at work, revealed that monitoring and collecting information takes up the greatest portion of their time, followed by teaching and coaching sports activities. Willis (1982) reports that a great deal of the principal's work is devoted to external affairs. In 1988, Pellicer et al. (Cited in Turney, 1992) reported that American school principals considered formulating and implementing policy, leading to educational innovations and sharing decision-making, as the three most important issues. Bezzina's (1998) study of Maltese school principals suggests that they spent most of their time as chief executives, rather than as leading professionals. Gamage (1998b), based on his research on teaching principals, suggests that their three most important concerns were school leadership, teaching, and school management.

3.5   Roles of Administrators

Another way of viewing an administrator's work is from the standpoint of role. A role can be defined as a set of behaviours associated with an office or position. Mintzberg (1973) points out that administrators play 10 different roles, and categorized these into three major headings:

- Interpersonal Roles: figurehead, leader, and liaison;
- Information Roles: monitor, disseminator, and spokesperson; .
- Decision Roles: entrepreneur, disturbance handler, resource allocator, and negotiator.

Simpkins (1982) grouped the roles of the administrator into two categories: *Group Representative:* group symbol, diplomat-ambassador, and warrior-knight; *School Executive:* staff patron, judicial role, conciliator/ arbiter, internal adversary, task controller and coordinator, agent of rationality, decision democrat, and considerate supervisor. In the same year, Sungaila (1982) claims that the administrators perform four roles, namely: symbolic fitness, policy advocate, mediator, and crisis manager.

However, it can be pointed out that there are two key roles that all administrators have to perform effectively. These twin tasks are — decision-making and communication. When the leader portrays the roles of figurehead, leader, disseminator, spokesperson and liaison, s/he performs these roles more as a *communicator*. On the other hand, when s/he portrays the roles of entrepreneur, disturbance handler, resources manager and negotiator, s/he is a *decision-maker*. Often, these two tasks have to be performed in combination as decision involves communication and each communication involves a decision.

3.6   Strategies for Time Management

Peter Drucker (1966), the foremost expert in management in the 20th Century, has stated that time is the scarcest resource, and unless it is managed, nothing else can be managed. Another management expert, Alan Lekein (1974) opens his best-selling book: *How to Get Control of Your Time and Your Life*, with a statement that "time is life". It is irreversible and irreplaceable. To waste your time is to waste your life, but to master your time is to master your life and make the most of it.

Based on a study in 1998, Freeston and Costa Sr suggest an approach for school principals to determine whether they are devoting their time towards the realization of the key goal of the school i.e. creation of learning. They categorize the activities of the school principal into three, namely: value-added work, waste work, and necessary work. Value-added work, encompasses such activities as doing research on effective instructional practices, conducting classroom observation, and keeping professional dialogue focused on learning, which are all activities that enhance teaching and learning. On the other hand, waste work such as correcting mistakes, dealing with teacher, parent or student complaints and conducting a meeting in the absence of the concerned personnel, does not contribute directly to learning. Necessary work like signing purchase orders, supervising bus duty, and ordering supplies, keep the school running, but does not have a direct impact on learning. If the educational leader/manager is to be considered effective in utilizing time, s/he will strive to do more value-added work, while seeking to reduce waste work.

Most journal articles on time management have referred to a circular process that includes the following four steps:

- Goal setting, which leads to prioritizing.
- Keeping a daily time log, which leads to the identification of time wasters.
- Management of time wasters, which leads to increased discretionary time.
- Wise use of discretionary time, which leads to the accomplishment of those goals identified in step one.

Goal Setting and Prioritizing — Just as a competent teacher does not teach without a course outline, a competent administrator needs a written outline of his/her professional goals, to effectively conduct the administration of the organization for which s/he is responsible. According to Drucker (1966), a competent administrator needs to get "the right things done", rather than "doing things right", those right things directly relate to the advancement of the organizational goals. For a school principal, one of the most important right things is the instructional leadership, but most school leaders, have displaced this activity by doing other tasks. In 1983, a survey conducted in 51 schools in Texas, Hughes (1983) has found that ideally the principals wanted to allocate 30% of their time for instructional leadership, but in actual practice, they were able to allocate only 10% of their time. Heading the list of their time constraints were telephone interruptions, preparing sometimes unimportant or useless reports, on excessive number of meetings, paper work and spontaneous interruptions. In this context, it is important to prioritize one's short-term, medium-term and long-term goals, and to list the relevant activities, to organize time allocation and proper time management with an appropriate identification of time wasters.

A Daily Time Log — All effective administrators need to know where their time flies. It is better to document how the time is used on a daily basis, for this purpose, a time log can be used for 1–2 weeks. To gain the maximum benefit, it is better to practice this at least 2–3 times a year. This process is likely to enhance self-awareness and self-development to minimize time wasters. It is important to track the activities that the administrator is engaged in, and to prioritize each on the basis of its significance. To be an effective administrator, it is very important to recognize and manage the time wasters, so that planned time allocations can be assigned to key responsibilities enabling the achievement of one's personal, as well as, organizational goals.

Managing Time Wasters — Time wasters can be considered a two-headed dragon. External time wasters include; visitors, phone calls, meetings, paper work and the needs of the coworkers. Internal time wasters can be the administrator's inability to say "no"; inability to schedule and prioritize, inability to delegate, and the tendency to postpone work. *Telephone calls* and *visitors* are two of the worst daily time wasters, while meetings come a close third. When these act as interrupters, they destroy one's concentration and momentum. The management of these time wasters is both an attitude and a skill of an administrator. It is necessary to set aside time for reflection on one's responsibilities and important tasks, and to make this time inaccessible to staff, visitors and telephone calls. Such a time could be treated similar to a meeting time, when interruptions are not allowed or tolerated. *Paper-work* needs to be sorted out as *action items, information items, and throw away items.* The secretary can help the administrator in this work. The action items can be attended to as they are being read on a priority basis, whereas, information items can be dealt with by adopting a good office filing system, to be recalled if and when required.

Inability to say "no" is a big time waster for many administrators.

Drucker (1996) has suggested asking oneself, "What would happen if this were not done at all?" Then what the administrator needs to do is to say "no" if an activity contributes nothing to one's organization, to him or her. An administrator's primary purpose is likely to be enhanced by the ability to schedule the activities, such as planning, prioritizing, clustering and delegating. For a variety of reasons, most administrators are reluctant to *delegate authority* to subordinates. Again, an attitudinal change must precede learning new skills, to trust and place confidence in others and delegate. A system of monitoring and follow-up, and a relaxed attitude towards staff member's work procedures is needed for this purpose. The inclination of most administrators to postpone or procrastinate, difficult decisions and challenging activities, is a very bad practice. It is important to pursue such work with the least possible delay, however difficult they are, as they could contribute significantly to the development of the organization.

3.7 Stress Management

In USA, it has been estimated that stress related dysfunctions cause around 20 billion losses each year, in industrial productivity. Stress affects workers' performance in several ways. Stressed employees lose their concentration and make mistakes, resulting in injury or loss of property. It could also cause bad workmanship, resulting in bad quality products, affecting the business reputation of the organization. They are also susceptible to illness. On the other hand, leaders under stress are likely to make bad decisions. Based on their study, Clark and Clark (1992) have pointed out that "[s]tress degrades the use of intelligence in leadership performance". In the circumstances, it is important for administrators to avoid stress if they want to be effective.

The data support the common observation that administration is a very stressful occupation. Administrators are not only required to make decisions themselves, they are also in charge of the decision-making processes. It is often more difficult to involve others in the decision-making process than to make a unilateral decision. Either way, the decisions need to be influenced by facts and once made, they need to be rational and logical. However, decisions are also influenced by the values of the people and groups involved, as well as, dominant opinions. On many occasions, the value-based decisions may seem to be irrational. The values of those participating in the decision-making process are frequently affected by their own self-interests. Consciously or unconsciously, many leaders perceive the organization from their own perspective. Thus, even when there is agreement on the facts pertinent to a decision, the meaning of those facts or the consequences of taking one course of action or another, is open to interpretation. It is in this welter of human behaviour, that educational administrators must make decisions and such a decision-making role is stressful.

The administrators need to understand the common factors affecting both time and stress management. Such a step can help minimize the negative effects of stress. Specific areas of time and stress management are identical. For instance, paper work, telephone calls, visitor interruptions, excessive meetings, lack of planning and preparation time and procrastination, are all time wasters and stress producers. In fact, during a visit to a Newcastle primary school by the first author in August 2000, the principal explained how his deputy had to counsel him when a death threat was received over the phone and he was badly stressed. Mismanagement in one area can lead to mismanagement in another. Similar to that of time management, stress management requires the administrators to:

- Shift his/her attitudes and level of awareness;
- Self-analysis and identification of stresses via the daily stress log; and
- Practical techniques for managing stress.

Leaders/managers also could gain helpful insights from Allison's research in 1997, on the stress coping strategies employed by principals. He reports that principals who cope with stress maintain a realistic perspective, keep a positive attitude, adopt a good physical health regimen, and get involved in activities that promote intellectual, social and spiritual growth.

3.8 Managing Conflict

Gamage (1998c) states that in spite of the fact that conflict is an inevitable part of human experience, for most people, conflict has a negative connotation. Indeed, many situations involving conflict are disturbing and stressful to the participants and observers alike. However, conflict can also be a source of creativity and constructive action and can be a valuable source of organizational renewal. It exists at many levels and takes different forms. Conflict is inherent in the roles played by most educational administrators. It is important for the administrators, especially in the case of schools, not to seek the elimination of all conflict. Instead, they should attempt to manage conflict in a proper and positive perspective. This conforms to what Burton (1990) refers to as "Conflict Prevention," which is defined as doing something about problems before they cause [dysfunctional] conflicts.

Schmidt and Tannebaum (1972) identifies the following stages of conflict development:

- Anticipation — for example, a manager knows of an impending change and projects its consequences.
- Conscious but unexpressed difference — word leaks out about the change, and a feeling of tension begins to build in the organization.
- Discussion — information is formally presented about the change and different opinions begin to emerge.
- Open dispute — differences become more sharply and explicitly defined.
- Open conflict — each disputant tries to force his or her view on the others. The only possible outcomes now possible are win/lose solution or compromise.

Lippitt (1983) lists both the negative and positive effects of a conflict as follows:

Negative Effects
- Diverts energy from the task at hand
- Destroys morale
- Polarizes individuals and groups
- Deepens differences
- Obstructs cooperative action
- Produces irresponsible behaviour
- Creates suspicion and distrust
- Decreases productivity.

Positive Effects
- Opens up an issue in a confronting manner
- Develops clarification of an issue
- Increases involvement
- Improves problem solving quality
- Provides more spontaneity in communication
- Is needed for growth
- Strengthens a relationship when creatively resolved.

Techniques for Managing Conflict — There are many approaches to resolving conflicts, as there are different types of conflict. No one method or approach works best in all circumstances. It is important for administrators to be aware of all possible approaches and techniques enabling them to select the best in a given situation. Some of the techniques are:

- Avoiding conflict — most natural manner in which all animals including humans eliminate conflict is by avoiding it.
- Individualizing or compartmentalizing conflict.
- Creating super-ordinate goals: super-ordinate goals are popular because of their promise of "win-win" solutions.
- Creative problem solving — mutual problem solving is often the best means of resolving social conflict, which usually stems from communication problems.
- Compromise and use of a third party — compromise is probably the most widely used technique for resolving conflict, which can be generated internally in a problem solving session, or externally by a mediator or an arbitrator.
- Changes in organizational structure — conflict can often be managed by making changes in the organizational structure.
- Authoritative command — individuals in organizations with rare exceptions, recognizes and accepts the authority of their superiors.
- Finding common ground — especially in the context of public schools when there is a multiplicity of values, cultures and opinions finding common ground is the best way to resolve conflict (Adapted from Smith & Piele, 1997, pp. 394–400).

3.9 Different Expectations

School principals have at least six major reference groups — teachers, students, non-teaching staff, parents, local community and the district or regional office. Teachers expect the principal to be interested in what they do in their classrooms, by providing active support. Students, on the other hand, expect the principal to be interested in them as individuals and available to them if someone tries to deny them playground rights or cause other problems. Non-teaching staff expects the principal not to ignore their place within the school. Parents expect the principal to provide the best possible education for their children. The local community expect the principal to manage the school in such a fashion that teachers and students are orderly and do not leave messes to be cleaned up. The superiors from the district or regional office expect the principal to conform to departmental policies, in the organization of instructional programmes and in other areas, by keeping within the budgetary provisions (Sergiovanni & Carver, 1980). In this context, the modern approach of school-based management (SBM) is a very good compromise, as it provides a forum, where all relevant stakeholders can have their input to decision-making and policy formulation.

These different expectations sometimes run counter to one another. Administrators must strive to reconcile them, and in so doing, bring their own expectations to bear on each situation. In the struggle to find a resolution to these divergent expectations, administrators are likely to experience considerable stress.

Getzels and his colleagues (1968) have presented one of the more insightful treatments of the sources of conflict, and thus stress in organizations. Noted in that study are conflicts between cultural values and institutional expectations, role expectations and personality dispositions between roles and within roles, conflicts arising from personality disorders, and conflicts arising from the perception of role expectations. For instance, a school leader's choice between pursuing an advanced training programme (professional expectations) and the desire to spend extended periods of time with family, during the school holidays (personal dispositions) can be cited as a case in point. Perhaps, even more common is the conflict between the long hours of administrator's job and expectations of spouse and children, that he or she be a participant in family activities.

3.10 Power, Influence and Prestige

Such things as power, influence and prestige constitute the rewards of doing the job of an administrator. Power or authority, may either be vested or entrusted. Vested power is power derived from the official position that a person occupies. Principals and school administrators have some power by virtue of the positions they hold. Entrusted power, on the other hand, must be earned from the followers. When an administrator demonstrates breadth of knowledge and understanding, fairness, decision-making skills, and consideration for people, additional power accrues from the followers or from the staff working for him or her. New administrators who try to rely entirely on vested power are probably in line for some rude shocks, as staff cannot be pushed around as machines.

On the other hand, an administrator who goes to the other extreme and tries to be just a good gentleman or a lady and ignores the power of his or her office may also be in line for some shocks. It is likely, that some staff could take advantage of such kindness and not perform as expected.

Prestige is a psychological phenomenon; it exists only when people think it exists. Thus, those who look for prestige can find it in the administrative office due to the authority vested in such an office. Still another reward in administration is financial compensation. In most instances, administrators are paid higher salaries or hidden allowances, while enjoying various fringe benefits and other perks, which are not available to ordinary members of staff.

3.11 Accomplishment and Achievements of Others

Still another source of satisfaction for administrators is the feeling that they can get things done. Administrators are generally people of action and they find satisfaction in coordinating the work of an organization in such a way as to accomplish the organizational goals. Administrators are charged with creating the structures, procedures and processes, for making decisions, as well as, making the system work. Many groups are involved, data must be collected and organized, some assessment of the values and dispositions of those affected must be made, long range implications must be considered, recommendations must be formulated, and implementation plans must be developed. All of these activities can find fruition with the approval of a faculty board or school council. With such approval, the administrator could shift the focus from planning to implementation. For most administrators this process is rewarding.

Finally, administrators often find pleasure in fostering the achievement of others. It is the students who achieve in arts, in the sciences, athletics, and in other activities. But the administrators have so much to do with the daily regimen, which establishes the climate or atmosphere of a school, that they can claim partial credit and be proud of such student achievements. Administrators can also find satisfaction in teachers' achievements. Moreover, teacher achievement, like student achievement, comes mainly from internal motivation and not from external supervision. Recognition of potential and encouragement of greater service in the organization can and should bring satisfaction to the administrator.

3.12 Conclusion

This chapter examined the status of some of the school systems and the profession of educational administrators, including the very nature of their responsibilities and tasks. It also examined the importance of time and stress management, with discussions of common factors affecting both issues. The need for an administrator to develop strategies to minimize and avoid time wasters in order to have time for reflection and planning and the development of strategies for organizational self-renewal is also stressed in this chapter. It also raises the importance of avoiding stress and strain and the need to develop strategies to avoid stress, as it would lead to better decisions and development of a healthy organizational regimen. Then it examined the inevitable nature of conflict, different stages of development and how to manage conflict by taking appropriate steps, depending on the nature of the conflict and the circumstances. The interrelationship of time, stress and conflict management and how the mismanagement of one can lead to mismanagement of another is also emphasized. Finally, readers are reminded that if an effective administrator dealt with issues properly, s/he is likely to feel accomplished and satisfied.

3.13 Review Questions

1. Undertake a critical examination of the responsibilities and tasks of educational administrators in a given organizational context.
2. Discuss the importance of time, stress and conflict management in becoming an effective and accomplished administrator.

CHAPTER 4

Organizational Behaviour as a Management Perspective

4.0 Learning Outcomes

Based on a systematic study of this chapter, the readers will:

- Gain an understanding of organizational behaviour from a management perspective.
- Comprehend the main theoretical contributions made by scholars and how those concepts can be used in refining one's own practice in adapting to the changing needs of organizations.
- Recognize the importance of leadership styles in creating an appropriate organizational culture and management as integrating activities.
- Appreciate the complex nature of the behaviour of personnel (individuals and groups) within working organizations and the necessity of a healthy organizational climate and culture.

4.1 Focus

This topic examines the vital role that organizational behaviour plays in determining an organization's efficiency and effectiveness. It provides a general overview of the concept of organizational behaviour, specifically in terms of its relationship to management. The development of the concept of organizational behaviour is discussed, with an emphasis on its integration to both scientific and behavioural approaches. Various perspectives on the essential nature of organizations are presented and the factors, which influence organizational behaviour, are described. Importantly, the organization is viewed as a complex entity, within which interrelationships between behaviour and other variables occur.

4.2   What Is an Organization?

It is important to begin the study of organizational behaviour with an understanding of the nature of organizations. The organization of people into effective working groups has always been at the heart of the management process. In a simple definition, two or more persons can form an organization for the purpose of achieving a common goal or goals. Formal organizations have objectives, which are explicit, limited and announced. They are formed with a common purpose and require people to enter into formal relationships, which have some contractual basis. More specifically, organizations are formed to achieve aims and objectives, which are difficult to be achieved as individuals. The study of organizational behaviour can provide an insight into all types of organizations, whether they are private, public, business, industrial, educational, voluntary or mandatory.

Organizations exist as means of achieving goals through group efforts. Hence, organizations are mechanisms through which many people combine their efforts and work together to accomplish more than any one person can achieve on his/her own. In this context, the purpose of forming an organization is to utilize the talents and efforts of those involved to the fullest, and achieve outcomes that are beyond the reach of an individual.

4.3   What Do We Mean by Organizational Behaviour?

In the contemporary world, organizations play a significant and a continuing role in the lives of all human beings. People are born in and into organizations. They play, study, work and die in organizations as we live in an organizational world. Organizations are an essential part of our society and they serve many important needs. The decisions and actions of management have an increasing impact on individuals (both staff and customers) and the wider community. It is very important for the educational administrators to understand how organizations function and how they influence the behaviour of individuals and groups. This knowledge of human behaviour is useful in both daily operations and in the accomplishment of organizational goals.

Organizational Behaviour (OB) is the study of individuals and groups in organizations, including private, public or educational organizations. It has implications for the ways in which leaders and managers interact with and manage staff/employees in any working environment, while striving to improve organizational performance. Increasing attention has been focused on organizational behaviour since the release of the report *A Nation at Risk* by the National Commission on Excellence in Education of USA in 1983. William Ouchi's book *Theory Z* (1981) also contributes significantly to highlight the lack of international competitiveness of American business enterprises. *A Passion for Excellence* by Peters and Austin (1985), deals with similar concerns, whilst, *Karpin Report* (1995) takes a critical view of managerial competencies and practices in Australia. The tendency for decentralization and devolution in contemporary education, accompanied by an increasing emphasis on performance and accountability, necessitates the study of OB, to assist in dealing with the diverse and shifting demands of a modern society.

4.4 Evolution of Organizational Behaviour

The historical evolution of organizational behaviour can be traced back to ancient civilizations, such as Egyptian, Indus-Valley, Mesopotamian, Chinese and Sri Lankan, where archaeological excavations have revealed massive engineering works, requiring huge managerial responsibilities (Gamage, 1996b). The foundations of modern organizational behaviour however, are rooted in the efforts during and after the industrial revolution. The necessary impetus to systematic studies in OB was provided by such works as: Taylor's pig iron study in the early twentieth century, and his book *The Principles of Scientific Management*, of 1911 and Henry Fayol's *Principles of Management*, of 1916 (English translation in 1949). Mary Parker Follett's studies (Metcalf & Urwick, 1941) on the impact of psychology in human behaviour at work places added another dimension. Max Weber's notion of *bureaucracy* in 1925 (translated into English in 1947); Chester Barnard's *Functions of the Executive* of 1938; Elton Mayo's Hawthorn studies from 1927–1932 and the application of behavioural science approaches added further momentum. However, it was only in the late 1940s that OB emerged as a separate field of study.

Organizational Behaviour is an interdisciplinary body of knowledge that draws from a variety of other disciplines, to build its theoretical concepts about human behaviour within organizations. OB has strong ties to behavioural sciences, such as psychology, sociology and anthropology, as well as, economics and political science. OB promotes a better understanding of human behaviour in organizations, through its integration of insights from these diverse disciplines. Its applied focus, its contingency orientation, and its emphasis on scientific inquiry characterize OB. It is an applied scientific discipline, which attempts to answer practical questions, in particular contexts and situations. The ultimate aim of OB is to help people and organizations to achieve high performance levels, with better understanding of individuals and groups. It also seeks to understand how to lead an organization, to get the best out of its members, while establishing appropriate structures and processes, in order to motivate and energize organizational members, hence ensuring job satisfaction.

Organizational Behaviour does not assume that there is "one best way" to manage people and organizations. A contingency approach is encouraged using scientific methods to develop and test its generalizations empirically. OB emphasizes the need for systematic and controlled data collection processes; rigorous and careful testing of its explanations; and accepting only those explanations which can be scientifically verified.

4.5   The Need to Study International Organizational Behaviour

Francesco and Gold (1998) stress the importance of the study of organizational behaviour, with an international perspective. The forces of globalization and multinational corporatism stress the need to understand organizations in the context of the various societal cultures prevailing in the world (Walker & Dimmock, 2000). Studying international organizational behaviour brings three benefits: competitive advantage, organizational analysis, and analysis of culture. When organizational managers base their practices upon theories based on cultural explanations, provided by the study of international organizational behaviour, managing people whose cultural backgrounds are diverse is likely to improve. Competitive advantage is likewise enhanced when leaders/managers are aware of the technologies and practices of competitors. Studying international organizational behaviour also enables leaders/managers to discover potential partners for collaboration towards higher levels of effectiveness.

Since formal organizations pervade the contemporary society, doing systematic analysis of organizations promote the understanding of the social control and economic production mechanisms existing in different countries.

Data derived from organizational analysis serve as useful inputs in the adoption of more effective global management practices. Studying international organizational behaviour fuels a sense of intellectual curiosity about the cultures of other countries. When management techniques are examined, under specific conditions, an understanding of how people interact and relate to others can be gained and, thereby, can be put into practice

Vecchio and Norris (1996) point out that studying OB provides new insights into the human element of organizations, as well as, hastens the development of interpersonal effectiveness. The study of OB, likewise, provides an understanding of a range of organizational practices, which guide everyday decision-making of organizational leaders/managers. As argued by Dunford (1992), one acquires improved skills in analysing action in organizations by employing a range of perspectives, which are supplied by studying organizational behaviour.

4.6 Factors Influencing Behaviour in Organizations

The formal organization is a constantly changing network of interrelated activities, which makes it difficult to study the behaviour of people in isolation. It is necessary to understand the interrelationship between human behaviour and other variables, which together comprise the total organization. The study of OB considers the interaction of individuals and tasks within the formal structure, how the tasks are performed, the technology is employed and how these factors affect the organizational processes, the behaviour of people and the effects of the external environment. Thus, the individual, the group, the leadership, the organization and the environment, collectively influence behaviour in work places, which in turn affects OB.

The individual — Organizations are made up of individuals who work within them. The individual is the central feature of OB and a necessary part of any sort of behaviour in isolation, or as a member of a group, which in turn responds to organizational expectations, or to the influences of the external environment (Lam, 1989). It is the responsibility of the leader/ manager to have a good understanding of the individual members of the organization, especially, their personality, experiences, competencies, potential in order to provide opportunities to tap their full potential. Whenever individual needs and organizational expectations are incompatible, it could lead to conflicts and frustration. It is the responsibility of the leadership and/or management to provide a working environment, which accomplishes organizational goals while satisfying individual needs resulting in a healthy organizational climate leading to job satisfaction.

The group — Groups exist in all organizations and is essential to their operation and performance. Every member of an organization belongs to one or more groups. Organizing compatible and cohesive groups to work together, with complementary roles, in achieving the organizational goals, is again, a responsibility of the leadership and management. Informal groups meet social needs and can affect the behaviour and performance of group members as they interact with other individuals and groups, within the formal organizations. The structure and influences of informal groups add another dimension to OB. Good leadership should know how to achieve congruency between formal and informal organizational roles.

The organization — Individuals and groups interact within the structure of an organization. The organizational leadership and management direct the relations between individuals, groups and the organization, in order to accomplish the organizational goals. Leadership establishes the structures, procedures and processes for its effective operations. It is through the formal structure that staff carries out their duties and responsibilities towards the realization of the organizational aims and objectives.

Behaviour is affected by organizational structures, leadership styles, technology and the management system, through which, organizational procedures and processes are planned, directed and controlled. Organizational structure and design and systems of management impact on the behaviour of staff within an organization.

The environment — Organizations, particularly, the social organizations such as educational institutions, function as part of the broader community, or the external environment. The environment affects the organizations, through technological and scientific advancement, economic and social activity and government actions, as well as through the cultural influence of people who join the organization (Pang & Lam, 2000).

Effective operation depends on how the organization achieves its goals and objectives, and how it takes risks and how it responds to opportunities. The rate of change in environmental factors, in addition to increasing societal demands, highlights the need to study the approaches and processes through which the organization operates.

These different dimensions provide contrasting, but related, approaches to the understanding of human behaviour in organizations. These factors present a number of alternative pathways for the study and analysis of OB. One of the alternatives is to adopt a psychological approach, focusing on the individuals within the organization. But, such an approach is too narrow, as it isolates the individual from the organizational setting. Another alternative is to adopt a sociological approach, which is concerned with a broader emphasis on human behaviour in society. Yet, such an approach also limits a thorough understanding of OB. Fish and Wood (1997) emphasize the importance of cross cultural management competence in societies such as Australia.

4.7 A Behavioural Science Approach to OB

There is broad agreement that a study of OB cannot be undertaken entirely in terms of a single discipline. The term "behavioural science" originally encompassed all social sciences concerned with the study of the behaviour of people. Now, it is more frequently used to refer to attempts in which a selective, interdisciplinary approach is applied to the study of human behaviour. In this context, the study of behaviour is viewed in terms of three main disciplines — psychology, sociology and anthropology. It is also evident that economics, political science, and cultural systems have influenced the development of OB.

Psychologists are concerned with the study of human behaviour, with traits of individuals, and with individuals as members of social groups. Focus is on the whole person (personality system), including individual perceptions, attitudes and motives.

Sociologists are more concerned with the study of social behaviour, relationships among social groups and societies, and the maintenance of order and discipline. Here, the main focus is on social structures and positions, especially the behaviour of leaders and followers.

Anthropologists are concerned with studying the science of mankind and human behaviour as a whole. Here, the main focus is on cultural systems, including the values, belief patterns, customs and ideas within a group or society, and the comparison of behaviour among different cultures. Most people depend on their culture to provide security and stability.

Contributions from psychology, sociology and anthropology help us to better understand behaviour within organizations. Behavioural science attempts to structure organizations for the purpose of securing a healthier working environment. It endeavours to reconcile the expectations of an organization to maximize productivity, meets the needs of members of the organization and encourages them to realize their full potential. The focus is on psychological and sociological concepts and practices, as well as cultural influences on organizational and managerial problems in organizational situations. Most rational decisions are based on some form of theory, while theory contains a message as to how a leader and/or manager needs to behave in a given situation. Receptiveness to theory can lead to changes in attitudes, which in turn leads to changes in actual behaviour. Theory contributes to the development of generalized models within a wide application, and conceptual frameworks, which provide a perspective for practical study of the subject.

4.8   Contrasting Perspectives of Organizations

Organizations are complex social systems, which can be defined and studied in a number of different ways. Morgan (1997) has provided a broader perspective on the nature of organizations and OB. He identifies eight different approaches to organizations, using metaphors. According to Morgan the following metaphors are descriptive of an organization:

Machine,	Political system,
Organism,	Psychic prison,
Brain,	Flux and Transformation,
Culture,	An Instrument of Domination.

Machine — In this approach, an organization is viewed as an efficient entity, which operates in a routine and predictable way. An organization is necessarily bureaucratic in nature and provides form, continuity and security. It may also have negative characteristics, which are likely to limit the development of human capacities. A "machine" is more likely to thrive in a stable and protected environment.

Organism — An organization is viewed as a living organism or a system. As the biological system adapts to changing environments, the organization needs to adapt to changes in the environment in which it exists, by appropriate restructuring. An "organism" exists in an open systems and turbulent, dynamic environments.

Brain — An organization is seen as rational and inventive. Depending on the type of organizational structure instituted, an organization promotes flexibility, creativity and autonomy.

Culture — An organization is a complex system, which is characterized by its own unique philosophy, values, belief patterns, rituals, heroes and practices. It is evident that the organizational culture affects the behaviour of those who function within it (Hofstede, 1993).

Political System — An organization is intrinsically political. This is based on the interaction of authority and power, and how they are influenced by superordinate and subordinate relationships.

Psychic Prison — An organization and its members become constrained by their shadows or "psychic prison" and get trapped by constructions of reality. Because of particular values and belief patterns, which influence organizational culture, viewing them as psychic prisons provides an understanding of the reality and illusions of organizational behaviour.

Flux and Transformation — An organization exists in a state of constant flux and transformation, and this is more so in the contemporary world, due to the rapid advances in technology. To understand the social life of an organization, one needs to understand the logistics of transformation and change.

Instrument of Domination — An organization is associated with the processes of social domination, where individuals and groups impose their will on others. In most organizations, small groups wield so much power and authority, they impose their decisions on the large majority of others, who have no option but to conform. Here, an organization is best understood as variations in the mode of social domination and control of their members.

4.9 Organizational Effectiveness

Every organization aims to be effective by accomplishing its set goals. The survival of an organization depends on its success in the achievement of the set goals and objectives. Gauging the effectiveness or the success of an organization is a complicated and complex issue (Cheng, 1996). The criteria for measuring success may differ from one type of organization to another. It becomes more complex in the case of public organizations, particularly educational institutions. Unlike in business and industry, realization of set goals of an organization is not easy to measure and takes a much longer period to make a proper judgement.

Studying successful organizations in Japan and America for a period of ten years, Ouchi (1981) observes that productivity is achieved through the effective management of people and influenced by their involvement and their commitment to stay with the organization. Effective human relations within the workplace and efficient management necessarily coexist.

4.10 Orientations to Work

In an examination of the inner workings of an organization, it is clear that staff members differ in the manner and the extent of their involvement with work. In a study undertaken by Goldthorpe, Lockwood, Bechhofer, and Platt (1968), involving 200 manual workers from three different firms, they suggest that responses to work resulted largely from the individual's orientation to work, and identified three types of orientation to work, i.e. instrumental, bureaucratic and solidaristic.

The workers with an *instrumental orientation* defined work not as a central life issue, but in terms of a means to an end. There was an economic consideration with work and a clear distinction between work-related and non–work-related activities. The workers with a *bureaucratic orientation* considered work as a central life issue. There was a sense of obligation to work and a positive involvement, in terms of a career structure, with a close linkage between work-related and non–work-related activities. The workers with *solidaristic orientation* considered work situations in terms of group activities. There was ego involvement with work groups, and group loyalties were high rather than to the organization. Work was more than just a means to an end, while non-work activities were linked to the work-related activities. Goldthorpe and associates suggest that some people who are intrinsically motivated may have a set orientation to work, irrespective of the nature of the work environment. Different work situations also influence the individual's orientation to work.

4.11 Managerial Responsibility in Integrating Staff within the Organization

Irrespective of the individual's orientation to work, it is management that is responsible for the coordination, guidance and direction of staff efforts towards the realization of organizational goals. In this context, management can be considered as the cornerstone of organizational effectiveness, and is responsible for the execution of organizational decisions as well as the institution and implementation of organizational processes. If the management is not effective and breeds nepotism, does not recognize or reward good contributions and provide opportunities to tap staff potential, then it could lead competent staff to withdraw active support and might result in status-quo. Peter Drucker (1954) emphasizes that it is management that enables an organization to contribute to societal advancement, the economy and the individual. A successful leader and/or a manager must possess the competency to manage, develop and lead people effectively. S/he should be competent in human and social skills, and have the ability to work with, and through, other people to achieve organizational goals. It is important to remember that every action and document in an organizational setting is the work of people.

It is the responsibility of management to get things done through other members of the staff. This involves treating staff as individual human beings and not as extensions of the machines, as was done in the past during the era of efficiency. Unlike physical and financial resources, human resources are not owned by the organization. The leaders/managers should not try to control its human resources but to develop, motivate, energize and tap its potential in the best interests of the organization and the staff. Staff brings their own perceptions, feelings and attitudes towards the organization. This can be influenced by systems and styles of leadership and management, as well as, the duties and responsibilities assigned and working conditions. Conflicts, informal groups and unofficial work practices are inevitable within organizational settings. Human behaviour is influenced by many factors, most of which are hard to identify and even harder to measure and control.

Figure 4.1 depicts the complex combination of individual, social and cultural factors that influence the patterns of human behaviour. It is believed that a vast majority of people joins organizations with expectations of performing their jobs competently. When actual performance fails to match

Figure 4.1   Role of Management as an Integrating Activity

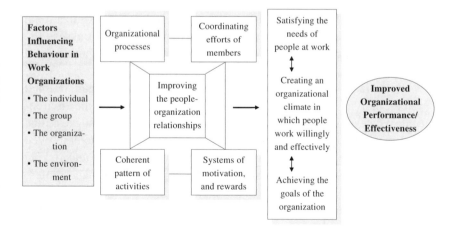

(Source: Adapted from Mullins, 1999, p. 22)

expectations, it may impact on the individual's perceptions of management and the management function.

Most industrial issues arise not so much from what management does, but the manner in which it is done. Often, it is the manner of implementation, which is the cause of staff unrest and dissatisfaction. For example, staff may agree on the need to introduce reforms to improve their performance, and through that, the organizational efficiency, but, may feel resentment towards lack of consultation, pre-planning, intransigence, and ineffective communication in servicing the implementation of reforms. A heavy responsibility falls on leaders and/or managers to create the appropriate work environments, systems of motivation, rewards and job satisfaction. They must endeavour to create a healthy organizational climate and culture, which is conducive to staff participation and commitment. Leaders and managers should encourage staff participation and involvement, with frank expression of their views and opinions on issues affecting the organization, to ensure their commitment for implementation. It should be remembered, however, that staff is unlikely to express their views and opinions on vital issues, unless, they feel that the management is receptive and appreciative of such views. Guidance can be found in McGregor's (1960) Theories X and Y, Likert's (1967) Systems 1–4 and Ouchi's (1981) Theory Z, in terms of adapting their leadership or managerial style to suit the context, situation and the maturity levels of staff.

4.12 Diagnosing Organizations

Management scholars agree that the first step in solving organizational problems or increasing organizational effectiveness is to assess the organization's current state. This assessment is called organizational diagnosis.

Organizational Diagnosis may focus on the whole organizational system, individuals, groups, leadership, power relations and the environment. Whatever is the focus of the diagnosis, Harrison (1994) suggests that the diagnostic process, methods and interpretations must be employed objectively. In addition, there are dilemmas that confront those undertaking the diagnosis. These dilemmas may be about goals, politics and professionalism.

The goal dilemma may involve the choice between the pursuit of modest objectives that can be achieved immediately, and ambitious aims that entail more effort and risk. The politics of the organization may involve the choice between the search for benefits for all or for a favoured or chosen few. The professionalism dilemma may involve a choice between maintaining strict professional standards or catering to the personal needs and interests of a few.

4.13 The Importance of Psychological Contract

A key foundation of harmonious relations, between the individual and the organization, is the concept of psychological contract. Even though it is not part of the employment contract, there is a process of giving and receiving by the employee and the organization, which relates to rights, privileges, duties and obligations, that in turn influence the behaviour of organizational members.

When an individual joins an organization, s/he may expect the organization to:

- Provide safe and healthy working conditions;
- Make every reasonable effort to provide job security;
- Provide satisfying and challenging jobs;
- Adopt equitable personnel policies and procedures;
- Allow staff genuine participation in decisions which affect them;
- Provide reasonable opportunities for career advancement;
- Treat staff with respect; and
- Demonstrate an understanding and accommodating attitude, towards personal problems, wherever possible.

These expectations can be considered as a social responsibility of management. Similarly, the organization will also have implicit expectations of staff, expecting them to achieve a high degree of congruency between their individual goals and organizational goals. Staff is expected to:

- Accept the organizational philosophy or ideology;
- Work diligently towards the realization of organizational objectives and goals;
- Not to abuse goodwill shown by the leadership and/or management;
- Uphold the reputation of the organization;
- Show loyalty; and
- Not to betray positions of trust (Adapted from Mullins, 1999, p. 12).

At times, organizations may place emphasis on expectations, requirements, and constraints, which often differ from, and may be in conflict with, the expectations of the staff. However, congruency between organizational and individual goals and expectations can influence the willingness of staff to stay with an organization, and of the organization to continue to employ them.

4.14 Interrelatedness of Management and OB

The activities of an organization and the job of management cannot be isolated and treated in separate categories. The majority of actions are likely to involve a number of simultaneous functions that relate to the total processes of management. For instance, think of a situation where a leader or manager briefs staff on an unexpected, urgent and important task. The action could include elements of the organization's mission and goals, organizational structure, management systems, process of delegation, systems of communication, motivation, leadership styles and managerial control systems. The behaviour of the staff can be influenced by a combination of individuals, groups, and organizational and environmental factors. This makes it difficult to consider the topics studied in OB as separate entities.

Any study of organizations and management covers multiple aspects, whilst, each study can be used to confirm generalizations made about specific topic areas. The absence of one right answer can make the study of OB complex and frustrating. But this area of study also can be interesting, challenging and stimulating. It can provide innovative ideas and actions relating to our own work experiences. The open systems approach views the organization within its broader, external environment, and places emphasis on multiple channels of interaction. It provides a means of viewing the organization as a whole, and of embracing different dimensions of analysis. The open systems model provides a perspective for a managerial approach to OB. It helps us to search for the most appropriate ways of influencing the behaviour of individuals and groups within an organization.

4.15 How Could Management Practices Lead to Improved Performance?

OB is concerned not only with employee and staff behaviour, but also, the behaviour of the leaders and/or managers. The values and beliefs that are embedded in the organizational culture, and more specifically, the assumptions about the nature of human beings, influence managerial behaviour. Effective managers know how to motivate and energize individuals and groups through empowerment in order to improve their performance, thus enabling them to experience job satisfaction. The creation of opportunities to tap individual and group potential forms the basis of this empowerment. Often, they do this by employing the management processes of planning, organizing, leading and controlling the use of organizational resources to achieve high performance. These management processes apply to any organizational setting, whether it is a private, public, business or an educational institution. An organization is unlikely to successfully achieve its desired goals, if the leader/manager does not possess the necessary skills and competency required for the planning, organizing, leading and controlling of the organizational resources (Wood et al., 1998).

On the basis of their research, Mintzberg, Raisinghani, and Theoret (1976) have concluded that a manager's job in any organization is a busy and demanding one. A working week of at least 50 hours is not uncommon, in larger and complex organizations up to 90 hours is often the case. Depending on the position held in the hierarchy, and responsibilities entrusted and the working week is likely to be shorter or longer. Depending on how higher is one's position within a hierarchy, and more intense the workload becomes, on any given day, requiring a wider skill base. Often, they have to work without breaks, sometimes having to participate at lunch and dinner working sessions. Mintzberg (1973) has identified three key roles, played by a leader/manager. These are:

- Interpersonal roles — working directly with other people, playing the sub-roles of figurehead, leader and liaison.
- Informational roles — exchanging information with other people, playing the sub-roles of monitor, disseminator and spokesperson.
- Decision roles — making decisions that affect other people, playing the sub-roles of entrepreneur, disturbance handler, resources allocator and negotiator.

In order to be an effective leader/manager, a person needs to develop the appropriate skills and competencies. A skill can be defined as an ability to translate one's knowledge and understanding into action strategies that lead to desired performance. It is an ability that enables a person to achieve superior performance in one or more aspects of his or her position. Robert Katz (1974) has categorized managerial skills into three areas: (1) Technical skills — ability to perform specialized tasks; (2) Human skills — the ability to work well with other people; and (3) Conceptual skills — ability to analyse and solve complex problems. Technical skills enable a leader/ manager to apply specialized knowledge and expertise to plan the strategies to perform the job, with a high degree of success. Human skills enable a leader/manager to work well with people, to get the best out of them, with a spirit of trust and empowerment, to enthuse and energize staff with a genuine involvement in interpersonal relationships. Conceptual skills enable them to view the organization as a whole and solve problems for the benefit of everyone concerned, including the organization. This depends on one's mental capacities to diagnose and analyse the problems, opportunities and threats, to gather and interpret the relevant data and make good decisions. The development of these three skills is more relevant and important to the higher level leaders and managers.

What is managerial competency? Competency could be defined as the underlying characteristic of a person (i.e. ability and skills), which enables him/her to perform in a particular area, in an exemplary manner with superior performance and greater effectiveness. Competency can be based on a sound knowledge and understanding of the relevant theoretical concepts and best practices, and the ability to develop technical, human and conceptual skills in translating them into appropriate practice, combined with experience in effectively facing possible challenges.

4.16 Conclusion

In a competitive environment, which demands efficiency and productivity, an understanding of organizational behaviour can assist the organizational leaders and managers in dealing with diverse pressures. Its emphasis on human behaviour in the workplace provides the key to organizational effectiveness. Whilst, organizations were initially studied in terms of improving efficiency, it was the recognition of human behaviour, in achieving efficiency, that gave impetus to a formal theory of organizational behaviour. Organizational behaviour is based on an integration of scientific and behavioural approaches, thus, allowing a number of alternative pathways, through which it can be studied and analysed.

Organizations are viewed as complex social systems, within which behaviour is influenced by various interrelationships between individuals, groups and the environment. Leaders and managers have a specific responsibility in ensuring that these interrelationships are coordinated in the pursuit of common goals. They also need to be aware of the roles they play in determining organizational effectiveness, through the creation of appropriate work environments and a culture of achievement and vitality. Finally, the leaders and/or managers require not only an understanding of the concept of organizational behaviour, but the range of technical, human and conceptual skills needed to effectively influence that behaviour.

4.17 Review Questions

1. Explain your understanding of organizational behaviour and how it was developed as a separate field of study.
2. Discuss the role of management as an integrating activity in an organizational setting. Express your views on managerial responsibility and how it should be exercised.

CHAPTER 5

Organizational Climate and Culture

5.0 Learning Outcomes

Based on a systematic study of this chapter, the readers will:

- Understand the concepts of organizational climate and culture, including their definitions;
- Understand their importance and relevance to organizational life;
- Distinguish the main characteristics of organizational climate and culture and the relationship of one to the other; and
- Develop the skills needed to improve the organizational climate and culture, using the knowledge and understanding gained.

5.1 Focus

In organizational behaviour, a number of perspectives compete for the attention of scholars and practitioners. The most well known ones are structural, human, political and cultural. These reflect concerns for efficiency, relations, politics and meanings in managing organizations. Most practitioners realize the importance of an organizational climate, and how it affects organizational effectiveness. The cultural perspective is the most recent view of theory and practice. Underlying the cultural perspective is the concept of community, and the importance of shared meanings and values. The organizational culture refers to the character of an organization, as it reflects deep patterns of values, beliefs, and traditions that have been formed over the course of its development. Beneath the conscious awareness of everyday life, there is a stream of thought, sentiment and activity that affects organizational life. Organizational climate refers to the surface feelings and relations with the organization, while the culture refers to what is embedded in organizational life, including values, beliefs, heroes, rituals and stories build over a period of time. This chapter provides a fairly comprehensive understanding of these concepts and how they can be employed to improve organizational effectiveness.

5.2 The Need to Understand the Concept of Organizational Culture

Any leader/manager who needs to improve the organizational effectiveness of his/her institution should be able to diagnose the organizational climate and culture. After recognizing the strengths and weaknesses of the organizational climate and culture, necessary steps should be taken to effect the changes to create a positive and healthy working environment. Perhaps, the assumptions and belief patterns relating to human beings, as well as, interpersonal relations, group dynamics and leadership styles need to be changed. The leader should discard the old assumptions of controlling the staff, instead looking up to the staff as a resource to be empowered, developed, energized and lead, thus, creating a whole new organizational culture. The latest and the most controversial approach is the cultural perspective (Sergiovanni & Corbally, 1984; Deal & Peterson, 1990). It is the most recent view of theory and practice amongst the four approaches and the view is likely to receive more attention in the near future. This view looks to phenomenology, symbolic-interactionism, anthropology, ecology, and critical theory as relevant scholarly traditions (Geertz, 1973; Louis 1985; Westoby, 1988).

Underlying the cultural perspective is the concept of community and the importance of shared meanings and values (Pettigrew, 1979; Deal and Kennedy, 1982; Sathe, 1983; Schein, 1992; Erickson, 1987; Pang, 1995). Leadership effectiveness is not viewed merely as the instrumental summation of the link between behaviour and objectives. Instead, the objective of leadership is the stirring of human consciousness, the interpretation and enhancement of meanings, the articulation of key cultural strands, and the linking of organizational members to these concepts (Sergiovanni, 1984).

The notion of organizational culture re-surfaced in the early 1980s. During these years, a trend in the study of organizational culture was created.

Undoubtedly, this trend began with Ouchi's (1981) book, *Theory Z*, which examined the challenges that Japan posed for American industry. The trend continued with Deal and Kennedy's (1982) book, *Corporate Cultures*, which focused more closely on American industry itself, and reached an early peak, with Peters and Waterman's (1982) book, *In Search of Excellence*, which perhaps best exemplified this trend. Afterwards, much attention has been focused on the culture of an organization as a significant component towards reaching excellence.

The concept of culture is meant to describe the character of a school or an organization, as it reflects deep patterns of values, beliefs, and traditions that have been formed over the course of its development. Beneath the conscious awareness of everyday life in any organization, there is a stream of thoughts, sentiments, and activities, which influence the culture. This invisible, taken-for-granted, flow of beliefs and assumptions give meaning to what people say and do. It shapes how they interpret hundreds of daily transactions. This deeper structure of life in organizations is reflected and transmitted through symbolic language and expressive action. It is a culture that consists of the stable, underlying social meanings, which over time shape beliefs and behaviour.

The instances of practice in the contemporary world are constantly and continuously turbulent. Traditionally accepted management theory and techniques are inadequate when school principals deal with increasingly complex tasks. Most principals find themselves entangled with conflicts of values, goals, purposes and interests. Gamage (1996b), in referring to the complexity, uncertainty, instability, uniqueness and value of conflicts, inherent in organizational practices in the past, suggests that it is necessary for school principals to employ new strategies and leadership styles in facing these new challenges.

Sergiovanni (1984) describes leadership, metaphorically, as a set of five forces available to school administrators, supervisors, and teachers as they set about influencing what goes on in their schools (Sergiovanni, 1984). He refers to the five leadership forces: such as, technical, human, educational, symbolic and cultural. But he points out that some of these forces have received too much attention in comparison with others. He argues that the vital component of leadership activity is the meaning the leaders communicate to their colleagues. He provides a valuable insight, into the dynamics of leadership, enabling school principals to act as culture builders in order to create conditions within which the beliefs and value systems of the school, and their visions, are accepted and encouraged.

5.3 Definitions of Organizational Culture

The concept of culture is not new, as "cultural anthropology" has been a focus of study for many years (Geertz, 1973). Within organizations researchers have focused on a related notion of "organization climate", for decades (Halpin and Croft, 1962; Likert, 1967; Litwin and Stringer, 1968; Tagiuri and Litwin, 1968). As culture is a complex and dynamic phenomenon, it is not easy to define. Kroeber and Kluckhohn (1952) find 164 different definitions of culture. Smircich (1983) points out that the concept of culture in organizations has been borrowed from anthropology, where there is no consensus on its meaning. Despite the cautionary attitude adopted in defining the concept, she suggests that the usual elements of most definitions depict it as the:

> ... Social or normative glue that holds an organization together ... it expresses the values or social ideals and the beliefs that organization members come to share ... Symbolic devices such as myths ... ritual ... stories ... legend ... and specialized language ... manifest these values or patterns of belief (1983, p. 344).

Thus it is not surprising that definitions of the concept are almost as numerous as the researchers engaged in its study. The definitions range from simple to complex, with no single definition acceptable to all researchers. The following definitions of organizational culture are widely accepted:

> Culture is the system of such publicly and collectively accepted meanings operating for a given group at a given time. This system of terms, forms, categories, and images interprets a people's own situation to themselves (Pettigrew, 1979, p. 574).

> The organizational culture consists of a set of symbols, ceremonies, and myths that communicate the underlying values and beliefs of that organization to its employees (Ouchi, 1981, p. 41).

> The elements of that make up a strong culture are those as environment, values, heroes, the rites and rituals, and the cultural network ... A strong culture is a system of informal rules that spells out how people are to behave most of the time ... A strong culture enables people to feel better about what they do, so they are more likely to work harder (Deal & Kennedy, 1982, pp. 13–17).

> A pattern of basic assumptions invented, discovered or developed by a given group as it learns to cope with its problems of external adaptation and internal

integration that has worked well enough to be considered valid, and to be taught to new members as the correct way to perceive, think, and feel in relation to these problems (Schein, 1992, p. 12).

Thus, it is clear that there is no universally accepted definition, and the preceding definitions cannot be neatly collapsed into a composite one. The organizational culture perspective has focused on the basic values, beliefs, and assumptions that are present in organizations. The patterns of behaviour that result from these shared meanings, and the symbols that express the links between assumptions, values, and behaviour to an organization's members, could be considered as the organizational culture. The organizational culture concept is, thus, generally seen as a phenomenon, which can permeate the operations of the entire organization.

Indeed, culture is a deep phenomenon. It is complex and difficult to understand, but the effort to understand it is worthwhile, because much of the mysterious and irrational norms in organizations suddenly become clearer when it is understood. Culture is a deeper level of basic assumptions and beliefs that are shared by members of an organization. These operate unconsciously in a "taken-for-granted" fashion of the organization's view of itself and its environment.

5.4 Levels of Organizational Culture

One way to grasp the essence of organizational culture is to view culture at different levels. Schein (1992) has summarized, from various typological studies of cultures, a model of levels of organizational culture. He proposes an operational definition of organizational culture that appears to be gaining acceptance from other researchers, scholars and readers. He presents a model: "levels of culture", which is helpful for sorting through some of the conflicting viewpoints arising from different definitions of organizational culture. The levels of culture as defined by Schein are shown in Figure 5.1.

The most tangible and observable level is that of norms as manifested in what people say, how people behave, and how things get done. Verbal norms include the language systems that are used, stories that are told, and examples that are used to illustrate certain important points. Behavioural norms are manifested in the ceremonies and rituals and other symbolic practices of the organization. Though these manifestations are readily visible, they are merely symbolic of the culture itself, which is not visible and which is not even in the awareness of the people we observe. To make

Figure 5.1   Schein's Model of Levels of Organizational Culture

Artifacts and Creation
Technology, Art, Visible and Audible
Behaviour Patterns
e.g. Support your colleagues;
Don't criticize the principal;
Handle your own discipline problems;
Be available to give students extra help;
Get to know your colleagues.

Visible but often
not decipherable

Values
Testable in the physical environment
Testable only by social consensus
e.g. Openness, Trust, Cooperation,
Intimacy, Teamwork

Greater level of
awareness

Basic Assumptions
Relationship to environment
Nature of truth and reality
Nature of human nature
Nature of human activity
Nature of human relationships

Taken for granted
invisible
preconscious

(Source: Adapted from Schein, 1992, p. 17; and Hoy & Miskel, 2001, p. 177)

sense of these norms and the behaviour, it is necessary for us to decipher their meaning.

The next level is that of values. Values are the shared conceptions of what is desirable. They refer to the shared rules and norms to which people respond, the commonness that exists among solutions to similar problems, how people define the situations they face, and what constitutes the boundaries of acceptable and unacceptable behaviour. Schein states that they reflect someone's sense of what "ought" to be, as distinct from what "is". Values provide the basis for people to judge or evaluate the situations they face, the worth of actions and activities, their priorities, and the behaviour of people with whom they work. Shared values define the basic character of the organization and give the organization a sense of identity. Sometimes values are encoded in written language such, as "mission statement", or a statement of philosophy.

The above categories provide researchers with a useful analytical framework with which to search for patterns amongst different underlying assumptions of groups, and allow them to identify the paradigms with which the members of a group perceive, think about, feel about, and judge situations and relationships. At the least, this paradigm framework enables one to answer, systematically, whether or not real consensus exists among group members, in certain areas.

Underneath the values and artifacts are the basic assumptions. They are more abstract than each of the other levels, as they are typically tacit and implicit. These assumptions deal with what the people in the organization accept as true in the world and what is false, what is feasible and not feasible. People in organizations are usually unaware of them. They are tacit, unconsciously taken for granted, not talked and discussed, and mostly accepted as truth and principles.

Schein (1992) has summarized, from various typological studies of cultures, five categories of basic underlying assumptions around which cultural paradigm is formed. Dyer (1985) modifies these categories created by Schein, and makes them simpler and applicable to organizational studies. These categories are useful in research and provide a framework for analysis, as they can be used to build coherent patterns of core organizational beliefs.

5.5 A Comparison of Organizational Culture and Climate

The roots of the climate concept can be considered Lewinian. Lewin (1951) states that the concept of behaviour as the product of individuals acting in given contexts providing the basic metaphor and conceptual framework for climate research. The use of the term organizational climate, and elaboration of this principle in organizational research, began with the study completed by Halpin and Croft in 1962. Almost all researchers presented formulations that specified a number of dimensions of organizational climate.

Halpin and Croft define organizational climate as follows:

> The organization climate can be construed as the organizational "personality" of a school; figuratively, "personality" is to the individual what "climate" is to the organization (1962, p. 1).

To assess the school climate, Halpin and Croft developed a descriptive questionnaire (with a final set of sixty-four items), called Organizational Climate Description Questionnaire (OCDQ). Using statistical techniques and factor analysis, the sixty-four items were grouped into eight factors. Four of the factors referred to the characteristics of the faculty group, and four described various components of the teacher-principal interaction. These eight clusters of items were named the eight dimensions of school climate. They then used the scores of the eight dimensions of OCDQ to identify six basic school climates, which are arrayed along a rough continuum: open, autonomous, controlled, familiar, paternal, and closed. In the years following its publication, the OCDQ has been widely used as a measure of school climate. However, it has at least two weaknesses:

- Since OCDQ was originally developed in a sample of elementary schools, the open-to-closed continuum, or the prototypes of organizational climate, may not be applicable to secondary schools.
- Halpin and Croft's conceptualization of organizational climate was narrowly limited to the behavioural relationships between principals and teachers, and between teachers and teachers, whereas, the relationships between teachers and pupils, as well as, between pupils and pupils were ignored.

Different researchers have proposed different perspectives in the conceptualization of school climate. While Halpin and Croft (1962) perceive school climate as the behavioural relationship between principals and teachers, Likert and Likert (1976) perceive it as different management styles, which comprise four systems ranged on a continuum. These are:

- Exploitative authoritative (System 1);
- Benevolent authoritative (System 2);
- Consultative (System 3); and
- Participatory (System 4).

The organizational health of a school is another framework for conceptualizing the general atmosphere of a school. In Hoy and Feldman's (1987) study, organizational profiles of schools were assessed in terms of seven dimensions: institutional integrity, managerial level, consideration, initiating structure, resource support, technical level and academic emphasis. More recently, the emphasis in school climate research has shifted from a management orientation to a student orientation. This perspective focuses upon teacher-pupil relations, rather than upon principal-teacher relations. Willower and his associates (1973) describe pupil control as existing along a continuum from humanistic to custodial. On the other hand, instead of measuring the pupil control ideology and behaviour of teachers, Pang (1992) measures the school climate directly on aspects of school life with respect to discipline. In his study, the school discipline climate was evaluated, compared and predicted on a continuum, in terms of a positive-negative typology. Thus, organizational climate may have many different facets in schools, and they are the visible and tangible artifacts. No one conceptualization could capture the complete picture of organizational climate in schools. The conceptualization of organizational climate is determined by how and in what way it is defined.

Tagiuri and Litwin offer the following conceptual definition:

> Organizational climate is a relatively enduring quality of the internal environment of an organization that (a) is experienced by its members, (b) influences their behavior, and (c) can be described in terms of the values of a particular set of characteristics or attitudes of the organization (1968, p. 27).

Hellriegel and Slocum (1974) also contend that organizational climate refers to a set of attributes, which can be perceived about a particular organization and/or its subsystems, and that may be induced from the way that an organization and/or its subsystems deals with these members and environment. Further, Brookover and his colleagues (1981, p. 19) refer to school climate as the "composite of norms, expectations, and beliefs, which characterize the school social system as perceived by members of the social system". Ellis (1988, p. 1) defines climate as "the aggregate of indicators, both subjective and objective, that convey the overall feeling or impression one gets about a school". These typical definitions of organizational climate seem to be mainly sets of shared perceptions of behavioural norms and attributes of an organization.

As these sample definitions indicate, the meaning of school climate varies in range and focus. Halpin and Croft (1962) and Ellis (1988) describe the climate in global terms, whereas, the others use climate synonymously with culture (Tagiuri and Litwin, 1968; Hellriegel and Slocum, 1974; Brookover et al. 1981). The definition issue is further complicated, when some scholars use the term without defining it, or use it interchangeably with such other terms as atmosphere, environment, ethos, milieu, setting, or context (Anderson, 1982).

However, contemporary researchers focus mainly on the primacy of the culture of an organization in defining the character and quality of the climate. Even though the definitions of organizational climate and culture may be diverse, Cheng (1989) believes that, to a certain extent, there is consensus that organizational culture is a system of shared assumptions, beliefs, values, and behaviours in an organization. According to Dyer (1985) and Schein (1992), culture should have three different levels: shared assumptions, values and norms (overt attitudes and behaviour) arranged from abstract to concrete and from deep to superficial.

From the definitions provided by Halpin and Croft (1962), Tagiuri and Litwin (1968), Hellriegel and Slocum (1974), organizational climate seems to be mainly a set of shared perceptions of behavioural norms and attributes of an organization. If we agree with the above concepts, we can see an important difference between organizational culture and organizational climate. Climate is a set of overt, perceptible, and behavioural norms, but culture may be multi-levelled, including implicit assumptions, beliefs and values and also explicit behavioural norms. In other words, organizational climate seems to be the overt part of organizational culture, partly reflecting the implicit assumptions, beliefs and values shared among members. This relationship between organizational culture and organizational climate is illustrated in Figure 5.2.

From the works of the different scholars referred to above, a comparison between organizational culture and organizational climate has conceptual considerations and has a reciprocal relationship. It could be summarized as follows.

Figure 5.2 Relations between Organizational Culture and Climate

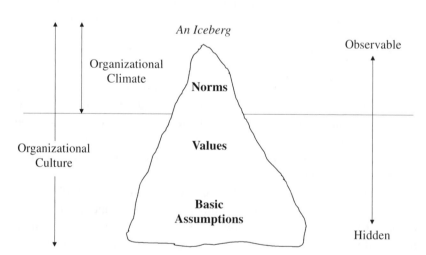

Climate is broadly defined as the shared perception of "the way things are around here". It is a concept that is indicative of the organization's goals and appropriate means to goal attainment. Thus, most studies of organizational climate have focused on the shared perception of organizational policies, practices, and procedures, both formal and informal. Culture is widely defined as a common set of shared meanings or understandings about the organization and its problems, goals, and practices. It is an interpretive scheme, or way of perceiving, thinking, and feeling in relation to the group's problems. Thus, the studies of organizational culture have focused on the basic values, beliefs, and assumptions that are present in organizations, the pattern of behaviour that results from these shared meanings, and the symbols that express the links between assumptions, values, and behaviour to an organization's members.

Actually climate and culture are very similar in many aspects. The concept of climate focuses on an organization members' perceptions of the way things are, but perception includes the idea that meaning is attached to the perceived event or thing. Thus, climate is a manifestation of culture. Culture is a deeper, less consciously held set of meanings. However, at a general level, there is substantial overlap between the two concepts. This is especially true when climate and culture are viewed as reciprocal processes, the one causing the other in an endless cycle over time. In this manner, climate is both the manifestations of culture and the data on which culture comes to be inferred and understood. In the methodological considerations, culture and climate are found to be very diverse.

Organizational culture researchers and organizational climate researchers come from different scientific traditions. Reichers and Schneider (1990) state that a key methodological distinction in science concerns is the familiar oppositions between subjective/objective and qualitative/quantitative approaches. These differences are reflected in the type of research conducted on culture and climate. Climate researchers have been contented to use the nomothetic, quantitative procedures that encompass an etic perspective. The etic perspective imposes meaning on a set of data, rather than letting the meaning emerge from the members of the group under study. Barley (1983) believes that the latter approach is termed emic. The focus on organizational culture has, in contrast to climate research, been more qualitative and ideographic in approach, and has employed methods that have been predominantly clinical, ethnographic and anthropological.

Despite the conceptual and methodological diversities, culture and climate are both found to have a number of similarities. Reichers and Schneider (1990, p. 29) summarize the similarities as follows:

- Both climate and culture deal with the ways by which an organization's members make sense of their environment. These shared meanings form the basis for action.
- Both climate and culture are learned, largely through the socialization process and through symbolic interaction among group members.
- Climate and culture are at the same time both monolithic constructs and multidimensional ones. Thus, we can correctly speak of organizational climate, cultures, and subcultures.
- Culture and climate are both attempts to identify the environment that affects the behaviour of people in organizations. Culture exists at a higher level of abstraction than climate, and climate is a manifestation of culture.

The relationship between culture and climate is diffused and complex but interlocked and reciprocal. Organizational climate is a Lewinian concept that emphasizes the impact of a social context on a member of the group or organization. The concept developed in response to the organizational behaviour literature of the situational and contextual factors that influence individual behaviour. According to Reichers and Schneider (1990), if culture is the next attempt to explain the E in Lewin's famous equation $B = f (P, E)$ (behaviour is a function of the person and the environment), then the culture concept must add something beyond climate's previous contribution. The research on organizational culture can focus on the assumptions and values that underlie the policies and procedures that are indicative of climate. Culture is at the next, higher level of abstraction, and thus, captures additional influences (overtly or covertly) on behaviour and on lower-level context variables, such as climate.

5.6   How to Improve School Culture and Climate

What should school administrators do to improve school culture and climate? The findings of the following studies may shed light on this question. According to Ouchi (1981), the secret to the success of Japanese companies was not technology, but a special way of managing people. It is a style that focuses on a strong company philosophy, a distinct corporate culture, long-range staff development and decision-making by consensus. Ouchi refers to these companies as Type Z organizations. The strategies behind Z organizations are based on participatory approaches to decision-making, strong orientation to collective values, particularly a collective sense of responsibility, and a holistic concern for people. In Z organizations, when they have reached consensus that is supported by the organizational members, they become committed to the implementation process and work well with each other, ensuring that employment is lifelong.

In a study investigating the causal relationship between organizational values and teachers' feelings, Pang (1996) has found that cultural linkage in Hong Kong schools promotes teachers' feelings of commitment, job satisfaction, sense of community and order and discipline, whereas, bureaucratic linkage undermines such feelings. The important strategies of cultural linkages in schools include participation and collaboration, collegiality and achievement orientation. An important implication of the study is that school principals should resort to the cultural linkage strategy in order to bind people together and to give meaning to their work. Further studies into organizational cultures of Hong Kong schools (Pang, 1998b, c) shows that schools can be classified into those of "strong culture", "moderate culture", "weak culture" and "conflicting culture". The implication of these studies is that if school administrators are to build a quality management culture in schools, they should decentralize school management to the teacher level and emphasize rationality, participation, collaboration, collegiality, goal orientation, communication and consensus in their daily managerial practices. A preliminary study of managerial practices of high schools in Shanghai by Pang (2001a) also supports the thesis.

Likert and Likert (1976) also support the importance of participatory approaches in schools, in their System 4 of management style. The finding, in their study of high schools, where System 4, participatory management style operates, is associated with effective schools. In schools operating on a System 4 model, group participation is emphasized; superior and subordinate relations are very close; communication flows upwards, downwards and horizontally with peers; and decisions are made through group processes. Gamage (1993), based on his research on school-based management, has pointed out how new organizational cultures, similar to System 4, are emerging in Australian schools.

The findings of the above four studies are also consistent with Purkey and Smith's (1985) review of literature. They suggest in their review of effective schools literature that collaborative planning, collegial relationships, sense of community and order and discipline are some of the crucial factors that define a school's culture and lead to the development of school climate. These four factors will evolve organically in each school and, over time, the outcome will be a school culture and climate that supports and nourishes academic success. Thus, adopting Ouchi's (1981) Theory Z, Likert's (1967) System 4 of management style and Pang's (1996) cultural linkages in school administration are the effective ways of improving school culture and climate.

Peterson and Deal (1998) have listed three important steps to improve school culture and climate. First, the leaders and managers should read the organizational culture (its history and existing condition), in order to discover the deeper meanings embedded in the school. Second, school leaders/managers should uncover and articulate core values, in order to determine the school's strengths and weaknesses. Third, school leaders should redesign the school context into a positive working/learning environment, by reinforcing the positive cultural elements and modifying the negative and dysfunctional ones.

School leaders/managers should never forget that any attempt to improve the school climate involves the exertion of conscious efforts that will enable the teachers to teach better and the students to learn more. Boyd's (1999) typology of school cultures encourages school leaders/managers to promote integrative culture, which stresses the need for high concern for both people and performance, so that every employee who works hard can experience success. Figure 5.3 suggests that different school cultures yield different results. In contrast to integrative culture, apathetic culture leads

Figure 5.3   Four Types of School Culture

Concern for Performance

	HIGH	LOW
	Integrative Culture "No one fails here who works hard."	**Caring Culture** "No one fails here who shows up."
	Exacting Culture "Some will fail here no matter what they do."	**Apathetic Culture** "No one fails, whether they show up or not."

Concern for People — HIGH (top row), LOW (bottom row)

(Source: Adapted from Boyd, 1999, p. 290)

to negative results, because the school leader/manager does not care about the employees and the organization.

5.7 Characteristics Associated with the Climate of Effective Schools

Pashiardis (2000) identifies the characteristics associated with the climate of effective schools. She notes that schools, which have climates that are conducive to learning, have principals who actively portray their instructional leadership roles. In addition, school policies, procedures, rules and regulations are clearly set and known to all stakeholders of such a school. Another characteristic is the existence of a plan, which spells out the school's goals and objectives, and inspires positive behaviour from all school stakeholders. Effective schools have teachers who possess a strong sense of responsibility for the students' learning. Moreover, emphasis on open communication and collaboration between and among the members of the school staff characterize the climate of effective schools. Inside the classrooms, a climate of optimism and high expectation pervades. Finally, the professional working climate within an effective school encourages an awareness and acceptance of the community in which it exists.

Gamage (1996b) based on research conducted by him and his associates in three different Australian school systems, refers to many instances of the positive effects of changed school climate and emergence of collegial cultures resulting from participatory decision-making with community participation. Many school leaders, teachers and parents refer to positive effects resulting from partnerships that they have built over the years.

Is it possible to determine school climate through measurement? Freiberg (1998), responding to this question, has presented practical ways of measuring school climate. One approach is to administer the Student Concerns Survey. This survey provides the administrators and teachers with concrete ideas on student concerns, thereby, enabling the school staff to design curricular and co-curricular experiences that are designed to address these concerns. Another approach is to obtain student views by conducting interviews. Through the interviews, the sentiments of the students can be determined and the appropriate modifications introduced to improve the school climate. Freiberg suggests using the cafeteria noise checklist as another measuring tool. If the noise is great, the school climate can be said to be unfavourable. On the other hand, a relatively quiet school cafeteria reveals a desirable school climate.

5.8 Conclusion

In conclusion, we would like to emphasize the primary importance of organizational culture and climate in school improvement. The types of values, beliefs, assumptions, attitudes, norms, ceremonies, rituals and heroes that are built into the organizational culture, affect the operational effectiveness of the organization. The leaders and managers have key roles to play in shaping the organizational culture and climate. Periodic evaluation of ones own organization is a very good approach in effecting organizational improvements, through gradual adjustment to its cultural assumptions. Of course, it is a slow and difficult process, but, if the leaders happen to neglect this aspect of their responsibility, it can be harmful to the productivity and effectiveness of the organization. In this context, the school leaders/ managers should pay greater attention to the establishment and maintenance of a positive school climate and culture, in order to hasten the success of a school's efforts towards excellence. When school leaders need to create a positive healthy school climate and culture, they should select the most appropriate approaches, based on theoretical concepts and best practices. What counts most, is how such efforts lead to the promotion of a desirable school climate and culture that consequently produces improved teaching and learning.

5.9 Review Questions

1. If organizational values are defined as the "taken-for-granted values and beliefs about how an organization should be operated", what are the organizational values and beliefs commonly found and shared in your school/organization? Elaborate your response with practical examples.
2. Different scholars may have different perspectives in perceiving organizational climate in schools, try to adopt or formulate one to define and describe the organizational climate in your school by your own insights and experience.

PART II

Structures and Processes of Educational Administration

CHAPTER 6

Understanding Administrative Structures and Processes

6.0 Learning Outcomes

Based on a systematic study of this chapter, the readers will:

- Understand the meaning and nature of administrative structures and processes;
- Identify levels of organization and dimensions of administrative structures and the significance of good structures for organizational effectiveness;
- Identify reasons why organizations are downsized to create flat structures; and
- Gain a better understanding of the components of the administrative processes available for leading and managing organizations.

6.1 Focus

This topic focuses on the importance of appropriate administrative structures, for the creation of efficient and effective organizations. The structure depends on the type and objectives of the organization concerned. Attention is paid to the designing of good structures, job designs and the definition of roles, and the assignment of appropriate personnel to the roles, within the administrative structure. Also discussed are modern approaches of downsizing and the creation of flatter structures, strategies for right sizing, the advantages and disadvantages of flat structures. Finally, the scope and the components of the administrative process, i.e. decision-making, planning, organizing, communicating, influencing, coordinating, and evaluating, are discussed, including some practical approaches to participatory management.

6.2 The Meaning and Nature of Administrative Structures

For the purpose of accomplishing the organizational goals and objectives, the work has to be divided amongst its members. But, to coordinate these efforts, an administrative structure is essential to enable the effective performance of key activities and to support the staff. Structure provides the framework of an organization and its pattern of management. It is through the structure that the purpose and work of the organization is carried out. Leadership and management need to have a good understanding of the importance and impact of the administrative structure. According to organizational behaviour and management scholars, designing the appropriate organizational structures, processes and procedures is very important (Murningham, 1982; Bennis & Nanus, 1985; Crespi, 1982 in Parkin, 1994; Micklethwait & Wooldridge, 1996; Wageman, 1997).

Administrative structure is the pattern of relationships between administrative/executive positions and amongst the staff within the organization. The purpose of structure is the division of work amongst the staff and the coordination of these efforts towards the accomplishment of organizational goals and objectives. The structure defines tasks and responsibilities, work roles and relationships, and channels of communication. Structure enables the application of the process of management and creates a framework of order and command, through which the activities of an organization can be planned, organized, directed and controlled. In very small organizations, structure can take a simple form, but in large, complex organizations, there is a need for a carefully designed and purposeful formal structure. The structure needs to be reviewed regularly, to ensure that it effectively meets the changing demands arising from the growth and development of an organization.

6.3 Categories of Organizational Structures

Management writers categorize organizational structures in different ways. A good understanding of these classifications helps the administrator choosing the design that suits his/her specific situation. Bennis and Nanus

(1985) suggest three categories, namely: collegial, personalistic, and formalistic organizational styles.

- *Collegial organizations* rely on participatory decision-making.
- *Personalistic organizations* count on trust between the employees and managers, and utilize informal policies.
- *Formalistic organizations* utilize clearly set rules and division of labour.

Mintzberg (1993) claims that there are five categories of organizational structures, namely: simple, machine bureaucracy, professional bureaucracy, divisional form, and adhocracy as described below:

- *Simple structure* relies on direct supervision as the primary co-ordinating mechanism.
- *Machine bureaucracy* coordinates jobs through the standardization of work processes.
- *Professional bureaucracy* involves the standardization of skills as the mechanism for coordination of performance.
- *Divisional form* standardizes outputs in coordinating performance.
- *Adhocracy* relies on the coordinating amongst staff mechanism for task performance.

Vecchio and colleagues (1996) refer to three categories: functional, product form, and hybrid design.

- *Functional organization* groups personnel according to resources needed in producing outputs.
- *Product form* considers organizational outputs as a basis for grouping.
- *Hybrid design* involves a dual hierarchy.

6.4 Why Should We Have an Administrative Structure?

Some of the key objectives of an administrative structure are as follows:

- Effective performance of the work, and the economical and efficient allocation of resources;
- Monitoring the activities of the organization;
- Ensuring individual and group accountability;
- Coordinating different parts of the organization and different areas of work;

- Providing flexibility to meet future demands and adapt to changing times and environments; and
- Meeting the social needs of the members working within the organization (Adapted from Mullins, 1999, pp. 520–521).

Peter Drucker (1989) suggests that the administrative structure should satisfy the following requirements:

- *The structure should be designed to maximize the main or core-business of the organization.* To achieve this, the structure needs to be direct and simple. It should not be based on past achievements, but on future demands and projected growth. The type of structure needed depends on the type of core-business of the organization. Thus, the structure of an educational organization differs from that of a business or an industrial concern.
- *The chain of command should be as short as possible.* This should be so, because, complexity distorts objectives, increases stress, creates inertia and slack increasing the difficulties in training future leaders and managers.
- *The structure should facilitate the training and testing of future leaders and managers.* Besides the provision of training, the structure enables the organization to place management trainees in positions of authority, with autonomy of operation, to gain experience at the organizational level, as well as, to test their abilities and preparedness to take responsibility. For example, a head teacher of a high school faculty can be placed in a position of head-teacher/administration or deputy principal to gain organizational level experience before appointing as a principal.

6.5 Levels of Organization

Organizations consist of several layers. The determination of policy, decision-making, the execution of work and the exercise of authority and responsibility, are entrusted to different positions throughout the organizational structure. An organization can be examined in terms of interrelated levels in the hierarchical structure such as technical level, managerial level and institutional level.

The Technical Level: The technical level is concerned with the actual job or tasks or core-business, to be performed. For example: the actual manufacture of goods in an industrial firm; rendering of services for the needy, by the Department of Social Security; the actual processes of teaching and learning in an educational institution.

The Managerial Level: The technical level interrelates with the management of the organizational level, which is responsible for the coordination and integration of work at the technical level. The managerial level is responsible for:

- The decisions relating to the provision of suitable buildings and acquisition of machinery and equipment, raw material and allocation of resources, as required for the production process;
- Mediation between the organization and the external environment; and
- The administration of the internal affairs of the organization including the control of the production processes, or the provision of services, as the case may be.

The Institutional Level: The managerial level interrelates with the institutional level, which is concerned with the organizational objectives, goals and broad policies of the organization as a whole. Examples of institutional or community level within an organization are, the board of directors of a public company, or the board of governors, or the council of an educational institution, which include external members.

However, these levels need to work more closely with each other. For example, the managerial level would not be able to plan and supervise the execution of work at the technical level without the knowledge, expertise and the practical know-how of the people closest to the actual tasks. In this context, the people at the technical level should brief and help the managerial level with problems and issues confronting them. It is also the duty of the managerial level to take appropriate action based on the information and advice. It should also consult those responsible at the institutional level. It is possible to have a greater or a fewer number of levels, but, these three levels provide an appropriate basis for an analysis of interrelated activities within an organization. A larger number of levels will increase the complexity and distort the communications and objectives, while a fewer number will overburden those in charge.

6.6 Dimensions of Structure

The variables, which determine the dimensions of structure, can be identified in a number of ways. According to Blackburn (1982), the dimensions of a structure usually include: the grouping of activities, the responsibilities of individuals, levels of hierarchical authority, span of control and formal organizational relationships. On an examination of the literature, Pugh, Hickson, Hinnings, and Turner (1968) refer to six primary dimensions of organizational structure as described below:

- Specialization or division of labour and the allocation of tasks amongst different positions.
- Standardization — standardized procedures or bureaucratic rules to cover regularity of occurrence, which is a basic aspect of organizational structure.
- Formalization denotes the extent to which rules, procedures, instructions and communications are organized in the form of written documents.
- Centralization or decentralization is concerned with the locus of authority to make decisions within the organization i.e. that is empowered to determine or approve before legitimate action is taken.
- Configuration is the shape of the structure, whether there is a short or a long chain of command. This can be illustrated by an organizational chart, which shows all key roles of an organization.
- Traditionalism is the extent to which an organization is standardized by customs or rules.

On the basis of another study, Child (1984) suggests the following six major dimensions, as components of an organizational structure:

- Allocation of individual tasks and responsibilities, job specialization and definition;
- Formal reporting relationships, levels of authority and spans of control;
- Grouping together of sections, departments, divisions and larger units;
- Systems for communication of information, integration of effort or participation;
- Delegation of authority, including procedures to follow, monitoring and evaluating mechanisms and guidance in using discretion;
- Motivation of employees, through systems for the appraisal of performance and reward.

An additional dimension of structural design is information technology (IT). Computer-based information and decision support systems influence choices in the design of production or service activities, hierarchical structures and the organization of support staff. Robey (1991) states that IT also influences the centralization vs. decentralization of decision-making and control systems. Work Research Unit has pointed out that IT has typically resulted in "flatter" organizational structures, with fewer levels of management. The role of the supervisor and/or manager is also changing, resulting in the number of managerial and/or supervisory positions declining.

6.7 The Imperatives for a Good Administrative Structure

The administrative structure of an organization affects not only the effectiveness or productivity and efficiency of the organization, but also the morale and job satisfaction of the staff. This leads to the conclusion that the structure should be designed so as to encourage not only the willing participation of the organizational members, but also the efficient allocation of limited resources resulting in high performance and effective realization of organizational goals. Drucker (1989) expresses the view that the appropriate structures influence organizational performance most significantly. Good structure by itself does not however, produce good performance, but a poor organizational structure makes good performance impossible, no matter how competent the individual managers are.

The functions of the formal structure, the activities and the defined relationships between positions exist independently of the organizational members who perform the roles. But, personalities are a significant part of the organization. In practice, the actual operation of the organization and its success in meeting objectives will depend upon the behaviour of personnel who work within the structure and who provide shape and personality to the framework. Meyer (1977) is of opinion that the organizational structure is a simplification of complex patterns of human behaviour.

The overall effectiveness of an organization is affected both by sound structural design, as well as, the personnel who occupy such positions within the structure. As all organizations are social systems, the people who work within them establish their own norms of behaviour, social groupings and relationships, irrespective of the formal structure. Management needs to acknowledge the existence of these informal organizations.

The operation of an organization and its actual work arrangements are influenced by the existing styles of leadership, the formal organizational structures, managerial team and the informal organization. These factors are likely to lead to differences between the formal structure and what happens in practice. The hallmark of many successful organizations is the attention given to the human element and the organizational culture, which helps to create a feeling of belonging, commitment and satisfaction. In the final analysis, structure must be designed so as to maintain the appropriate balance between the socio-technical system and the effectiveness of the organization as a whole.

6.8   How to Design an Administrative Structure?

In the final analysis, to successfully accomplish the goals of an organization, it is necessary to establish a framework/system of control. This suggests that attention should be given to certain basic principles and considerations when designing an organizational structure, or when reviewing the effectiveness of an existing structure. Some of the key principles that should be considered are:

- Clarification of objectives;
- Task and element functions;
- Division of work and grouping of employees;
- Centralization vs. decentralization;
- Principles of organization;
- Span of control and scalar chain;
- Formal organizational relationships;
- Line and staff organization; and
- Project teams and matrix organization (Adapted from Mullins, 1999, pp. 526–543).

In this context, it is important to maintain the appropriate balance of the socio-technical system and effectiveness of the organization as a whole. The structure of an organization provides the framework, which in turn needs to harmonize with the goals and objectives. The first step in setting up an organization, or in reviewing an existing one, is to examine the organizational objectives. Only when the objects are clearly defined, can alternative structures be developed and compared in order to select the best structure.

6.9   Effects of a Deficient Structure

The negative effects of a poorly designed structure can be identified more easily than the positive effects of a successful organizational structure. In his discussion of the principles of organization and coordination, Urwick (1952) suggests that the lack of a good design is illogical, cruel, wasteful and inefficient.

- It is illogical — First, a design should be considered, both in terms of good social practices and good engineering practices. For example, it is considered that no senior person should be appointed before the identification of responsibilities, relationships and the role attached to the position within the structure.
- It is cruel — Usually, it is the individual members of the organization who suffer most as a result of a bad design or lack of design. If personnel are appointed without a clear identification of their responsibilities and the qualifications required in performing these duties and responsibilities, they can be blamed for poor results.
- It is wasteful — If the jobs are not designed to be within the lines of functional specialization, new members cannot be trained properly. It is very important to see that the right person is assigned to a job, rather than attempting to design a job to suit a person.
- It is inefficient — If an organization is not established on well-designed principles, the managers will be required to fall back on personalities. This will enable managers to play politics resulting in staff frustration and disappointments, affecting the organizational health and staff morale.

In another study, Child (1984) refers to the following consequences, arising from structural deficiencies:

- Low motivation and morale can be the result of inconsistent and arbitrary decisions; lack of or insufficient delegation; lack of clarity in job descriptions and assessment of performance; competing pressures from different parts of the organization; and work overloads for supervisors, resulting from inadequate support staff.
- Late and inappropriate decisions can result from lack of relevant, timely information to the right people; poor coordination of decision-makers located in different divisions; work-overload for decision-makers, due to insufficient delegation; and inadequate procedures to evaluate the effectiveness of past decisions.
- Conflict and lack of coordination can result from conflicting goals and staff working at cross-purposes, due to lack of clarity on objectives and priorities; failure to bring organizational members

into teams; and breakdowns in planning and actual operational work.

- Poor responses to new opportunities and change can result from failure to establish specialist jobs, concerned with forecasting environmental changes; failure to give adequate attention to innovations and planning of desirable changes.

6.10 Organizational Downsizing and Creation of Flatter Structures

DuBrin (1994) states that organizations attempt to create flatter structures (with fewer levels in the hierarchy) through downsizing or right sizing, in order to achieve, among others, organizational effectiveness. A primary reason for the elimination of one or more levels is to reduce personnel costs. Usually, payroll costs being around 75–80% of the operating costs of most organizations, reduction of staff is one of the prime aims of downsizing in order to reduce unit costs or improve efficiency. For businesses to be competitive, both in domestic and overseas markets, cost reductions are essential. In the case of public institutions, downsizing helps to cope with dwindling budgets. Reduction of costs, by eliminating a layer or layers of managerial staff and laying-off other staff, is now an accepted turnaround strategy for many organizations, both private and public. Decreasing managerial layers also helps to speed up the process of decision-making, effecting further savings in time and resources while improving customer services.

Business concerns stay lean by decentralizing as many functions as possible to local units, with a high degree of autonomy of operations. On the other hand, some organizations use the flatter structures in accordance with modern approaches. Because of the current belief that downsizing and creation of flatter structures leads to more effective, more competitive, world-class organizations, the concept persists even when institutions improve their performance. For example, in the mid-1990s, Broken Hill Private (BHP) in Australia downsized its steel works in Newcastle to prepare itself to enhance organizational effectiveness and become a world-class steel manufacturer.

6.11 Strategies and Tactics for Downsizing

Researchers and consultants have developed several strategies and tactics for downsizing and creating flatter structures, to improve effectiveness and minimize human trauma. Right sizing is used to create a leaner organization in an attempt to maximize productivity. The organizational restructuring strategies are grouped into two categories: (1) those dealing with structure, job design and policy; and (2) the other dealing with the human aspects resulting from downsizing.

6.11.1 Restructuring, Redesigning Jobs and Developing New Policies

The first step is to *identify the need for trimming the managerial staff*. Poor managerial practices are responsible for much of the top-heavy organizational structures. Organizational diversification breed hierarchy as senior managers create positions to assist them in specialized areas, in order to cover their lack of expertise. Another sign of managerial overstaffing has been identified with the title "manager" to avoid pay limitations on support staff positions. In one factory, it was revealed that each supervisor was responsible for only four workers, whereas, in a rival company supervisor's control extended to 20. The Tom Peters Group (1986) suggests that senior executives should examine the prevailing span of control. He suggests reducing the managerial layers in order to increase the span of control and states that today, many institutions have moved towards an organizational structure in which the ratio of managers to non-managers is 1 to 100 at the bottom and 1 to 20 at the top.

The second step is to *change the organization structure to a simpler design*. Once the need to reduce the number of managerial layers is identified, a simpler structure should be designed. With the restructuring when one managerial level is eliminated, the incumbents of eliminated layer have either to be reassigned to lower level positions, and/or offered early retirement.

The third step is to *make the changes quickly, rather than gradually*. It is argued that in times of layoffs, it is better to plan the reductions at once, rather than over a protracted period. If alternative replacements are not available, cuts become much less disruptive when done quickly as the survivors deal with the situation better, rather than prolonging the agony of not knowing what comes next. The problem with the gradual approach is that competent staff, who feel insecure, will find jobs elsewhere and less competent staff will also spend time on job search and contribute less, as the morale will be low. On the other hand, some others argue that it is better to do the layoffs gradually, as it is less painful than shock treatment. It is easier for an organization to find several alternative jobs at a time, rather than many. It is also possible to do it through natural attrition and voluntary retirement packages (VRP), without sending shock waves through the whole organization.

After creating flatter structures, it is natural for the workloads to increase. To cope with post-downsizing, leaders and managers need to put in more hours, late in the evenings or at night. One remedy is to undertake regular reviews on what sort of activities could be cut, without affecting productivity, and *streamline the work to match the reduced work force*, for example, reducing the number of staff meetings, organized lunches, ceremonial functions and so forth.

Finally, *a task force can be used to solve special managerial problems*. After restructuring, as fewer managers are available, they may not be able to solve complex problems. Then, a special task force or forces can be formed, with some top level and first level managers to investigate the issues on a full-time or part-time basis. Once the problem is sorted out, the task force can either be disbanded or leave as an operational ad-hoc body, to be used whenever a need arises.

6.11.2 Strategies for Dealing with Human Aspects of Downsizing

It is important to *deal openly and honestly with the problems* arising from downsizing. Lies and half-truths by top management foster employee rumours and negative accusation by the media. It is noted that no one can avoid the painful experience associated with a major downsizing. Even those who escape staff cuts, feel a sense of loss for departed workmates. Management should honestly acknowledge the widespread pain and suffering. A public statement about when, and under what conditions, the staff cuts will occur will help reduce anxiety. For example, it is better if the Chief Executive Officer (CEO) releases a statement to the effect: "Our downsizing will end when the firm returns to profitability. With the reduction in work force that has already taken place, we hope to be in the black by the end of the year."

It is better to *use performance appraisal information to make fair layoff decisions*. An important strategy for staff cuts is to base downsizing decisions on merit, rather than seniority or political favouritism. Poor performers should be the first people to be laid off, or offered early retirement. Retaining those favoured by senior managers, but generally incompetent, damages morale and deprives the organization of needed skills. A reliable performance appraisal provides objective data, to determine which employees need to be downsized. Human resources information systems (HRIS) can assist in downsizing and redeployment of staff, by analysing each position by title, salary grade, skills, and location. HRIS also can identify new positions within the system and match them with available employees for redeployment as well as for termination.

It is also important to *pay adequate compensation and support for the displaced persons.* The managers and professionals being people, who are more dedicated and attached to their jobs, need more help to minimize stress as a result of losing their jobs. Middle managers also need more help to cope with layoff. Developing support mechanisms should begin with the completion of planning for downsizing, in order to treat staff with dignity and respect, rather than pushing them out. Offering early retirement or severance packages, depending on the number of years of service, with other appropriate benefits, is desirable to reduce stress in coping with layoffs. It is also necessary to offer each staff member who is laid off, a candid, but sympathetic statement of why he or she was chosen to be laid-off. For example, "We have decided to lay off 50% of staff at your level. Your performance has been above average, but we are only retaining those with excellent performance appraisal and who have critical skills in our core-business. You will receive a very favourable employment reference."

Human resources balancing also can be used to minimize layoffs. A comprehensive programme of human resources balancing may be implemented for surplus employees by: (1) regional redistribution, (2) relocation, (3) loaning to divisions, which have temporary shortages, (4) reclassification, and (5) voluntary retirement with incentive packages.

It is also important to *provide job security to those who are retained.* One way of shoring up the prospect of job security is to explain, to those who are retained, that they are a select cadre, on whom the organization hopes to build its future. Comforting words should be matched by appropriate action, by improving performance in such a way as to show that job security is high. Temporary or casual staff can be hired to attend to urgent and seasonal work, suggesting that the permanent staff is an elite group whose services are highly valued. This strategy also gives the impression that if staff layoffs are needed, it is the casual and temporary staff who will be laid off.

Further, *flexible benefits could be provided to offset long working hours.* DuBrin (1994) states that naturally, in a downsized organization, those who are retained have to assume the additional responsibilities of the laid off staff members. In order to compensate for this, by way of incentives, the organizations need to offer flexible benefits to help blend their family and work lives. Some of these benefits could be flexible working hours, child-care or dependent-care facilities, job-sharing and part-time work.

6.12 Advantages of Flatter Organizational Structures

Downsized organizations with flatter structures offer several advantages. Downsized organizations usually produce large dividends when it results in a leaner organization. The reduced payroll costs may increase profits for private business, while public service organizations stay within the budgets. Good examples of this are: the big three Australian banks (Australian National Bank, Australia New Zealand Bank, and Commonwealth Bank of Australia), which announced billions of dollars in net profits, in the year 2000, after restructuring into leaner organizations. Flatter structures contribute to organizational effectiveness, including increased productivity. Flatter structures hasten effective decision-making as a result of fewer managers, and top managers can communicate directly with lower levels of management.

Sometimes, a downsized organization improves teamwork because thin staffing makes it necessary for people to work collaboratively on an array of projects, to pool their resources and potential. Flatter structures enable more effective communication with improved facilities for horizontal communication. Operations become less bureaucratic and more collegial. Downsizing also contributes to the social good, as laid off managers start helping smaller organizations with their expertise to grow, thus, creating more jobs.

6.13 Disadvantages of Downsizing and Flat Structures

Severe downsizing can lead to financial losses rather than gains. The confusion, inefficiency, cost of early retirement and severance pay, legal expenses in defending against court cases combine to offset the gains from savings in payroll costs. Downsizing also can be self-defeating in several ways. Even though payroll cost may come down, they do not bring increased revenue. The organization may be understaffed and unable to capitalize from new ideas and a rapid recovery. Profitable units may be required to cover loses of uneconomical units. Because of the layoffs, customer services can suffer and sales can be adversely affected delaying recovery.

Very often, downsizing results in expensive lawsuits especially when laid off staff claim that they were discriminated against on various grounds. Flatter structures also have their own problems, due to the shortage of sufficient numbers to contribute to particular tasks, and not having a variety of inputs to make better decisions. Most great organizations have been built on pyramid-shaped, rather than flatter structures. In pyramid-shaped organizations, middle managers provide very useful information and ideas for top-level decision-making, as well as, providing badly needed relief to the top managers. Crisis situations can be better met by pyramid-shaped organizations. In flat-shaped organizations, where managers are badly stretched, it becomes more difficult to cope with such situations. Flatter structures reduce opportunities for promotions, which can affect the morale of the staff. Multi-layered structure, also facilitate the training of future executives.

6.14 Scope of the Administrative Processes

In a discussion of general administration, Gulick (1937), who was one of the earliest and best known organizational analysts, in defining administrative process, posed the question: "What is the job of a chief executive?" and answered it as "POSDCORB". POSDCORB is made up of the following activities: planning, organizing, staffing, directing, co-ordinating, reporting and budgeting. Readers are referred to p. 9 for the details of these activities.

Tead (1951) comments that literature and best practices reveal the following essential elements of administrative processes:

- Defining purposes and objectives;
- Developing the broad plan for the structuring of the organization;
- Recruiting and organizing executive staff;
- Delegating and allocating authority and responsibility;
- Overseeing the delegated activities;
- Ensuring quantity and quality of performance;
- Achieving coordination through committees and conferences;
- Stimulating and energizing the entire personnel;
- Evaluating the total outcome in relation to objectives; and
- Forecasting the organization's aims, as well as, the ways and means of analysing them.

The *1955 Yearbook of the American Association of School Administrators* described the following as the functions of an administration:

- Planning or the attempt to control the future direction, of the organization, based on careful analyses and estimates, and setting new goals;
- Allocation or the procurement and allotment of human and material resources, in accordance with the operational plan;
- Stimulation or motivation of behaviour, in terms of the desired outcomes;
- Coordination, or the process of fitting together the various groups and operations into an integrated pattern of work, for the purpose of achieving the goals; and
- Evaluation or the continuous examination of the effects produced by the ways in which the other functions are performed.

6.15 Components of Administrative Processes

A study of literature, relating to the administrative processes, reveals the following list of action words and phrases:

Identifying the needs, exploring problems, defining purposes, determining resources, initiating planning, involving people, formulating policy, seeking information, formulating courses of action, collecting data, solving problems, predicting, making decisions, setting goals, organizing, determining roles, delegating, empowering, allocating resources, budgeting, providing materials, staffing, implementing, utilizing resources, communicating, reporting, directing, controlling, influencing, stimulating, overseeing, coordinating, appraising, evaluating, and reviewing.

However, when allowance is made for the overlap of the meanings, it appears that the administrative process may be described in terms of: (1) Decision-making, (2) Planning, (3) Organizing, (4) Communicating, (5) Influencing, (6) Coordinating, and (7) Evaluating.

6.15.1 *Decision-making*

Decision-making is at the very heart of administration. McCamy (1947) has stated that "the reaching of a decision is the core of administration, all other attributes of the administrative process being dependent on, interwoven with, and existent for the making of decisions" (p. 41). All administrators are required to make decisions of an organizational nature. Much of the literature in the administrative field, in general, and particularly in educational administration, has been concerned primarily with "doing" rather than with "deciding". But, as Herbert Simon (1957) has pointed out, a theory of administration should be concerned with the processes of a decision, as well as, with the processes of action.

6.15.2 Planning

Planning is widely recognized as essential to organizational success. Organizations, which do not plan, are often characterized as meaningless and ineffectual. It is through planning that goals are established and strategies developed and coordinated, to accomplish the set goals. Planning is an essential component of the administrative process. Nowadays, most schools implementing school-based management resort to strategic planning and global budgeting.

6.15.3 Organizing

One of the most important responsibilities of an administrator is that of developing an organization in which the coordinated efforts of staff result in the accomplishment of the accepted educational purposes. Dissipated effort, wasted resources, and poor results can be attributed to poor organization. It is through an organization that administration must act. Without an organization, administration is inconceivable. Organization implies the coordinated activities of a group of persons, in the pursuit of a common goal. An organization comes into being when there are people who are able to communicate with each other and who are willing to contribute coordinated and regulated behaviour towards the accomplishment of a common goal or goals.

6.15.4 Communicating

Organizational communication is a crucial component of the administrative process of any organization, particularly in social organizations, such as schools and universities. Communication is a word like "organization". Everyone knows what it means until asked formally to state its definition. It may be useful to think of communication as an interpersonal process of sending and receiving symbols with meanings attached to them. When problems arise in organizations, their cause is frequently identified as poor communication. This is because leaders and managers use communication to obtain necessary information in making decisions that affect the organization. When poor decisions result, bad communication is frequently to blame. Communication is the glue that binds the different parts of an organization into one.

6.15.5 *Influencing*

The very nature of an organization requires some systemic control, in order to maintain order and stability. Control or power is expressed in terms of authority, which may be necessary for the maintenance of an orderly environment. Indeed, power can be used as a motivating force in maintaining the organization's vitality and impetus. Successful administrators use a number of methods of influence, in guiding and coordinating the behaviour of members of an organization. The test of administrative leadership is always the degree to which members of an organization can be influenced to contribute spontaneous, ordered, and cooperative efforts, in order to accomplish the mission of the organization.

6.15.6 *Coordinating*

Coordinating is the process of unifying the contributions of people, material and other resources, towards the achievement of a recognized purpose. In every organization, the problem of coordinating the efforts of individuals and groups, into an integrated pattern of activity, is of utmost importance. Newman (1951) has stated that achieving coordination is one of the primary goals of every administrator. It should not be regarded as a separate and distinct activity, but, a part of all phases of administration, whether it is planning, organizing, developing executives, directing and controlling, all should contribute to coordination.

Without coordination it is unlikely that there will be an orderly arrangement of the efforts, of two or more people, in the pursuit of a common purpose. It is a process through which different parts of an enterprise are put together in an integrated and harmonious relationship to each other (Moore & Walters, 1955).

6.15.7 *Evaluating*

All organizations, particularly public organizations, are likely to be subjected to continuous evaluation. This evaluation may be informal and sporadic, rather than purposeful and planned. It is the responsibility of leadership to have well conceived continuous evaluating activity, to ensure satisfactory accomplishment of the purpose, and objectives of the organization. Evaluating is an important and integral component of the total process of administration. Evaluation of a public agency such as a school is of legitimate concern to a wide variety of individuals and organizations, such as the Department of Education and Training or Education Department, parents, teachers, students, PTA, School Council, school management committee, and local community, etc. Logically:

- The first step in an evaluating process is the selection and definition of the particular phase of the total activity, which is to be evaluated.
- The second, the development and acceptance of criteria and basic assumptions on which interpretations and judgements will be made.
- The third, collection of data pertinent to the criteria; and
- The final step is the analysis and interpretation of the data and drawing of conclusions.

6.16 Restructuring and Participatory Approaches in School Settings

Experiences in participatory management in school settings have revealed that its benefits are likely to accrue to the organization only if it is supported by structures designed to maximize the involvement of all those concerned. Further, such structures need to be nurtured by a climate and culture that promotes participation. Different structures and strategies can be organized for participation. It may be as individuals, groups, through representatives or the whole group. The structures that are established depend on the perception of the leader, with regard to the degree of control s/he should retain and his/her own attitudes, relating to the contributions that others can make. If the administrator feels strongly about hierarchical models, s/he will be slow in moving towards broader participatory approaches. Gamage, Sipple, and Partridge (1995 & 1996), especially in Victoria and the Australian Capital Territory, and Gamage's research (2000a) in England, suggest that extensive use of sub-committees of the school councils, boards or governors, enabling wider participation of relevant stakeholders, lead to motivation, ownership and commitment.

A number of approaches to participatory management have been developed because of increasing dissatisfaction with administrative techniques associated with the bureaucratic model. One of the best-known models is the team management concept. This approach is implemented by forming an administrative team to meet and bring its collective wisdom to issues that relate to the responsibilities they share. In most large schools, the school executive, consisting of the principal, deputy/assistant principals and faculty heads, meet as an administrative team in sorting out organizational problems and issues.

On the basis of research on effective schools, schools have started to develop various approaches to widening the involvement of organizational members. School site and school-based management models require the involvement of staff, as well as, parents and community members, and in the case of secondary schools, students. New structures known as school boards, councils, school management committees or school governors, consisting of representatives of relevant categories of stakeholders, have been established to broaden the participation for organizational decision-making. Gamage, with his extensive research on school-based management, points out that educational systems in different parts of the world (such as Australia, the United States of America, United Kingdom, New Zealand, Spain, Canada, Czech Republic and Hong Kong), have developed different models of participatory management, to suit their special needs and situations (1996c; 2000a, b). When the local governance gives a school direct access to the expertise of its key stakeholders — the sponsoring body, the principal, teachers, parents, alumni and members of the community, it empowers the stakeholders themselves to work effectively for the educational welfare of the students under their care. When the stakeholders of different backgrounds come to exchange views of school improvement and participate in decision-making in formulating school development plans, it is inevitably that numerous conflicts and serious disagreements will arise. Pang (2001b) opines that giving top priority to students' welfare should be the paramount principle, in coping with disagreements and resolving conflicts arisen from participatory decision-making.

6.17 Conclusion

This topic examined the importance and the relevance of the administrative structures. Structure is the frame of an organization, which determines the key positions. It also includes the job design and clear description of the roles. A structure of an organization can be summarized in the form of an organization chart, showing the hierarchical structure. The administrative structure needs to be designed to accomplish the objectives of the organization, while the structure has a big impact on the operations of an organization. A well-designed structure can lead to an efficient and effective organization, whereas, a poorly designed structure can lead to a less effective organization. Traditional organizations are known for their pyramidal bureaucratic structures, with several layers of management. Currently, most organizations resort to restructuring towards the creation of flatter structures. Researchers and consultants have developed several strategies for downsizing organizations. There are both advantages and disadvantages in flatter organizational structures. It can be said then, that it is very important for the leaders and managers to have a sound understanding when designing appropriate structures, jobs and roles to create efficient and effective organizations. Finally, a knowledge and understanding of the different administrative processes such as decision-making, planning, organizing, communicating, influencing, coordinating and evaluating enables a leader/manager to develop the skills to act effectively within the given constraints.

6.18 Review Questions

1. Why do organizations resort to downsizing? Discuss the different strategies developed for downsizing and creation of leaner organizations.
2. Examine the key components of the administrative process and how a sound understanding of these processes can make you a more effective leader/manager.

CHAPTER 7

Organizational Communication

7.0 Learning Outcomes

Based on a systematic study of this chapter, the readers will:

- Understand the concept of communication and its significance to organizational life and effectiveness;
- Understand the types and processes of organizational communication, and how to employ them to the best advantage;
- Encourage interpersonal communication and identify the barriers to communication; and
- Establish the structures, procedures and processes for effective organizational communication.

7.1 Focus

Communication is a process by which information is exchanged between individuals and groups, through a common system of symbols, signs and behaviour. It includes all the procedures by which one mind may affect another. However, no communication is received without a certain degree of distortion. Hence, all efforts are needed to minimize the degree of distortion. Communication is the glue that holds an organization together. Despite tremendous advances in communication and information technology, communication amongst people in organizations, leaves much to be desired. This topic examines organizational communication in all relevant aspects, providing a sound understanding, to develop the skills for the improvement of organizational communication.

7.2   What Do We Mean by Organizational Communication?

Efforts to find a universally acceptable definition of organizational communication have been frustrated by the multifaceted nature of the process, which is characterized by subtlety, variety, and ubiquity. In a review of literature, Frank E. Dance (1970) has discovered 95 definitions containing at least 15 themes that suggest different and contradictory approaches to understanding communication. Traditionally, communication has been defined as the transfer of thoughts and feelings from one person to another. Communication enhances understanding of information exchanged between individuals, through symbols, signs or behaviour. Complexities suggest that communication include "all the procedures by which one mind may affect another". Porter and Roberts (1976) have defined communication as the sharing of messages, ideas, or attitudes that produce a degree of understanding between a sender and a receiver. In everyday usage, communication implies an attempt to share meaning, through the transmission of messages amongst people. Coursen, Irmsher, and Thomas (1997) claim that communication is the art of listening carefully and expressing views clearly and concisely.

Since our focus is on educational organizations, we need to assume that the sharing of messages, ideas or attitudes occurs in educational contexts amongst administrators, teachers, students, parents, and other interested parties. From this perspective, Herbert Simon's (1957, p. 154) definition that "communication is any process whereby decisional premises are transmitted from one member of an organization to another", is an appropriate one. As pointed out by Drake and Roe (1999), accurate transmission and understanding of the messages are essential for effective organizational communication. Understanding, however, is a relative concept. Low levels of understanding can develop between people who do not speak the same language or even amongst those who suspect each other. Body motions, facial expressions, tone of speech, and speech rapidity, convey useful information. In this context, in an organizational setting, communication requires a high level of understanding.

Coordinated action by all concerned is needed in achieving organizational goals and it becomes more complex in the educational contexts. Goal-directed behaviour is generated through communication. Therefore, greater clarity of the messages is needed to direct the actions of the administrators, teachers, students and parents in a more fruitful manner. A school principal may want the teachers and students to understand and accept their ideas and act upon them. But, unless the principal can communicate in such a way as to get the staff to share the validity of the goals and explain the procedures relating to implementation accurately, s/he is unlikely to achieve the desired results. Thus, in an educational setting communication becomes successful only when the sender of a message and the receiver, have a very similar comprehension of the content of the message.

Some scholars argue that we are in an age of exploding knowledge and communication systems. Mass media has influenced the awareness and horizons of school-age children, in new heroes and value systems, capturing their imagination and influencing the shaping of their life goals. These have affected the classroom environments, forcing educators to compete with television commentators, in interpreting world events. In this contest, the educators have lost their aura of authority to the mass media. Communication occurs only to the extent that the message sent is received. No message is ever received without an element of loss or distortion. In a sense, therefore, "communication" is a relative term, for only the essence of a message can be received since the reception can never be perfect in completeness or accuracy.

7.3 Significance of Organizational Communication

Communication is the glue that holds organizations together. Communication assists organizational members to achieve both organizational and individual goals; implement and respond to organizational change, coordinate organizational activities, and engage in virtually all organizationally relevant behaviours. Similarly, a breakdown in communication leads to disastrous repercussions. The success or failure of an organization is largely dependent upon the communication process (Hargie, Dickson & Tourish, 1999). Without effective communication, employees cannot be made aware of what is expected of them, how they should do their jobs, and what others think about their work (Orpen, 1997 cited in Hunt, Tourish & Hargie, 2000).

It would be extremely difficult to find an aspect of a manager's job that does not involve communication. Serious problems arise when directives are misunderstood, when casual kidding in a work group leads to anger, or when informal remarks by the leader are distorted. Each of these situations is a result of a breakdown in the process of communication.

Thus, communication is unavoidable in an organization's functioning; only effective communication is avoidable. Every manager must be a communicator. In fact, everything that a leader/manager does, communicates something in some way to somebody or some group.

What communication does for an organization resembles what the bloodstream does for an organism. The bloodstream supplies all the cells of the organism with oxygen; the communication system supplies all the units i.e. departments and the people of the organization, with information. Deprived of oxygen, the cells malfunction and die, similarly, deprived of necessary information, individuals and departments within the organization malfunction, which can certainly lead to a sort of terminal ineffectiveness for them and for the organization as a whole. Communication amongst people does not depend on technology, but rather on forces in people and their ability to listen and understand message and their surroundings.

7.4 Theories and Concepts in Organizational Communication

In the study of organizations and their behaviour, communication has taken a central focus. Frederick Taylor's (1911) functional mode was designed so that each worker had eight specialized bosses to provide information on job functions such as speed, quality and other details of the shop. Bureaucratic theory emphasized the need for detailed communication (usually in writing), so there would be no doubt or confusion regarding limitations of a position. Subsequent studies by Chester Barnard (1938), Herbert Simon (1957) and Rensis Likert (1967) deserve more careful attention.

In *The Functions of the Executive*, Chester Barnard (1938) has suggested that the first responsibility of a leader, in the context of an organization, should be to provide for a system of communication. Bernard defines an organization as "that kind of co-operation among people which is conscious, deliberate, and purposeful." He sees the success or failure of the organization as being directly related to the success of communication facilitation in establishing and maintaining the processes of cooperation. In order to become effective and efficient, organizations have to deal continuously and successfully with individuals and groups, in such ways that a common set of goals are perceived and attained. For this purpose, he points out that communication is central to the development of healthy interactions between and amongst the individuals and groups within an organization. The mechanistic approaches of the bureaucratic theory (Weber, 1947) are rejected and a concept of the individual is emphasized as the prime actor in bringing harmony to the organization. It is pointed out that coercion is self-defeating, whereas, persuasion through rational processes could guarantee continued cooperation. As against the belief of many others, he sees the informal organization as a vital and positive force for cooperation.

Barnard (1938) also advocates a communication network, both formal and informal, which is well known to the staff. Distributed information must be definite and minimize ambiguity. The messages should be direct, short and simple, free from administrative jargon. Each transmission should be complete in itself, so that understanding and compliance are enhanced. Finally, the need to have a close loop feedback system was emphasized.

Thus, it is clear how communication becomes essential to improve the operational efficiency and effectiveness of an organization. Communication becomes the bridge between individual participation and group identification. Models of adaptive behaviour need to be developed, to facilitate the development of alternative processes and networks, to provide closer realization of intended consequences, while avoiding the most problematic of the unintended results. In formulating his "bounded rationality" Barnard sought, through communication processes, to look for satisfactory choices, rather than optimal ones, to replace global goals with tangible and measurable sub-goals, and to divide up decision-making among many specialists by means of a structure of effective communication and authority relationships. Thus, communication was considered to be the key tool, with which organizational decisions are made and problems are solved.

The downward flow of communication is complicated by the reactions people have towards a person in authority. Downward communication, from someone in authority, tends to assume the form of directives whether or not they were so intended. Administrators, generally, make the assumption that when a message is sent it will be accurately received, even though very often it is not the case.

Rensis Likert (1967) proposes a new foundational concept of participation and a new formulation of the executive or administrative role, called the link-pin concept. Taken together, these two propositions magnify the importance, as well as, the contributory effects of organizational communication. Likert sees the importance of participatory decision-making through the communication process, not only for the idiographic dimension and outcomes of individual and group morale, but also as essential in attaining the organizational goals in terms of outcomes and effectiveness.

He is of the opinion that deeper involvement in communication — participation leads to a natural growth process, which is necessary for continuing cooperation and adjustment. In this respect, Likert's work is closely aligned with that of Argyris (1964) and Maslow (1970), in terms of personality, motivation and organizational growth. All three of these theorists (Likert, Argyris and Maslow) believe that individual growth and organizational development are closely connected and interrelated. They suggest that greater maturity in individual decision-making, communication, and time perspective can lead to greater cooperation amongst staff, efficiency and organizational effectiveness.

Likert (1967) in his link-pin concept advances the need for group processes that overcome natural obstacles to improve superordinate-subordinate relationships, and offer alternative ways, in which participation is encouraged within organizations. Essentially, this means each administrator deals with a group of subordinates, whose combined perspective and persuasive powers, can offset the natural imbalance of traditional organizational power relationships, by creating a more collegial environment.

7.5   Understanding the Need for Effective Communication

Because of the central role that communication plays in educational organizations, such as schools and tertiary institutions, the key issue is not whether the educational leaders/managers engage in communication or not, but whether they communicate effectively or poorly. This means that communication is unavoidable in the functioning of organizations; yet, effective communication is avoidable. In other words, people within a school or tertiary institution is unable to avoid exchanging information, but to develop shared meanings requires positive efforts by the educators and other participants, which is a difficult process.

In an organizational situation, communication amongst those involved depends on a combination of personal and environmental factors. In a basic generalization, it could be said that the meaning of a message is to be found in what people take it to mean, and not necessarily in the intended content. Because the same word means different things to different people, an administrator can convey only words and not the meanings. The same word may have a wide variety of meanings, as organizational members have different communication abilities, knowledge levels, and backgrounds and also different perceptions about the person sending the message. The words assume alternative meanings as the individuals have personally experienced varying environmental or social forces. Thus, the socio-psychological theory of communication considers an individual's personal and social context as basic to the communication process.

In the traditional bureaucratic model, formal communication channels traverse the organization, through the hierarchy of authority. Chester Barnard (1938) suggests that several factors must be considered when developing and using the formal communication system. These are:

- The channels of communication must be known;
- The channels must link every member of the organization;
- The lines of communication must be as direct and as short as possible;
- The complete lines of communication need to be used; and
- Every communication needs to be authenticated and should be from the person who is empowered to issue such messages.

Accuracy is ensured, by placing emphasis on formal written communication. The implicit assumption of this model is that by strictly adhering to the assigned duties and also in view of the fact that the bureaucratic model requires the selection of personnel on technical competence, the context is the same for all organizations. In this context, communication in a school system has to flow from the Director General/Director to the Regional Director/District Superintendent and through the Principal to the classroom teacher.

Barnard (1938) believes that the objective of communication is co-ordination of different parts of the organization. March and Simon (1938) assume that the capacity of an organization, such as a school, to maintain a complex and highly interdependent pattern of activity is limited by its ability to handle the communication needed for coordination. However, Gamage, Sipple and Partridge (1995, 1996) have argued that with the introduction of school-based management, the Victorian and the Australian Capital Territory (ACT) school systems in Australia have been able to establish effective networks of communication with their school communities. If the organizational communication is effective, the ability to coordinate interdependent activities, such as curriculum and instructional procedures would be greater.

Lee Bolman and Terrence Deal (1984) refer to four purposes that are served by communication. These are manipulating and transmitting facts and information, exchanging information, influencing others, and telling stories about the organization. Three characteristics of school bureaucracies seem to be critical to the formal system of communication. These are:

- The degree of centralization in the hierarchy;
- The organization's shape; and
- The level of information technology.

The external environment also affects the communication within a school. As uncertainty and complexity increase two factors emerge that require heightened information processing by individuals, groups and the organization itself. First, in the face of uncertainty, strategies have to be developed to obtain some degree of predictability. Second, in conditions of high complexity, elevated levels of communication must be carefully processed. In this context, organizations such as schools need to monitor critical factors in their external environments, process information carefully to make accurate decisions and to coordinate and control sub-units and members. The ability to receive information, process it, and communicate what is needed in a timely and an accurate fashion, becomes crucial to organizational performance in schools.

One of the key functions of the organizational structure is to facilitate communication. Organizational structure and communication are interrelated. This interrelationship needs to be understood if administrative communication is to be effective. Therefore, it is very important to consider the implications of organizational structure, on communication.

7.6   Directional Flow of Communication

To be effective, any organization needs to utilize three kinds of communication within the administrative hierarchy: downward, upward, and horizontal. Information is transmitted in a downward direction in the administrative hierarchy to provide for coordination of effort, directed towards achieving the organization's mission. Such coordination is promoted through statements setting forth and explaining policies, procedures, and administrative directions governing the entire operations and flow of information to all parts of the organization. The exercise of administrative power necessitates the downward flow of communication, and the use of power is essential if an organization is to be effective. The downward flow is the most consistently used and most effective. It is the easiest to utilize, whether the message is received and understood is another matter.

Katz and Kahn (1966) have identified five types of *downward communication*:

- Specific task directives, job instructions;

Figure 7.1 Typical Media for Communicating Information

Visual	Audio-visual
Written	**Sound Films and Film Strips**
Individual messages	Television
Circulars	Demonstrations
Manuals	Video Tapes
Handbooks	
Bulletin Board Notices and	**Audial**
Announcements	Face to Face Conversations
	Interviews
Pictorial	Meetings
Pictures	Conferences
Photographs	
Diagrams	**Intermediate Contact**
Maps	Telephone
Pictographs	Radio
	Intercom
Written Pictorial	Public Address System
Posters	
Silent Films	**Symbolic**
Film Strips	Insignia or Flags
Charts	Buzzers
Cartoons	Bells
	Other Signals

(Source: Adapted from Redfield, 1958, p. 72)

- Information designed to produce understanding of the task and its relations with other organizational tasks and job rationale;
- Information about organizational procedures and practices;
- Feedback to the subordinates about the performance;
- Information of an ideological character to circulate a sense of mission, such as indoctrination of goals;

Of the five types of downward communication, those, which administrators use most frequently in relating to staff within educational institutions, are probably those concerning job rationale, procedures and practices, and indoctrination goals.

In general, the opportunities for misunderstandings of communications will increase as the space within the organization increases between the sender and the receiver. A message is interpreted by the members of each organizational unit in terms of perceptions developed from a particular position within the organizational hierarchy. When the distance between the sender and the receiver is longer, a greater difference in perception is likely to occur. If a message is sent out from a large school system, provisions need to be made for interpretation of what the message means to each particular unit, and for feedback to determine whether the message is getting through. District, individual school and faculty level meetings constitute a device, which can serve those purposes admirably, on matters important enough to warrant such an investment of time.

The *upward flow of communication* is necessary in any organizational setting. It is especially important when resources are to be utilized, based on the most relevant information for making such decisions. The effectiveness and adequacy of the organizational communications need to be continuously evaluated. Upward communication provides for the transmittal of reports, opinions, ideas, suggestions, complaints, grievances, gripes and rumours. According to Katz and Kahn (1966), it includes what the person says (1) about himself/herself, his/her performance and his/her problems, (2) about others and their problems, (3) about organizational practices and policies, and (4) about what needs to be done.

However, Newell (1978) states that distortion in upward communication is inevitable. All of the information that goes up the line, has been coloured by the individual perceptions of the people doing the communicating; most of the information has been condensed and summarized, and much of it consists of inferences, rather than facts.

Horizontal communication is necessary to provide for consistency in the organization's actions. Horizontal communication is essential for the coordination of work effort among peers, unless the administration is dictatorial. Horizontal communication also fills in gaps that occur in downward communication. If and when information is not received from the superiors within the organizational hierarchy, a staff member typically consults a peer to obtain the information to decide upon a course of action. Finally, horizontal communication helps to meet many social and emotional needs.

Horizontal communication tends to be the most neglected type of communication, due to the fact that the need for such communication often goes unrecognized. One of the best ways of providing for horizontal communication is the creation of policy formulating and decision-making groups, which cut across the structural boundaries of a formal organization, with representatives from various organizational units. In the case of a school, the establishment of committees such as, Finance and Budgeting,

Buildings and Grounds, Curriculum, Time Tabling, Discipline, Canteen etc. would facilitate this requirement.

7.7 Communication Overload

Students, staff and members of the community use communication channels in a school. They are selected in terms of the appropriateness of the channel for serving a particular need or task. Some of the ways in which an overload can be constructively handled is through prioritizing and delaying responses, where necessary. This means responding immediately on matters of highest priority and responding to other matters when more time is available, or alternatively the diversion of messages into other communication channels (i.e. redirection of messages to other persons or units in the organization).

During the second week of February 2000, some of the prominent web-sites such as Yahoo and Amazon dot com, faced breakdowns as a result of an information overload by computer hackers. It was revealed that large numbers of messages were sent to these sites making it difficult to cope with the flow of information. In the light of huge web-sites, such as these being unable to cope with an overload of information, it would be wise for administrators to be selective in sending information to busy personnel. Categorizing information on the basis of importance, purpose, availability of time, relevance, mode, content etc. could encourage people to be more responsive to communication.

7.8 Formal and Informal Organizations

In all organizational settings, in addition to the formal organization, there is an informal organization, involved in communication. People talk together over coffee or at lunch, in the faculty room, in offices and in the corridor. A grapevine develops, through which information and rumours pass from one person to another.

Charney (1995) makes some suggestions to avoid rumours in an organizational setting. She encourages managers/leaders to believe that it is better to give abundant information as opposed to less than required, to hold regular briefings; to post a flipchart in the work area where news is written regularly; and also to anticipate potentially controversial issues in order to deal with them promptly.

Administrators learn to depend on various individuals for information. Individuals who may not even be shown in an organization chart are consulted and wield substantial power. The communication which occurs through the informal organization is desirable, and whether the administrator wants such communication or not, it is inevitable. Informal communication enables people to make friends, to express grievances, to pass information back and forth to one another, to explore ideas, which may later be introduced into the formal organization, and to obtain suggestions for solving specific problems. These functions are important to the life of an organization and can never be performed adequately by the formal organization alone.

7.9 Crossing System Boundaries and Administrative Competencies

If a school system is to be effective, two-way communication between the formal organization and the people outside the organization is essential. For example, information needs to go from the school to the parents and other citizens, and on the other hand, from individuals, groups, and organizations in the community to the school. Moreover, the school cannot carry out its mission effectively without information from the community at large.

As effective communication is essential for the successful functioning of a school, the school administrators are responsible for helping to facilitate communication. Meeting this responsibility adequately is possible only through a high level of administrative competence in a wide range of processes, procedures, and skills, which effective administrators utilize, in their day-to-day work on various kinds of problems (Newell, 1978). Most importantly, the administrator should be able to establish an effective network of communication in consultation with the staff and the local community. This could be done by means of school council members, parents and citizens associations (P&CAs), letters to parents, weekly or fortnightly newsletters, news reports and/or articles in local newspapers etc.

7.10 Organizing Communication

Mukhi et al. (1998) develop an information process model of an organization based on the three laboratory demonstrated propositions. Accordingly, task dictates information processing needs. Structure shapes the communication system, and a good fit between the task and the structure enhances effectiveness. In general research evidence supports the idea that increased uncertainty, complexity and interdependency intensifies organizational information processing needs. It also supports the idea that effective organizations, through appropriate organizational design and co-ordination mechanisms, provide organizational communication systems that fit those information-processing needs.

Research evidence, suggests that the distribution of communication time among the various relationships in the network vary, depending on the type of managerial job. If the manager at the centre is a functional manager, the lateral and diagonal relationships with other departments often consume the most time. Whatever the distribution, any single com-munication can be extremely important. Therefore, we need to consider the kinds of information communicated and the difficulties in com-municating up, down and across the organization.

Any effort to improve communication and understanding in the management team should focus as much attention upon the reception of messages, as it does upon the transmission of messages. Nearly all of us do more listening than speaking in meetings, yet, we are much more conscious of what we are saying than what we are hearing. Wynn and Guditus (1984) suggest that most of us need to listen more carefully and intensely, than we do now.

Hoy and Miskel (2001) have made an insightful analysis of communica-tion in organizations and have presented the following generalizations on communication theory:

- Communication is purposive.
- Meanings of messages are in people and not necessarily in the intended content.
- Feedback is essential for high levels of understanding.
- Formal and informal communication exist in all organizations.
- Formal and informal communication channels are potentially complementary.

Jehiel (1999) encourages leaders and managers to set up optimal communication structures in their organizations. An optimal network of communication is likely to maximize the chance of effective communica-tion, where no message is lost at any level of the communication process.

7.11 Interweaving of Organizational Tasks

In reality, the organizational tasks are closely related, interdependent, and inseparable. According to Wynn and Guditus (1984), they are like the warp and woof of a fabric; identifiable individual strands woven together, reinforcing and interacting with each other, while functioning together as a whole. We may pull them apart for analysis strand by strand, but it is the total fabric with properties derived from the interlocking weaves that separate strands.

Figure 7.2 illustrates this warp and woof relationship. This figure shows how communication and decision-making are paramount in organizations especially in the context of effective leadership and management. It is the management of communication and decision-making in an effective organization that differentiates it from other forms of management.

Figure 7.3 depicts another view of communication, as the critical interface of every administrative process. It refers the three most important administrative tasks of leaders and managers such as: policy formulation, allocation of resources and the execution of policies and in the context all three areas, how effective communication becomes paramount while decision-making plays almost a similar role.

Figure 7.2   The Interweaving of the Leaders'/Managers' Tasks

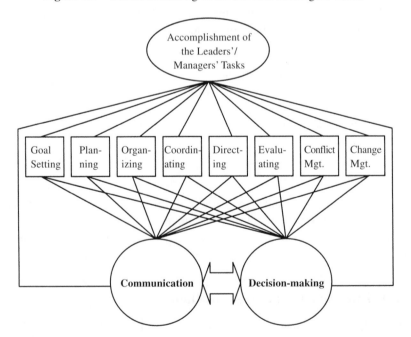

Figure 7.3 The Key Administrative Tasks Cycle of Leaders/Managers

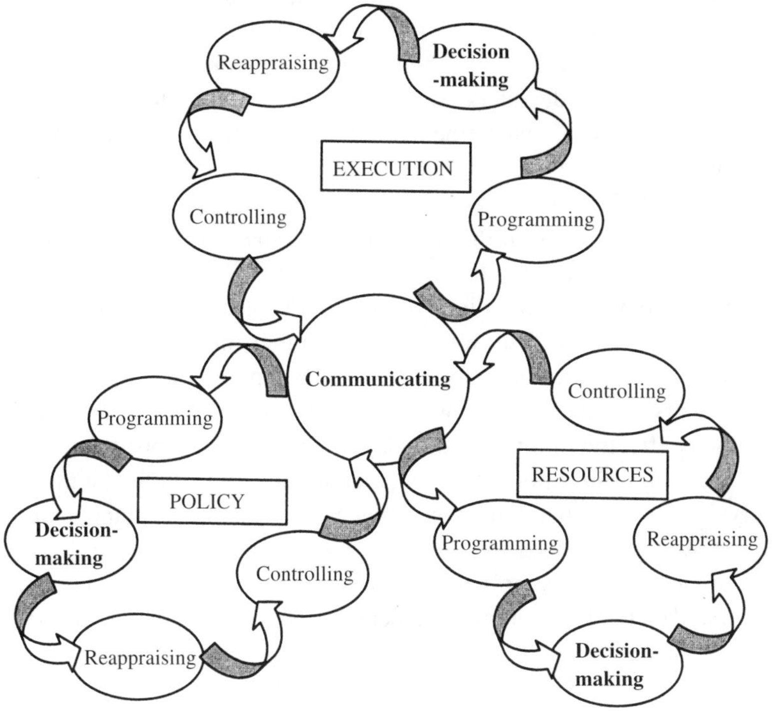

The Australian Capital Territory and Victorian government school systems in Australia (where SBM has been in operation since mid-1970s) have established appropriate linkages between communication and decision-making. School Boards and/or Councils are supplied with accurate and comprehensive information well in advance of the meetings of these governing bodies to facilitate effective decision-making. Similarly, the executive is made responsible to the governing body by requiring the principal to submit progress reports on a regular basis on the implementation of decisions already made. Effective communication flows to the stake-holders through the weekly or fortnightly newsletters and the representatives of different categories of stakeholders (Gamage et al., 1995, 1996).

7.12 Improving Communication

Leaders/managers, who are striving to become better communicators, have two separate tasks they must accomplish. First, they must improve the information included in the message that they want to transmit. Second, they must seek to improve their own understanding of what other people are trying to communicate to them. This means that they must become better encoders and decoders. They must strive not only to be understood, but also to understand what others are saying. In this context, it is better to assume that you are misunderstood and, whenever possible, attempt to determine whether the intended meaning actually was received. Very often, meaning is in the mind of the receiver. When the head of an organization passes notices of vacancies in other organizations to staff, it is possible that staff members who are familiar with the boss's intention may understand it as a friendly gesture. But, a new staff member might interpret it as an evaluation of poor performance and a suggestion to leave.

Leaders/managers may employ communication audits as a strategy in promoting effective communication in the organization. Kopec (1982) cited in Scott et al. (1999) points out that a communication audit is a thorough analysis of an organization's communications, both internal and external. This complete analysis involves the assessment of the organization's communication needs, policies, practices and capabilities, and uncovers essential data to allow top management to make informed and economical decisions about the future objectives of the organization's communication.

7.12.1 Regulating Communication Flow

The regulation of communication can ensure an optimum flow of information to staff, thereby, eliminating the barriers to "communication". Communication needs to be regulated, both in quality and quantity. The idea is based on the exception principle of management, which states that only significant deviations from policies and procedures should be brought to the attention of superiors. In terms of formal communication, superiors should be informed of only matters of exception and not for the sake of communication.

Feedback is an important element in effective two-way communication. It provides a channel for receiver's response that enables the communicator to determine whether the message has been received and has produced the intended response.

In a face-to-face communication, direct feedback is possible. In downward communication, however, inaccuracies often occur because of insufficient opportunity for feedback from receivers. A memorandum, addressing an important policy statement, may be distributed to all staff, but this does not guarantee that communication has occurred. It is important to encourage upward communication in the form of feedback.

7.12.2 Receiver Orientation of Empathy

When an administrator wants to communicate with his or her staff, s/he should be concerned with receiver orientation, rather than communicator orientation. The form of the communication should depend largely on what is known about the receiver. Empathy requires communicators to place themselves in the shoes of the receiver, in order to anticipate how the message is likely to be decoded. Empathy refers to the ability to place oneself in another person's role and to assume that particular individual's viewpoints and emotions. Whenever the gap between the experiences and the backgrounds of the communicator and the receiver are greater, the greater is the effort needed to find common ground.

7.12.3 Repetition

Repetition is an accepted principle of learning, especially, in the rote learning approaches. Introducing repetition to communication ensures that if one part of the message is not understood, other parts will carry the same message. Often, new staff members are provided with the same basic information in several different forms when first joining an organization. This is to ensure adherence to procedure.

7.12.4 Encouraging Mutual Trust

We know that time pressures often negate the possibility that leaders/ managers will be able to follow up communication and encourage feedback on upward communication. Under such circumstances, an atmosphere of mutual trust and confidence between superordinates and subordinates can facilitate communication. Leaders who have developed a climate of trust will find that following up on each communication, is less critical because of the mutual trust and confidence built over the years.

When trust is present, organizational members tend to share power and minimize control, in order to hasten the accomplishment of personal and organizational goals (Hackman, 1994). Trust, likewise, encourages members to share information and participate in the completion of tasks (Mishra & Morrissey, 1990). Moreover, McLain and Hackman (1999) argue that trust-building provides a social resource, that can be used to reduce unknown future risks in the organization.

Booher (1999) suggests the use of small talk as a powerful, although simple, strategy in building rapport and trust within an organization. To use small talk effectively, managers should engage the right person, choose the right timing, employ the right medium, and cover the right topic. Hunt et al. (2000) urge organizational leaders/managers to inform employees about all events within the workplace and to value their opinion as a way of building trust amongst the staff.

7.12.5 Effective Timing

Especially, with the advancement of information technology (IT), individuals are exposed to thousands of messages daily. Many of these messages are just received but never decoded. It is important for the leaders and managers to note that while they are attempting to communicate with a receiver, numerous other messages are being received simultaneously. Because of this, the message sent by the leader would not have been "heard". Messages are more likely to be heard when they are not competing with other messages. On an everyday basis, effective communication may be facilitated by properly timing major announcements. Poor timing is a barrier to communication.

7.12.6 Simplifying Language

Complex language has been identified as a major barrier to effective communication. Students often suffer when teachers use technical jargon that transforms simple concepts into complex puzzles. Leaders must remember that effective communication involves transmitting, understanding, as well as, providing accurate and timely information. If the receiver does not understand, then there has been no communication. Hence, it is important for the leaders/managers to encode their messages in simple, easy to understand language, avoiding technical jargon.

7.12.7 Effective Listening

It has been said that to improve communication, leaders must seek to be understood, but also to understand. This involves listening. One method of ensuring that someone expresses true feelings, desires and emotions, is to listen. During the process, distractions such as answering the telephone or talking to another person should be avoided, putting the speaker at ease, showing that you are actually listening, and even asking questions to show your attempt to understand the message accurately. Thus, it is important to make a conscious decision to listen.

7.12.8 Using Grapevine

The grapevine is an important communication tool that exists in all organizations. It serves a bypassing mechanism, and in most instances, is faster than the formal system it bypasses. Because it is flexible and usually involves face-to-face communication, the grapevine transmits information rapidly. The resignation of a key administrator may be common knowledge long before it is announced.

If the management knows how to utilize it, a grapevine can be an effective means of communication. It is likely to have a stronger impact on the receivers, because it involves face-to-face exchange and allows for feedback. Because of the ability of a grapevine to satisfy many psychological needs, the grapevine will exist in all organizational settings. More than 75% of the information on the grapevine could be accurate. Of course, the portion that is distorted can be devastating. What is important is, however, as the grapevine is inevitable that leaders should seek to utilize it or at least attempt to increase its accuracy. If the leaders and/or managers can communicate with the opinion leaders within informal groupings, making accurate and adequate information available, then the possibility for damaging rumours to arise could be minimized.

7.12.9 Promoting Ethical Communications

It is of utmost importance for organizational members to deal ethically with one another in their communications, especially with outsiders. First, those organizational members should not intentionally deceive one another. Second, organizational members' communication should not harm any other colleagues. Finally, organization members should be treated justly. Of course, internal communication is not the only area where ethical behaviour is important, as communication with the external contexts of an organization can be more ethically challenging (Ivancevich & Matterson, 1993).

7.13 Conclusion

Communication is very important in educational contexts, such as, in schools and tertiary institutions. It should be considered a fundamental and integrative process in educational administration and management. Communication expects to share messages, ideas or attitudes that produce understanding between the sender and the receiver. From a study of communication processes, four major conclusions seem clear. First, communication is purposive for both the initiator and the receiver. Second, communication is a socio-psychological phenomenon that is explained by information theory. According to this theory, people within an organization exchange ideas or facts with other persons, when interacting in social situations. The people who receive and interpret them determine the meaning of these messages. Third, messages traverse through formal and informal channels, using a variety of verbal and nonverbal media. Fourth, to ensure a high level of understanding, feedback mechanisms are essential.

Communication is the process that supplies necessary technical, coordination related and motivational information to all corners of an organization. The design of a communication structure should be contingent upon the nature of the task to be performed. Communication is a complex process, because several sources may send competing and conflicting messages, simultaneously. Information is also subject to distortion as it is transmitted through intermediate levels of supervision. It is also subject to distortion when interpreted by the receiver. Although, perfection is virtually impossible, several approaches can be adopted to evaluate and improve the communication process, both at the individual and the organizational levels.

7.14 Review Questions

1. Explain what do you mean by organizational communication and evaluate its significance in improving organizational efficiency and effectiveness.
2. Evaluate the current system of communication in your working organization and discuss possible approaches to improving the system.

CHAPTER 8

Organizational Decision-making

8.0 Learning Outcomes

Based on a systematic study of this chapter, the readers will:

- Have a better understanding of the significance of decision-making and administrators' responsibilities in making appropriate decisions.
- Improve the knowledge and understanding of different approaches such as rational, administrative, incremental, mixed-scanning, and participatory models of decision-making.
- Develop the skills to draw from the theoretical concepts and best practices in order to establish the structures and processes for decision-making by adopting the most appropriate approaches and strategies.

8.1 Focus

The topic focuses on the significance of decision-making as one of the key responsibilities of an administrator, along with communication, serving as one of the two pillars supporting the administration of an organization. It discusses different models of decision-making, employed by administrators, in different situations and different contexts. Readers' attention is drawn to the advantages and disadvantages of the classical, administrative, incremental, mixed-scanning and participatory models of decision-making. Then, the different styles of decision-making that can be adopted, depending on the complexity of the issue, time available and the maturity level of the participants, will be discussed. It also points out the advisability of creating structures and processes for others to participate in the process by minimizing the number of terminal decisions made by the administrator.

8.2 Significance of Decision-making

Decision-making is one of the most significant responsibilities of an administrator. It is widely recognized as at the heart of an organization and as central to administration. Policy making, itself, is a product of decision-making; it establishes the values and guidelines for operational decisions. What we describe as organizing is the distribution of authority to officers and groups, to make decisions within the organizational setting. The organizational structures are created for the purpose of empowering them to make decisions, relating to the areas or units that come under the purview of that structure or position. Even if we think of one's own family, which is the smallest organization, very often, husband and wife, either formally or informally, agree or empower each other to make decisions relating to different aspects of family affairs. Then, the transmission of information essential to decision-making is communication. Evaluation and even auditing is the process of making judgements relating to the quality of decisions. In fact, the quality of working (organizational) life is largely a function of the quality of decisions, whereas, the quality of administration is largely a function of the organization's capability to make quality and effective decisions. As Vecchio, Hearn, and Southey (1996) note, firms that can utilize creative ways of making decisions enjoy a key competitive advantage.

In a landmark book, published by Herbert Simon (1957), he observes that a general theory of administration must include principles of organization that will ensure correct decision-making. Daniel Griffiths (1959) further emphasizes this particular point, when he states that a theory of administration means decision-making. He, likewise, points out that an administrator's power and authority depends on the number of decisions s/he is empowered to make.

- *First, the structure of an organization is usually determined by the nature of the decision-making process.* For example, a business firm is structured with a small board of directors and a managing director, as its core-business is not that diversified and easy to handle, with a centralized smaller unit. But, a high school is structured with a principal, heads of faculties, year-coordinators and student counsellors, as the structure of decision-making relating to core-business, needs to be decentralized.

- *Second, the organizational rank of an individual is directly related to the degree of control s/he exercises over the decision-making process.* For example, a principal becomes the head of the school because of the control s/he has over the decision-making process.
- *Third, that the effectiveness of an administrator is inversely proportional to the number of decisions that he or she must personally make.* A principal who has a high degree of control is the head of the school. But, instead of creating the necessary structures to make shared decisions or making them by him or herself, if s/he allows his deputy to make most decisions, it is the deputy who will be more effective in the organizational setting (Adapted from Griffiths, 1959).

Especially in educational contexts, Griffiths' theory of administration has been highly influential, highlighting two important concepts. The administrator's first responsibility is to establish the structures and processes for decision-making, and second, once the structures and processes are established, an effective administrator makes only a few decisions by himself or herself. This leads to another important concept, that the administrator's influence resides more firmly in creating and monitoring the structures and processes, through which decisions shall be made by the organizational members, rather than making a large number of terminal decisions by him or her.

8.3 What Is Decision-making and How Is It Done?

What is decision-making? It is the process through which individuals, groups and organizations choose courses of action to be acted upon. It includes not only the decision, but also the implementation of that decision to take a particular course of action. When an individual or an organization is faced with a problem, a decision needs to be taken and acted upon to rectify the situation. If a particular individual's neighbour constantly organizes parties and creates noise, disturbing his or her sleep, the person has to take a decision to stop it. S/he can either speak to the neighbour or explain the problem, suggesting that the noise level be kept to a minimum, or can notify the police. Once she decides which course of action to be taken, she has to take the decided upon action in order to get the desired redress. Similarly, if a school is under threat because of declining enrolments, the school authorities need to decide what to do, and take the necessary action accordingly. In case of such a critical issue, naturally, the principal has to consult with his or her executive, and decide on preliminary causes of action. Then, s/he should involve the whole staff, and even the local community in examining the alternative solutions and acting upon the best course of action to solve the problem. When an issue is complex and affects others, it is always wiser to consult others affected, and even seek outside help in sorting out the problem.

Decision-making can be a painful process. It can lead to changes, conflicts, taking risks, resulting in success or failure. The administrator also has to cope with reading through documents, listening, researching, collecting data and consulting others or experts to make the best possible decision. Because of these complications, there are people, even top administrators, who try their best to avoid taking a decision. There have been high university officials, with whom the first author (Gamage) has worked, who have kept the files for 8–9 months and returned the papers, with no decision, even though the relevant information was made available. There have been occasions, when a problem affecting an employee could have been resolved with a simple solution. However, the issue remained unresolved up to 4–5 years, passing through the hands of several senior administrators, but none of them was prepared to take a decision, except to say that the matter was receiving attention. It is not difficult to visualize the frustration of the employee and how it affected his morale.

However, failure to take a decision is often worse than taking a decision on any of the alternative courses of action open for the decision. The unnecessary delay frustrates the subordinates, creating many more problems for the organization. When a problem arises, it is always wiser to examine the issues involved and to take the most feasible decision in the given situation. Later, if it is found that the earlier decision was faulty, it is necessary to take action to rectify the resulting situation. According to a survey conducted by Everard and Morris (1996, p. 40) at all levels of an organization, in which the staff were asked what change they would most like to see in their boss, the most frequent response by a clear margin was that "he should take decisions". In an analysis of the responses, some have stated "more clearly", "more rapidly". Some have gone to the extent of stating; "often it doesn't matter which decision, as long as s/he takes a decision". In fact, failure to take decisions can be considered as management by default, which might have more serious implications than a decision on any of the alternative solutions.

8.4 Influence of Organizational Culture

Organizational culture involves the norms that develop in a work group or an organization. The dominant values advocated by the organization, the philosophy that guides the organization's policies relating to staff and client groups, and the feeling that is evident in the ways in which people interact with each other influence decisions. Thus, organizational culture deals with basic assumptions and beliefs shared by the organizational members. Usually, these include, why it exits, how it has survived, what it is about. Organizational culture plays a key role in shaping the intuition, assumptions and beliefs of administrators, on a taken-for-granted basis and influences the decision-making process. The participants in most educational organizations have a long history of sharing common experiences. These shared experiences, have over time, led to the creation of a shared view of the world and their place in it. This enables them to make sense out of events, ascribe meanings to symbols and rituals and share common understandings of how to deal with the unfolding events in appropriate ways.

Karl Weick (1979) has described such sense making as central to understanding how people in organizations attribute credibility to interpretations that they have made, based on their experiences. Mintzberg's (1983) analysis supported by several other studies, relating to the functioning of educational organizations, points out that administrators, who are pressed for time due to numerous interruptions, have little opportunity to be alone, to be engaged in reflective thought. This, further, increases the dependence on intuition based on organizational culture. The role and power of organizational culture are to shape and mould the thinking, and therefore, decision-making is not a new concept. However, until recent times, not much emphasis was placed on its significance. But, now most organizational analysts, as well as, practitioners, not only admit its significant influence, but also try to improve decision-making by effecting changes to the organizational culture.

A good example is the significant changes to school cultures, revealed in Australian research by Gamage and colleagues (1995, 1996), as a result of two decades of school-based management, with community participation in the Australian Capital Territory and Victorian schools. Participatory approaches have made schools more open than closed to the parents and community, resulting in significant changes to organizational culture, leading to effective decisions and more effective schools. Pang's (1999d) study, which reviewed the effectiveness of school-based management in Hong Kong since its inception in 1991, also shows that when aided schools (the major sector in Hong Kong) which had implemented SBM, the schools' managerial practices in participatory decision-making, collaboration, collegiality, communication, and consensus were significantly improved. However, the impacts of school-based management on government schools (the minor sector in Hong Kong) in such respects were minimal (Pang, 2002). In the government schools, even when SBM was implemented, schools' goals and missions, school-based decision-making and teachers' work were not significantly enhanced. The government schools have failed to delegate authority for decision-making in keeping with the principles of SBM and decentralization. Even in 2001, the decisions relating to supplies, equipment, personnel, maintenance, utilities, payroll and policy and so forth were made at the headquarters of the Education Department and the Civil Service Bureau. On the other hand, no significant changes in managerial practices have been effected.

8.5   Decision-making Models

Organizational behavioural scholars have proposed different models of decision-making. These are the classical, the administrative, the incremental, the mixed-scanning, the contingency and the participatory models.

8.5.1   *The Classical (Rational) Model of Decision-making*

The most common approach to the analysis of decision-making is through the rational model. This strategy seeks "the best possible alternative to maximize the achievement of goals and objectives." Hoy and Miskel have referred to the relevant steps as follows:

- Identify that there is a need for a decision. If there is pressure to take action, the administrator should make sure that a problem does really exist.
- Identify cause. If circumstances exist that requires action, identify the causal factors, but not the symptoms.

- Develop criteria. Identify the criteria for the solution, including time and resource constraints.
- Evaluate alternatives. Seek and identify the alternative solution that seems to meet the potential needs.
- Evaluate alternatives. Compare the alternatives on the basis of the predetermined criteria.
- Select the best option.
- Implementation: Ensure that the selected option is implemented and action is in accordance with the decision.
- Review: Compare the outcome with the objective or intention and adjust actions as it is deemed necessary (Adapted from 2001, p. 317).

With regard to the use of information, it has been observed that the rational model assumes that:

- Relevant information will be collected and analysed, before a decision is made.
- The available information will be used in making the decision;
- Additional information will only be called for if available information is examined and found to be inadequate;
- Information needs will be determined, before requesting information; and
- The information relevant to the decision will be gathered.

However, based on their reading of research studies on decision-making, Feldman and March (1981) have found that what happens in practice is quite different and have made the following observations:

- Much of the information that is gathered and communicated, by individuals and organizations, has little relevance to decision-making;
- Much of the information that is used to justify a decision, is collected and interpreted after the decision has been made, or substantially made;
- Much of the information gathered in response to requests for information is not considered in the making of the decision;
- Regardless of the information available at the time, a decision is first taken to call for more information.
- Complaint that an organization does not have enough information to make a decision occurs while available information is ignored.

- The relevance of the information provided in the decision-making process, to the decision being made is less obvious than the insistence on information (1981, pp. 171–186).

However, the rational model is portrayed as the best method to make high quality decisions. But, the model has a number of difficulties in practice. Dunford (1992) has pointed out that the model can work only when there is a clear, commonly agreed objective; all options are known and the decision criteria, is clear. However, this rarely occurs in real world situations. The model does not adequately take into account the time constraints and cost limits that may hinder the analysis of all possible alternatives. Nor does it account for the divergent views that may influence the setting of objectives and decision criteria. Hoy and Miskel (2001), likewise, claim that this model is unrealistic, because of the fact that not all-rational and objective bases for making decisions are accessible.

8.5.2   The Administrative Model: A Satisfying Strategy

In the light of the fact that it is virtually impossible to optimize benefits under the strategy advocated by the classical (rational) model, in practice, other strategies have been developed. One of the models proposed, as an alternative is the administrative model. The basic approach in this behavioural theory of decision-making, proposed by Herbert Simon is to find a satisfactory solution with which the group or organization can live, rather than the best solution. Vecchio et al. (1996) have referred to the following steps involved in this model:

- A problem situation exists, which requires a decision to be made;
- The problem is recognized and analysed;
- Criteria to select a satisfactory alternative is drawn;
- Alternatives are evaluated as they become known;
- The first alternative which seems satisfactory and acceptable is selected;
- Chosen alternative is implemented; and
- Effectiveness of chosen alternative is evaluated (pp. 356–357).

Edward Litchfield (1956 cited in Hoy & Miskel, 2001, pp. 318–321) draws our attention to the following assumptions, when making organizational decisions:

- Decision-making is a cycle of events that includes the identification and diagnosis of a problem that an organization is confronted with, the development of a plan to solve the problem, the implementation of the plan, and the appraisal of its success.

- Administration is the performance of the decision-making process by an individual or a group in an organizational context.
- Complete rationality in decision-making is virtually impossible. This forces the administrators to seek a satisfactory solution, as they are unable to find an ideal solution to maximize the decision-making process.
- The basic function of administration is to provide each subordinate with an internal environment for decision-making. But this is done on the assumption that the behaviour of staff members is rational, from both individual and organizational perspectives.
- Decision-making is a general pattern of action found in the rational administration of all major functional and task areas.
- In most complex organizations, there is a significant similarity and generality in the decision-making process.

After the problem has been analysed and specified, the administrator must decide what constitutes an acceptable solution. What are the minimum objectives that are to be accomplished? What would be most essential, when compared to the current problems confronting the organization? As it is almost impossible to achieve a perfect solution, s/he needs to decide what would be good enough, or acceptable, to the majority of those affected? The answers to these questions will enable the administrator to establish a criterion for a satisfactory solution. It is better to analyse the available solutions, according to the degree of satisfaction gained. Naturally, once the compromises are made, with adaptations and concessions within the boundary conditions, it is unlikely to have a completely satisfactory solution for a decision. Accordingly, the administrator makes a satisfying decision.

8.5.3 The Incremental Model: A Strategy of Muddling Through

Even though, the satisfying strategy described above is good enough in most situations, to meet the demands in educational administration, there are some issues, which require an incremental strategy. This occurs when the relevant alternatives are difficult to discern, or when the consequence of each available solution is complicated, so as to elude analysis and prediction, to the extent that a satisfactory solution is also blocked. To meet this situation, Charles Lindblom (1968) and Lindblom and Cohen (1979) introduce and formalize the incremental model. Lindblom characterizes this model for decision-making, as the science of muddling through, and argues that it may be the only feasible approach, when issues are complex, uncertain and riddled with conflict. In this context, the process is best described by the method of successive limited comparisons.

The incremental model also reduces the number of alternatives, as it considers only those alternatives within the administrator's interest and control, which would be suitable to the current situation. This approach also can be considered as an alternative to theory. Usually, theory is viewed as a useful way to bring relevant knowledge to bear on a specific problem. However, when problems become too complex, the existing theoretical concepts may not be able to guide a solution, thus, requiring the updating of theory. The strategy of successive limited comparisons suggests that administrators can make more progress on such complex issues by employing this model.

Hoy and Miskel (2001, p. 331) indicate that the incremental model has the following features:

- It seeks to set objectives and generate alternative solutions simultaneously, which could be considered inappropriate.
- Decision-makers agree on solutions, which are considered to be good irrespective of the objectives.
- As the current situation becomes the pre-eminent consideration, only the alternatives relevant to the current context are considered.
- Evaluation is limited to differences between the current situation and proposed alternatives.
- The incremental method discards theory in favour of practical solutions available with ease.

8.5.4   *The Mixed-scanning Model: An Adaptive Strategy*

Hoy and Tarter (1995) have pointed out that the process of "muddling through" has its advantages and limitations, in view of the fact that it is conservative and goes on aimlessly. In real world situations, most administrators make decisions only with partial information especially when pressed for time. Etzioni (1989) advocates a pragmatic approach to decision-making, which can be employed in uncertain and complex situations. The Mixed-scanning model involves two questions, i.e. what is the organization's mission and policy? What decisions will move the organization towards its mission and policy?

This approach seeks to use partial information to make satisfactory decisions rather than getting bogged down in examining all available information or proceeding without any information. In summarizing Etzioni's (1989) basic principles of the mixed scanning model, Hoy and Tarter (1995) state the following:

- It is a trial and error approach. The model seeks limited, easy to find alternatives, selects what is considered reasonable, and implements and tests them. Modification is undertaken when the outcome becomes clearer.
- The administrator considers the decision as tentative and becomes more open to effect changes, when a clearer picture emerges.
- If and when the problem is complex and the situation is unclear, a decision is delayed until a better picture emerges.
- The administrator seeks solutions by stages. Time is taken to study the situation and take the next step, as and when it is warranted.
- Partial solutions are sought and implemented, committing partial resources, until the outcomes become more satisfactory.
- Competing alternatives are implemented and final decision is based on the results.
- As partial solutions are implemented on a tentative or experimental basis, it enables the administrator to reverse his/her decision when full information is available and outcomes are known.

As Etzioni's techniques enable a flexible, cautious and incremental approach, the educational administrators can easily employ them to find satisfactory solutions, especially in situations where they are confronted with difficult and complex issues.

8.6 Types of Organizational Decision-making Processes

Nutt (1984) has grouped decision-making into five categories, such as, (1) historical, (2) off-the-shelf, (3) appraisal, (4) search, and (5) nova. The historical decisions are taken routinely guided by the precedents already created. Off-the-shelf decisions involve choosing from a number of relatively obvious alternatives. Appraisal decisions entail a more comprehensive, in-depth evaluation of less familiar alternatives. Search decisions take place when no alternatives are available and the decision-makers lack knowledge of the basis for decisions. This could involve collection of data and analysis, to provide a better picture. Nova decisions involve the leader/

manager and the staff in generating and evaluating fresh ideas for implementation.

8.7 Styles of Decision-making

In an examination of the approaches employed by the leaders and managers in making organizational decisions, their approaches could be categorized as follows:

- *Autocratic:* The leader and/or manager on his or her own, without the input or consultation from those affected takes the decision. Then staff and/or those involved are informed of what and when the decision is to be implemented and what is expected of them.
- *Persuasive:* The leader and/or manager makes a decision without consulting those affected, and then sells the decision to them, with convincing reasoning and arguments, as to why it should happen that way and why it is important to proceed according to his/her recommendation.
- *Consultative:* The leader/manager seeks the views of others, through a process of individual consultation or a brain storming session with the group affected, and takes them into account in the decision-making process.
- *Co-determinate:* The leader/manager decides with the staff, either by consensus or majority vote, at a meeting convened for the purpose (Adapted from Everard & Morris, 1996, p. 45).

8.7.1   *Autocratic Decision-making*

Usually, within any organization, this style is acceptable on mainly routine and individual matters, where clear understandings and precedents have been established and the decision does not concern or affect others. This style is the usual practice in cases where the bureaucratic rules have laid down the conditions under which a decision could be made, on particular issues, such as leave of absence to a staff member. This style is also accepted without fuss, where the leader has a considerable track record of success, because of his/her expertise or charisma. Even though staff may be unhappy and grumble, they may grudgingly accept the decision, because of the belief that at times, decisions have to be handed down with no opportunity for input. For example, when there were allegations of child abuse in schools and much criticism by media and public, on the advice of the government, the Director General of Education issued a Code of Conduct for child protection, to be followed by school personnel.

8.7.2   Persuasive Decision-making

This style differs from the autocratic one, as the leader takes the decision, but rather than directing or expecting staff to follow it, s/he tries to sell it to those affected. Here, the leader uses his or her leadership skills of advocacy, to reason out and justify the decision taken as the right one, in the given set of circumstances. If the leader reveals that s/he was pressed for time and honestly did not have the time to canvass staff views, without trying to pretend that s/he wanted to consult the staff, it is an acceptable position and it occurs in most organizations. The persuasion can be interpreted as leader's understanding, and sincere respect for staff, especially when s/he explains why it was impossible or inappropriate to consult them before the decision.

8.7.3   Consultative Decision-making

This approach has advantages where the leader receives the input, opinions and suggestions of those who are affected and interested, while vesting authority to decide in the leader. The staff is assured that the decision will be in conformity with the established guidelines and precedents. In taking the decision, the leader is expected to evaluate of the majority views already expressed at private consultations or at group meetings. However, it may be interesting to note that many leaders and managers employ this approach, as a ploy, to impose their own decisions, irrespective of the majority views expressed in consultations.

8.7.4   Co-determinate Decision-making

This style is likely to be consistent with assumed collective responsibility and, thereby, avoiding individual responsibility. This method is unavoidable when there is no person vested with responsibility, but a group of people, such as a committee, is vested with authority to make the decisions. In terms of school-based management, the authority is usually devolved on to the particular school council, board, trustees, and school management committee or school governors. Whenever this style is adopted, it is important to see that the decision-making procedure conforms to the following criteria:

- The decision-making process is open and clear to all concerned.

- It is consistent with reality.
- Accurate and adequate information on complex issues are provided for making informed decisions.
- The leader/manager understands the concerns of others and establishes the conventions of the particular form of decision-making.

8.8 Participatory Decision-making

Participation can be defined as the mental and emotional involvement of an individual, in a group situation, that encourages him/her to contribute to the group process and share responsibility with the group. Gamage (1996b) as well as Blasé and Blasé (1999) have described this approach as a genuine involvement, with just and fair opportunities for all participants to have their input, rather than merely being present and going through the motions. Such involvement is motivational to the participant and it releases his or her own energy, responsibility and initiative, resulting in ownership and commitment. Participatory decision-making in schools is also called shared governance or school-based management.

Participatory decision-making leads to organizational success, as it ensures that the chosen solution is of a high quality (Hirokawa & Poole, 1986; Vecchio et al., 1996; Liontos & Lashway, 1997). In addition, participatory decision-making heightens learning and personal growth among the members of the organization, as a result of diverse and fresh ideas being generated by the other participants (Kelly, 1994; Oswald, 1997). Moreover, the members appreciate the reasons underlying chosen courses of action as their decisions are based on their interaction (Brown et al., 1974; Vecchio et al., 1996). This method of decision-making reflects Likert's (1961) System 4 approach and Blake and Mouton's team management approach (Lussier, 1993).

How does collaboration between the administrators and the employees in decision-making promote superior performance? Gamage (1998a) reveals how a genuine partnership resulting from participatory decision-making enables the participants to appreciate each other's points of view and consequently foster increased motivation and commitment enabling the accomplishment of organizational goals. In addition, Bandrowski (1990, p. 99) notes that "when executives and lower level employees are properly tapped for ideas and brought into the decision-making process, peak experiences occur and peak results follow". Moreover, it is reported that the employees' degree of involvement in considering alternatives and in planning are significantly related to their performance (Black & Gregersen, 1997).

The collaborative strategy of decision-making imbues the employees with a sense of empowerment and a feeling of importance that satisfies their motivational needs. Brown and Brown (1994) argue that team-based decision-making structures respond to Maslow's highest needs for creativity, self-expression and self-accomplishment.

In the process of implementing a participatory decision-making process, Owens (2001, p. 285) proposes that the following three factors should be considered as a practical guide:

- The need for an explicit decision-making process;
- The nature of the problem to be solved or the issue to be sorted out; and
- The criteria for the inclusion of staff members or their representatives (who are affected and/or interested in the issue being considered) in the decision-making process.

Yukl (2002) refers to several ways of how leaders and/or managers can encourage the staff to participate in decision-making. One way is to encourage people to express their concerns. Another is to describe any proposal as tentative. Likewise, ideas and suggestions from others must be placed on record. Moreover, ways and means to build on the ideas and suggestions of the participants should be discovered. When participation is drawn from the members, dissenting views should be allowed to surface freely. Finally, suggestions from members should be duly appreciated.

The literature has lots of information regarding research on participatory decision-making, some through laboratory experimentation, with ad-hoc heterogeneous groups, and others in real world situations. But, there are circumstances and variables, which can guide the choice of the most suitable approach.

The Nature of the Problem — Group decisions are often superior to individual decisions when the problem is not easily conceptualized, it requires reasoning through a series of interdependent stages. The problem requires continued coordination and interaction of a number of persons for effective implementation.

The Composition of the Group — The nature of the members of the group is an important variable. It is evident that often, an established committee or a group produces better decisions than an ad-hoc group. In an established group, the participants share common goals, a better sense of understanding, loyalty and higher motivation resulting in effective decision-making, hence, creating a better image for the whole group.

Consensual Process — The consensus approach to decision-making influences the nature of the decision in several ways. Such decisions reached, after discussion within a group situation, tends to be better than an individual decision with or without discussion. The need to communicate one's ideas and views to others, forces refinement of the views prior to expressing them to a group, due to peer review.

Impact of Leadership Behaviour — Leadership is crucial to determine the social factors affecting group problem solving. Leader needs to have an open mind, receptive to criticisms and group views, by encouraging frank expression of views on the subject. However, when a leader after making up his/her mind, pretends that s/he wants staff participation and wastes staff's valuable time, it leads to frustration and lower morale.

Impact of Circumstances — The existence of differences of opinions often results in high quality decisions. The presence of concerns and stress, also may increase the creativity of alternative proposals, put forward. Encouraging group performance, as against individual performance also improves the quality of decisions.

On a review of research literature, Likert (1967, pp. 61–62) have pointed out that group decision-making tends to have the following effects upon the participants:

- Increased productivity.
- Reduced resistance to change in one's own behaviour.
- Reduced resistance to organizational change.
- Higher task motivation.
- Higher job satisfaction.
- Reinforcement among group members of the values commonly accepted in the organizational or group culture.
- Better teamwork.
- Deeper sense of mutual interdependence among participants.
- Stronger commitments of participants to a decision.
- Cooperation increases the participants' subsequent ability to complain about decisions.
- Influence of participants towards uniform or similar behaviour and attitudes, is a phenomenon sometimes identified as conformity effect, which may lead to either desired or undesired behaviour.

- Greater satisfaction among participants, with management and with the organization.
- Greater satisfaction among participants with both the solution and the process.
- Establishment of higher performance goals for participants and for the organization.

However, participatory decision-making also has certain limitations, costs, and hazards. Some critiques of participatory approaches invoke these concerns as a basis for discrediting it, however, the reasons given are common issues affecting most other similar social interactions. In certain circumstances, in the event of certain problems group decisions are superior, but it is a *time consuming process*. Gamage's (2000a) research in Leicester in England, reveals that with 10 years of experience in implementing local management of schools, school leaders, as well as, teachers are happier with participatory decision-making. Teacher governors admit that it leads to ownership and a higher degree of commitment to the implementation process.

Critiques also refer to *loss of control of the organization by the hierarchy*. They say that "everybody's business is nobody's business", as shared responsibility for decision-making amounts to diluted accountability. However, once a culture of group decision-making is built into the organizational culture, the group becomes more cohesive, responsible and accountable. *Indecision* is another possibility, especially when a group is large. If the problem is too complex and the group lacks cohesiveness, it is likely that the group may fail to reach consensus. To make the process more effective, it is better to organize smaller groups or teams, such as sub-committees or standing committees of the school governing body or the whole staff meeting.

8.9 Contingencies Approach

In many situations, there are contingencies, which accompany a given problem and its relationship to the approach taken in decision-making or in the solution of a problem. It is wiser to evaluate the contingencies that apply to a given problem and determine the most effective mode of decision-making.

Kelly (1994) identifies several team-based decision-making techniques, which may be employed in organizations, depending on a given situation. Such techniques are the nominal group technique, the Delphi technique, the consensus card method, the paired-choice matrix, and the criteria rating technique.

8.9.1   The Nominal Group Technique

This decision-making technique combines the aspects of silent voting with limited discussions to help an organization to arrive at a consensual decision. The steps involved are:

- Definition of the problem, or difficulty, which requires resolution.
- Generation of ideas silently (in writing).
- Recording of ideas generated.
- Clarification of each item on the list.
- Ranking of items, silently, or listing the rankings.
- Tallying of all the rankings.
- Wrapping up the nominal group technique session.

8.9.2   The Delphi Technique

This technique involves the solicitation and comparison of multiple rounds of anonymous judgements from team members on a decision or a problem. This is used if and when the leader/manager wishes to ensure that the input of each member is anonymous. Likewise, using this technique minimizes face-to-face interaction, particularly if the issue is sensitive or needs to be taken up with confidentiality. The steps that can be followed in the Delphi technique are:

- Define the problem or difficulty to be solved.
- Request the participants to provide round-one input.
- Summarize round-one input, with no names attached, and ask for round-two input.
- Summarize the round-two input and ask for round-three input.
- Summarize the round-three input.
- Wrap up the Delphi technique session.

8.9.3   The Consensus Card Method

This method uses a visual aid, which is provided to every member. The visual aid is used to indicate the position of each member at any point in the discussion. This technique is applicable when situations arise where potentially opposing opinions may surface in a face-to-face setting. This also hastens the arrival at a consensus, when confronted with controversial issues. Moreover, everyone is provided with the chance to express his/her position on the different alternatives considered by the group. The steps are:

- Define the issue or issues involved and set the goal[s] for the session.
- Prepare necessary presentations and documentation for the session.
- Present and discuss the ideas.
- Wrap up the consensus card method session.

8.9.4 The Paired-Choice Matrix

This technique enables a group to select from a number of alternatives. This approach can be effective in situations where there is a complex set of alternatives to be evaluated in a short period of time. Similarly, in situations where the options to be considered are similar in nature, there is a need to break a complex issue into appropriate, simple steps. The steps involved are:

- Identification of the issue[s], options and goal[s].
- Preparation for the session.
- Making decisions between pairs.
- Tallying scores of paired choices.
- Discussion and clarification of the result.
- Wrapping up the session.

8.9.5 The Criteria Rating Technique

This is a decision-making technique, employed to arrive at a choice between alternatives, using clearly defined criteria. This is useful when there is a need to select from amongst a number of alternatives. When this technique is employed, more objectivity is built into the decision-making process. Finally, this strategy facilitates the building of consensus, as individual contributions are depersonalized. The steps are:

- Start the session and list all the available alternatives.
- Brainstorm on the criteria for decision-making.
- Determine the relative importance of each criterion.
- Establish a rating scale, then rate the alternatives.
- Calculate the final score.
- Select the best alternative.
- Wrap up the session.

However, a survey conducted by Savery, Soutar, and Dyson (1992) on ideal decision-making styles as indicated by a group of deputy principals in Western Australia and the Northern Territory, suggest a variety of preferred modes of decision-making. The mode of decision-making depends on whether a staff member wants to participate or s/he wants the leader to take the decision. The perceived importance of the decision to the person's job and the level of skill that an employee has to make contributions to the participatory process, are considered very significant.

Figure 8.1 shows a good guide for the administrators to determine their approaches to decision-making:

8.10 Strengthening Decision-making

Burke (1999) has introduced the 3 **E**'s model for the purpose of strengthening organizational decision-making. According to him, *Empathy* encourages stronger networking; *Evaluation* promotes accountability; and *Ethics* strengthens leadership. Burke and Miller (1999) have shown that intuitive decision-making is employed by some of the successful managers. Intuition, which they define as a cognitive conclusion, is based on the decision-maker's previous experiences and emotional inputs. This can be categorized as experience-based, affect-initiated, cognitive-based, and value-based decision-making. Experience-based decisions are drawn from accumulated successes and failures, in work and in personal life. Emotional and/or gut feelings drive affect-initiated decisions. Cognitive-based decisions are inspired by knowledge and skills learned from training, seminars/workshops and textbooks. Value-based decisions are guided by the decision-maker's own moral values, or the organizational cultures.

Organizational decision-making can, likewise, be strengthened if the makers of decisions are aware of the obstacles to effective decisions. Vecchio et al. (1996) identifies these as judgmental bias, escalation of commitment and groupthinks. Awareness of these obstacles will enable decision-makers to think of ways for minimizing, if not completely avoiding, such obstacles.

8.11 Conclusion

The significance of decision-making is such that it is considered to be at the very heart of an organization, and at the centre of administration. Decision-making and communication can be considered as the two pillars on which an administration rests. An administrator who wants to be effective

Figure 8.1 Modes of Decision-making

CONTINGENCIES	A	B	C	D	E	F	G	H
1. An emergency exists	X		X					
2. Little time is available to decide	X		X					
3. Considerable time is available to decide				X	X	X		X
4. Decision doesn't merit time for group deliberation	X							
5. Leader is unwilling to share decision with group	X							
6. Leader has necessary information to decide	X							
7. Leader lacks necessary information to decide		X		X	X	X	X	X
8. Leader wants counsel but wants to keep options open				X	X	X		
9. Leader is incapacitated			X					
10. Leader lacks confidence in the group	X							
11. Executive decision within existing policy	X							
12. Relevant information is indisputable	X	X						
13. One decision is likely to be eminently tight	X	X						
14. Problem can be defined and structured precisely	X	X						

(Source: Adapted from Wynn & Guditus, 1984, p. 109)
Legend for Decision-making Modes:
A – Leader decides
B – Leader decides after recommendation by expert or project team
C – Small executive body decides
D – Leader decides after consulting or polling individuals
E – Leader decides after consulting the group
F – Leader decides after using the Delphi technique
G – Group decides by majority vote
H – Group decides by consensus

has to prove that s/he is an effective decision-maker. The above discussion draws the attention of the participants to the different theoretical concepts developed, such as the classical, administrative, incremental, mixed-scanning, participatory and contingency models of decision-making.

However, an administrator needs to determine the particular mode and style to be followed, depending on the complexity of the issue and who is likely to be affected by the decision, whether it is an individual, a group or whole staff etc. S/he needs to consider the time available and the maturity levels of the staff. A wise administrator prefers to create the structures and processes for staff participation, rather than making a large number of terminal decisions by him or her. The organizational health and effectiveness depends on the capability of the organizational leadership/management to make effective decisions, leading to ownership and commitment of the organizational members.

8.12 Review Questions

1. Examine the different modes and styles of decision-making available to an administrator and how would you make use of such knowledge in decision-making within your own organization.
2. Undertake a critical examination of the structures and processes for decision-making, currently available within your working organization and examine the ways and means of improving the organizational effectiveness through effective decision-making.

CHAPTER 9

Educational Planning and Policy Formulation

9.0 Learning Outcomes

Based on a systematic study of this chapter, the readers will:

- Gain a better understanding of the importance of planning and policy formulation, in the context of educational management, including the types of planning available to administrators;
- Examine the process of planning and policy formulation, and develop the skills to be better leaders and managers, by creating effective educational institutions; and
- Improve knowledge and understanding of alternative models, developed in other systems, for designing more appropriate plans and policies for one's own organization.

9.1 Focus

This chapter examines the process of planning and policy formulation, in the context of educational management. The importance of planning is emphasized, with a specific focus on the benefits of strategic and management planning. Two models are outlined for policy-making in schools. The Collaborative School Model and the Outcomes Driven Development Model are presented to guide effective formulation of policy.

9.2 The Concept of Planning

Planning is a process that precedes decision-making. A plan can be defined as a decision, with regard to a course of action. A course of action is a sequence of acts, which are mutually related and viewed as a unit. All successful organizations develop plans. There are some organizations, or even countries, which develop plans that are not implemented. If an organization develops a plan, it must be implemented to be successful, and it is expected that all organizational members follow the plan. Planning can be said to be an intelligent preparation for action. The planning process is differentiated from other pre-decision activities, in that it is systematic, deliberate and continuous. The planning process can lead to:

- Democratic and open management, or autocratic and closed management; creativity and flexibility, or organizational and human arrangements of rigidity;
- More efficient utilization of financial and human resources, or wastage of these resources, particularly over a long period of time;
- Building identification and commitment, among students and staff, to institutional goals or a leading to demoralizing effects;
- Develop the institution as a professional organization, or reinforce the school's bureaucratic tendencies.

9.3 The Importance of Planning

In the context of educational management, there are two key reasons as to why planning is considered important. First, it often has "primacy", from the standpoint of its position in the sequence of management functions. Second, it has "pervasiveness" as an activity that affects the entire organization. With regard to "primacy", planning logically precedes the performance of all other managerial roles, especially in organizing and/or controlling an organization. Planning establishes the objectives to be pursued and strategies through which they are to be achieved. It should not be assumed that planning is the initial step in a linear process. The objectives may have to be modified, as action plans are developed and reviewed periodically, to suit changed circumstances and new developments. The pervasiveness of planning is evident in the performance of all other managerial roles, and potentially, the activities of almost all members of an organization.

Planning is considered a vital responsibility of a leader or manager in any organizational setting. According to Boone and Kurtz (1987), there are specific reasons for its importance:

- Planning is related to performance — organizational success and school effectiveness depend upon successful planning.
- Planning focuses attention on objectives — plans continually reinforce the importance of objectives. Planning help to ensure that decisions contribute to their achievement and that administrators do not become over-involved in less important and less relevant decisions and activities.
- Planning helps offset uncertainties and anticipate problems — by developing plans for future contingencies; leaders and managers become better prepared and proactive, providing the staff with better security of tenure.
- Planning provides guidelines for decision-making — as plans specify the actions necessary to attain set objectives, they serve as a basis for decisions about future activities.
- Planning is necessary to facilitate monitoring and control — reference to plans can help leaders and managers determine whether decisions are being implemented properly, and whether organizational objectives are being accomplished.

Planning is important in resolving the following issues, which arise in contemporary educational systems:

- How to make the best use of limited resources?
- How to gear the education system to meet the needs of the economy?
- How to make the educational system more effective?
- How to keep pace with the equity requirements?
- How to provide for the effective participation of the school community in educational decision-making? and
- How to make the curriculum more relevant to the changing environment in meeting society's needs?

Change needs to be systematically planned and coordinated. In the planning process, appropriate attention needs to be given to long-term goals and priorities, as well as, to the goals to be achieved in the medium to short term. Finally, those concerned with planning improvements in education need to recognize that competent educational and lay leaders must be involved, at least, in the process of determining goals and major policies. This arises, because the public must accept the goals and policies, before they can be utilized for guidance in effecting any significant changes in education.

Some basic concepts of educational planning that are worthy of consideration are as follows:

- Planning has to be a logical and systematic process.
- In a democratic society, the people should cooperatively determine their goals and appropriate ways of attaining them.
- In the context of a democratic society, the goals should be social and economic ones, concerned with the welfare and progress of all.
- Cooperation implies the active involvement of representative and perceptive community members, as well as educators, in studying problems and needs, and in agreeing on appropriate goals and optimum ways of attaining them, rather than merely accepting the goals and policies developed by a few educators, or community members.

Different scholars stress the positive effects of planning in different ways. Timmons (1999) points out that opportunities and changes can be anticipated when management thinks ahead. Bangs (1996) echoes this idea when he claims that planning makes possible the objective assessment of weaknesses, needs and problems, before they grow into damaging proportions. Bryson (1990) as well as Flavel and Williams (1996) are of opinion that when planning is carried out strategically, it yields a clearer direction to any organization.

9.4 Kinds of Planning

There are two models of interrelated systematic planning: Strategic Planning, and Management Planning.

9.4.1 Strategic Planning

It is the process of discovering effective and efficient ways of utilizing organizational resources, for the attainment of a desired future (Flavel & Williams, 1996). Weindling (1997) points out that strategic planning stresses evolutionary, or rolling planning, where the plan itself is altered to adapt to changing circumstances. Strategic planning, fosters and requires productive relations and linkages with public agencies and groups, other than those directly responsible for education. It involves the determination of policies and the establishment of new or revised goals. This concept should be of special interest to educational leaders, who have a major responsibility for developing and implementing plans, because, it will help to ensure the commitment and support that is essential in facilitating needed changes.

Kaufman (1995) expands the concept of strategic planning, using the term *strategic planning plus*. Strategic planning plus is concerned with identifying the future for tomorrow's children, while addressing the existing housekeeping problems.

9.4.2 Management Planning

It is concerned with the effective and efficient attainment of goals and objectives that have been agreed upon and accepted. It can be conceptualized as that portion of the planning process that is implemented after the basic decisions relating to goals and policies, have been determined. Through appropriate management planning, those responsible for implementation of decisions, maximize the realistic achievement of goals and objectives. Educational administration is the process of working with and through others, to determine and achieve educational goals with maximum efficiency and effectiveness. The pursuit of excellence in educational administration is a continuing challenge. In both Australia and Hong Kong, a number of issues highlight this challenge:

- The design and delivery of new approaches to curriculum and certification;
- The concern for quality in education;
- The expectation that these be accomplished under conditions of economic restraint.

There is a growing concern to achieve a high degree of effectiveness in the school systems (Cheng, 1999). The aim of the effective schools movement has been to identify the characteristics of those schools considered to be highly effective. In contrast to earlier views, expressed in the mid-1960s, that schools do not make a difference in a child's learning, there is now general agreement that they do, and there is consistency amongst the findings on the characteristics of highly effective schools.

Davies and Ellison (1998) re-conceptualize the planning process as involving three types of activities, which occur concurrently and interact and reinforce each other. The first type is *future thinking*, which involves the identification of longer-term fundamental shifts in the educational setting. The second is *strategic intent and traditional strategic planning*.

Strategic intent focuses on the less predictable areas of medium-term planning, while traditional strategic planning is used for the definable and predictable areas. The third type is the *operational target setting*, which enables the school to set measurable targets for the whole school, different faculties or sections and pupils.

9.5 Developing a Strategic Plan in an Educational Setting

In the contemporary world, similar to many other fields, education is undergoing unprecedented change, due to the advancement of technology, globalization and changing expectations of the society. Educational leaders find it extremely difficult to face the challenges and predict the future of their organizations. Strategic planning is a means by which they can establish and maintain a sense of direction. It is a continuous process by which an organization is kept on course, through making adjustments, when both the internal and external contexts change. Planning cannot be considered as having been completed when the written document is finalized, it is only a record of the process, at a given point of time, the difficult part is the implementation.

In strategic planning, the emphasis is on evolutionary or rolling planning, enabling adjustments to be made, to suit the changing circumstances. Strategic planning, which is a way of looking more systematically into the future, originated in the business world in the 1970s and has now become a standard part of management thinking in most organizations. The main purpose is to prepare the best fit between the organization and the environment, leading to the development of the best strategy, for the organization to move forward. Today, strategic planning is a technique, which assists leaders and managers in dealing with the increasingly turbulent environments and challenges, confronting organizations. The school development planning stresses the link between planning and school improvement. As strategic planning takes an overall view of the long-term development, many educational institutions have embraced the concept of strategic planning.

Once the shared vision and the goals are agreed to at the organizational level, it is important to organize the school development or strategic plan. In drafting a strategic plan, it is important to establish a strategic planning group involving all stakeholders. This group, or the working party, needs to be entrusted with the overall responsibility. Within the purview of this team, it is better to establish smaller teams, with the responsibility of organizing the strategic plan for the particular areas or faculties to be incorporated into the overall plan. When the final draft is ready, it is better to provide an opportunity for all those affected and interested in the organization to express their views and accommodate desirable and feasible amendments, before the governing body finally approves the plan.

Once the plan is approved, it becomes the responsibility of the Chief Executive Officer (CEO) to organize the implementation by those who have been made responsible for various faculties and/or sections, in keeping with the target dates. The same strategic planning committee can be entrusted with the responsibility of monitoring the progress of implementation, with monthly progress reports, by the principal, to the governing body. If and when problems arise, action needs to be taken to address them, without delay. On the other hand, at the end of each year, another year needs to be added, with necessary amendments to the goals, making it a rolling plan in moving the school forward.

In responding to a question whether her school had a strategic plan, a principal of a Community College in Leicester, England, responded:

> Yes, we have a strategic plan, which was prepared by consulting senior management, the teachers and to some extent, the students. We have very broad aims; we try to focus our plan on outcomes for students. With each of our aims and goals, we have targets to achieve, which we monitor. The governors are very much involved in each term, when I report to them in writing on the monitoring of the plan. So they have a very important role in monitoring — at the level of an overview (Cited in Gamage, 2000a, p. 10).

A primary school teacher governor described the procedure followed in the preparation of the strategic plan in her school as follows:

> It has evolved over the past few years. Everyone is involved in it. The members of staff put together their three-year rolling program and governors have their part to play. We meet in the summer and discuss what we have achieved or what we hope to achieve. We have interviews with the Head-Teacher, as well. I can say that we have ownership of this document (Cited in Gamage, 2000a, p. 10).

9.5.1 *Benefits of Strategic Planning in Schools*

According to the National Audit Office (1997) in UK, Strategic Planning brings the following specific benefits to the schools:

- Focus for clarifying the school's overall aims and objectives is provided by undertaking strategic planning;
- Ways of improving the school's educational services are identified, options are examined and tasks are prioritized;
- The financial requirements of the plan are identified, options are evaluated, and resources are allocated properly;
- The school is enabled to communicate the plan's objectives to the different stakeholders, to make them understand and get involved, and consequently, draw their commitment to outcomes;
- The completed plan serves as a basis for financial decision-making during the year; and
- Tasks are allocated across the school, and clear criteria for the evaluation of accomplishments at the end of the year, are established.

9.6 Strategic Planning vs. Long Range Planning

Valentine (1991, cited in Weindling, 1997) and Herbert (1999), differentiates strategic planning from long range planning in the following manner:

- Long range planning assumes that an organization is a closed system, within which relatively accurate 3–5 year plans of action can be designed while strategic planning assumes that an organization is an open system that is dynamic and perpetually changing, as it integrates the shifting situations.
- Long range planning is viewed as a separate function, while strategic planning is considered an integral part of managing the operation of the organization.
- Long range planning tends to focus on the final plan and the 3–5 year future organizational targets, while strategic planning focuses on the process.
- Long range planning is a mere internal analysis, while strategic planning employs both internal and external analysis, to move towards the shared vision.
- In long range planning, decisions about the future are based on the present data. In strategic planning, current and future trends are considered in making current, not future decisions.

9.7 The Process of Planning

In the planning cycle, there are seven key steps that can be followed. They are:

(1) Defining the planning problem;

(2) Analysing the planning problem area;

(3) Conceptualizing and designing plans;

(4) Evaluating plans;

(5) Specifying the plan;

(6) Implementing the plan; and

(7) Feedback on the plan.

Banghart and Trull (1973) have depicted these stages in a more comprehensive manner as shown in Figure 9.1, in the next page.

9.8 Different Perspectives in Strategy Formulation

Different explanations are given as to how strategies are developed. Bailey and Johnson (1997) have listed these perspectives as follows:

- The planning perspective;
- The logical incremental perspective;
- The political perspective;
- The cultural perspective;
- The visionary perspective; and
- The natural selection perspective.

9.8.1 *The Planning Perspective*

According to Bailey and Johnson (1997), this perspective strategy formulation involves a logical, rational and planned approach. Senior managers set clear strategic goals and objectives. Then, a systematic analysis of the organization and its environment is carried out. From the data, strategic options are generated. These alternative courses of action are assessed, before one is chosen. The chosen option is translated into specific action plans. In this systematic form of developing the strategy, the resources needed are identified and subsequently allocated, providing for monitoring and control systems.

9.8.2 *The Logical Incremental Perspective*

Lindblom (1959), cited in Bailey and Johnson (1997), argues that it is difficult for managers to consider all possible options in the process of shaping strategic actions, as organizations and their environments are complex. Rather, "successive limited comparisons" of the possible strategic

Figure 9.1   Different Stages of Planning

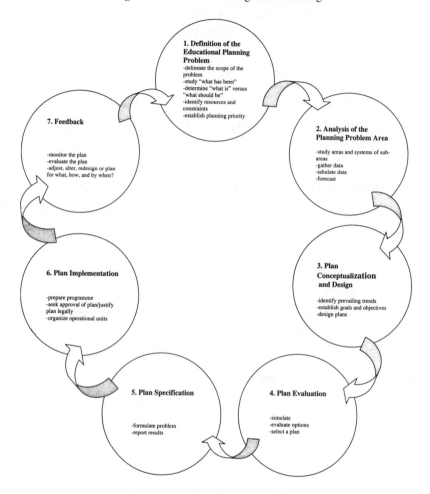

options are undertaken, in order to determine the best choice. When managers have a clear view of where they want their organization to be in the future, they work towards that desired future in an evolutionary process. This logical incrementalist view of strategic management considers the organization as a cyclical system, encompassing feedback loops to previous stages, where the problem may be redefined and the solution may be redesigned. Analysis is ongoing. Assessment is refined incrementally, to match the environmental changes with the procedures implemented in the organization.

9.8.3   The Political Perspective

The political explanation for the formulation of strategy, is that organizations achieve compromises between internal and external interest groups, with conflicting interests. Strategies are then formulated, through bargaining or negotiations. Both in democratic and autocratic systems, the general directives for the planning are formulated through a political process. Naturally, leadership has a big say in formulating such directives.

9.8.4   The Cultural Perspective

This perspective recognizes the significance of organizational culture in the formulation of strategies. This cultural perspective is built into the planning process through the history and past experience of the managers and the organization. The evaluation and choice of strategies are coloured by the values, attitudes and perceptions common among the organizational members and other stakeholders.

9.8.5   The Visionary Perspective

Especially in the current context, the choice of organizational strategies is influenced by an organizational vision, which is simply the desired future state of the organization. In terms of school-based management, all schools are expected to develop a shared vision. Accordingly, a leader is expected to use his intuitive or innovative acumen in dealing with strategic problems of the school and in articulating and communicating such a vision to other stakeholders. This well articulated idea then becomes a shared vision for resolving organizational concerns.

9.8.6   The Natural Selection Perspective

In the case of educational organizations, there are many environmental factors that influence, as well as, constrain the choice of strategies. These external factors impinging on the organization may occur unintentionally, in the form of conflicts over the control of limited resources, accidents, errors, tactical moves and vested interests. In the case of schools, the socio-economic status of the parents of the student population has a big impact on many aspects of schools' life, and leaders need to work hard in building a healthy positive organizational culture. If the variations are beneficial, the leader opts to retain them (Bailey & Johnson, 1997).

9.9 Policy-making

Policy-making is, in many ways, the key to successful implementation of development planning. Policy-making is the responsibility of the senior management team or the school executive. However, in systems where school-based management has been introduced, this group could be the school council, school board, school governors or the school management committee. Usually, this group should be broadly representative of the parents, teachers, the community, the principal and, in the case of secondary schools, students. Research on school-based management, in Victorian schools, reveals that school councils function as an effective instrument of policy formulation, assisted by a significant number of sub-committees, established for wider participation. A president of a secondary school council, referring to his own experience has stated:

> Our policy formulation begins with the sub-committee structure in the school, and many of the issues are thrashed out at that level, before it actually goes to the council. Then a recommendation is put to the council, with all the necessary support material and the information that needs to develop the policy. It seems to work most effectively. There isn't a power group on our council, there is opportunity for all members to contribute to that development. We do look to the principal to give some general direction. We respect and value his opinion, which he has generally arrived at after consulting various groups within the school, that is the staff in particular, and various committees in the school. So it really is, I believe, a very good and cooperative way of developing policy, here (Cited in Gamage, Sipple, & Partridge, 1996, p. 30).

On the other hand, the Australian Capital Territory (ACT) where the school board is smaller in size, more school level committees have been established to complement the governing body i.e. the sub-committees of the school board. With regard to the formulation of policies, a secondary college principal has stated:

> We only have two committees of the board: one on finance and the other on curriculum. We have another 15 committees in the school, which are administrative committees of the staff and students. Basically, committees take the nitty gritty of decision-making of the board. The curriculum committee deals with the entire course, ... and then it [board] relies on the expertise of the committee — so, straight board meetings on major policy decisions, rather than the nitty gritty. Same with finance, the finance committee deals with all the submissions and ranks everything and does all the preliminary work, so

the board is faced, then, with a set of priorities for the budget, and the decision-making is quite smooth (Cited in Gamage, Sipple, & Partridge, 1995, pp. 284–285).

A policy consists of a statement of purpose and one or more broad guidelines as to how that purpose is to be achieved, which taken together, provides a framework for the operation of the school, or the programme. A policy may allow discretion in its implementation, with the basis for discretion often stated as part of the policy.

A policy can also be referred to as a set of guidelines, which provides a framework for action in relation to a substantive issue. The guidelines include, in general terms, the action, which may be taken in regard to the issue. They imply an intention and a pattern for taking action. In a school, these guidelines provide a framework, often with some basis for discretion, within which the principal, staff and others in the school community can discharge their responsibilities with clear direction.

Croll and Moses (2000) note that in analysing public policy-making, there are two contrasting approaches, namely: the *rational approach* and the *incremental approach*. The rational approach to policy-making entails large-scale reform of the structures of the organization, while the incremental approach proceeds through small-scale changes to the status quo. Cheng and Cheung (1995) have designed a framework for the analysis of educational policies. According to them, educational policy analysis should be concerned with the background and underlying principles affecting the development of the policy, the policy formulation process, the educational policy implementation (identifying gaps between planning and implementation), and the policy effect.

Garn (1999) is of the opinion that if policy implementation is to be successful, the educational leaders/managers should consider the following variables: communication, financial support, will, and bureaucratic structure. His case study of Arizona charter schools, shows that the intent of a policy could be preserved via purposefully preserved policy instruments and supportive contextual environments.

9.10 Policy-formulation and Its Benefits

When a policy is established, usually, it is based on a set of beliefs, values and an educational philosophy on the issue concerned. The formulation of policies is not required to address all issues. Action on routine issues can usually be shaped by the formulation of simple procedures. A policy is a more appropriate framework for issues of some substance, for example, discipline, curriculum, admissions, credit standing, staff-leave and examinations. The benefits of well-written and continuously updated policies are numerous.

- Policies demonstrate that the school/institution is being operated in an efficient and businesslike manner. Written policies diminish ambiguity concerning school values and norms.
- Policies foster stability, goals and administration.
- Policies ensure, to a considerable extent, that there will be uniformity and consistency in decisions and in operational procedures. Good policy makes *ad hoc* decision-making difficult.
- Local policies must be consistent with system policies and legislation affecting school. Policies add strength to the position of the principal and staff.
- Policies help ensure that meetings are orderly. Valuable time will be saved when a new problem can be handled quickly and effectively, helped by policy documents.
- Policies foster stability and continuity. Policy documents indicate the general directions, enabling new staff members to familiarize themselves with school's directions.
- Policies provide the framework for planning in the school.
- Policies assist the school in the assessment of the instructional programme. Written and publicly disseminated policy statements make the policy group accountable.
- Policies clarify functions and responsibilities of the policy group, principal and other staff. When policies are well known, all can work with greater efficiency, satisfaction and commitment.

9.11 The Collaborative School Management Cycle

The model developed by Caldwell and Spinks (1988) is best described as a Collaborative School Management Cycle. The Cycle has six phases: (1) Goal setting and need identification; (2) Policy-making, with policies consisting of a statement of purpose and broad guidelines for action; (3) Planning of programmes; (4) Preparation and approval of programme budgets; (5) Implementing, and (6) Evaluating. There is a minimum of paperwork and documentation associated with the model:

1. Policy Statements: a maximum of one page.
2. Programme plans and budgets: a maximum of two pages.
3. Report of a minor evaluation: a maximum of one page.
4. Report of a major programme evaluation: a maximum of two pages.

9.11.1 *A Sample Strategy to Start Collaborative Management Cycle*

- It is important to introduce the change to the policy group and staff, by explaining and demonstrating its nature and purpose. There is no need to sell the approach, but it is necessary to reassure all concerned that adequate time will be allowed for its introduction.
- The policy group should determine the timetable for implementation.
- There is no need to introduce the different phases of the approach to all programmes, at a particular time. For example, there is no need to establish goals for each programme, at the same time, or programme plans and programme budgets, for the first time, in the same year.
- In the first year, volunteers can be involved to prepare programme plans and programme budgets for a few programmes, allowing time for integrating this work with other tasks and for consultation.
- In the first year, priorities can be set for policy-making, with a small number of high priority contentious issues addressed, along with a relatively large number of non-contentious issues.
- Programme planning and budgeting may be extended to all programmes in the second year, with time allowed for the activity, including the use of an in-service day, for adequate information gathering and consultation.
- The policy base may be completed in the third year.
- Programme planning and programme budgeting may be refined in the third year.
- Programme evaluation need not be addressed in the early stages. A cyclical approach to major and minor, evaluations among programmes may be commenced, as late as the fourth year, with the involvement of volunteers to initiate the process.
- Programme evaluation may be extended to all programmes in the fifth year (Adapted from Caldwell & Spinks, 1988, pp. 163–183).

9.11.2   *Benefits of the Collaborative School Management Model*

The prime beneficiary of the model should be the student. Successful implementation ensures that all resources — teachers, time, space, facilities, supplies, equipment and services — reflect plans to achieve learning and teaching priorities. Caldwell and Spinks (1988) suggest the following benefits:

- Collaborative School Management (CSM) provides teachers with a role in the management of education.
- CSM ensures that all teachers have the opportunity to contribute according to their expertise and willingness to participate.
- Distinction between policy-making and planning are made clear.
- CSM provides a framework (programme teams) for teachers to make a substantial contribution in resource allocations.
- Programme plans and budgets provide a source of information, regarding the work of colleagues.
- A well-implemented system of CSM ensures that goals and policies are translated into action.
- CSM provides a valuable framework for the management of conflict, because of the opportunities for collaboration and openness.
- The openness and systematic matching of resources to needs, provides an opportunity to detect areas of overlap and avenues for cooperation.
- CSM establishes the importance of teachers as a major resource in the teaching-learning process.
- CSM provides most teachers opportunities to exercise responsibility.
- CSM calls for a minimum of writing and documentation, for the purpose of easy communication, understanding and commitment (Adapted from Caldwell & Spinks, 1988, pp. 54–56).

Indeed, collaborative school management provides teachers with the opportunity to get involved in decision-making. Rice and Schneider (1994) find that this involvement is positively related to the job satisfaction of the teachers. Green and Etheridge (1999) conclude that collaboration energizes people, gives them a single purpose, and engages them in meaningful conversation, consequently, leading to improvements in academic achievements of the students. Tschannen-Moran, Uline, Hoy, and Mackley (2000) find that collaboration enhances organizational learning, by enabling administrators and teachers to discover ways of sharing their expertise, making their thinking explicit, and articulating their goals.

Mullen and Kochan (2000) suggest that joining a coalition of schools for improvement, which goes beyond collaboration within a school or district, is one way of expanding professional networks, for better educational outputs. This multi-institutional partnership fosters synergy, empowers shared leadership and organizational transformation for school improvement.

9.12 Barriers to Collaboration

Various barriers may thwart the efforts of educators to practice collaboration. Phillips and McCullough (1990), in Welch (1998), categorize these barriers into four, namely: conceptual, pragmatic, attitudinal, and professional barriers.

- Conceptual barriers include the notions of the various educational stakeholders about their roles, and the roles of others, which are shaped by entrenched cultural factors.
- Pragmatic barriers are normally associated with systemic and logistic factors within the school, such as lack of time due to overwhelming responsibilities.
- Attitudinal barriers take the forms of unrealistic expectations, fear of the unknown and attitudinal shifts.
- Professional barriers are brought about by the very nature of professionals. Their tendency to be isolated from each other, as well as, inadequate knowledge and skills in effective communication and conflict management, are some professional barriers to successful collaboration.

9.13 The Output Driven Development Model (ODDM)

Figure 9.2 shows how the Johnson City Central School District, in New York, found a way to coordinate decisions, so that new policies could be incorporated, without nullifying or conflicting with those already in place. Policies were based on research and consensus, rather than the expediencies of the moment. Albert Mammary, superintendent of the Johnson City Central School District, formulated the Output Driven Development Model (ODDM). ODDM is the only total school curriculum improvement model, validated by the National Diffusion Network, in the USA. Its success has been established by a number of research reports.

As shown in Figure 9.2, all members of the professional staff have agreed to the district's system of shared beliefs in ODDM's philosophical base through discussion, deliberation, and participation by all members of the professional staff. This is the basis upon which decisions are made. All can contribute to the process of consensus, but every effort is made to see that opinions rest on the research base, built from examination of the professional literature. Together these lead to a mission statement.

According to Vickery (1990), ODDM is participatory in every sense of the term, and it cannot be mandated. It is compatible with top-down management. However, it does require transformational leadership, by a person or persons, with a compelling vision of what can and ought to be, who can inspire action, secure resources, and remove obstacles. If aligned organizational change is to be achieved, administrative leaders must have a deep commitment to help staff develop individually and collectively, into competent professionals, who work successfully to achieve the school's mission. In other words, the leaders need to ensure that the professionals are developed and empowered to exercise influence within the system.

9.13.1 Administrative Support

The administrative support aspect of the programme includes five elements: (1) the process of change, (2) the staff development model, (3) a communication network, (4) problem solving procedure, and (5) the climate monitoring policies.

9.13.2 Community Support

This includes establishing clear policies that are consistent with the school's mission, developed with the participation of the representatives of the school community, to which they are committed and accountable.

9.13.3 Teacher Support

The third aspect of the programme — teacher support — includes five areas that directly affect instruction. These are (1) the instructional process, (2) organization of the curriculum, (3) school practices, (4) classroom practices, and (5) organizational structure.

9.14 Conclusion

In this chapter we examined the importance of planning, in the context of

Figure 9.2 ODDM Developed by the Johnson City School

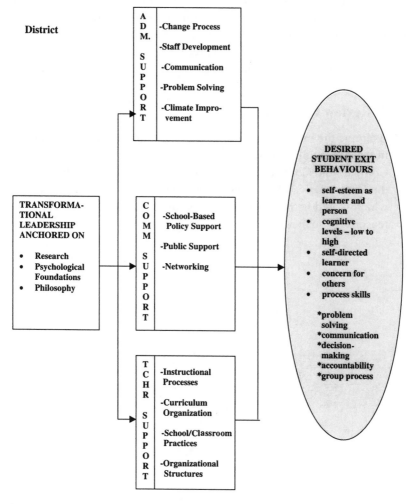

(Source: Adapted from Vickery, 1990, p. 68)

education, at which educational administrator needs to be competent. Planning is seen as a key function and the responsibility of the educational leader or manager. Similarly, the importance of policy formulation and the need to establish appropriate structures for policy formulation, such as, a policy group, a school council or a school management committee is recognized. To be an effective, proactive leader and/or manager require the development of the necessary skills and competencies such as the acquisition of a sound theoretical base, relating to planning and, more specifically, strategic planning and policy formulation. Two models for school improvement, developed in Australia and USA, and being implemented in many parts of the world, were also presented for consideration by school leaders, with whatever modifications needed, to suit one's own context.

9.15 Review Questions

1. Examine the importance of strategic planning and policy formulation in the context of educational management.
2. Compare the Collaborative School Management Cycle (CSMC) and the Output Driven Development Model (ODDM) and select the one, which would be more suitable for your own situation, indicating the reasons for such a selection.

CHAPTER 10

Management and Resolution of Organizational Conflicts

10.0 Learning Outcomes

Based on a systematic study of this chapter, the readers will:

- Understand the meaning of conflict, and also, the value and dangers of organizational conflicts;
- Identify different philosophies, techniques and approaches available for conflict management;
- Gain a sound theoretical knowledge and understanding in order to be a proactive leader/manager in conflict management; and
- Develop the skills necessary to handle and manage, as well as minimize conflict in organizational settings.

10.1 Focus

Considering the rapid changes that are taking place in the contemporary world, conflict can be considered as part of human existence. Educational institutions, being people-oriented organizations, are influenced by the changes taking place within society. This has given rise to many conflicting demands on school organizations. These conflicting expectations of different stakeholders, and funding cuts, have made the issues more complex. In this context, the following pages of this chapter examine the types of conflict, the value and dangers of conflict, and philosophies and techniques of managing conflict. Further, consideration is given to the different approaches to managing and solving problems arising from conflicts, guidelines for handling conflicts and the types of conflict management skills that are needed.

10.2 Conflict Defined

Most people's perception of "conflict" is one of existing incompatibilities with negative connotation. Most of us think of conflict as being unpleasant and resulting in consequences that are detrimental to some, if not all, of the participants. In contrast, we usually think of competition as a healthy process. Parents encourage their children to compete for awards and recognition in school. The Olympics is considered as one of the most important international events, occurring once in every four years, where sports men and women face very keen competition to win medals for their respective nations. Similarly, it is important to think of conflict as natural in one's individual and organizational life. At any given time, differences of opinions can arise between individuals and groups or within oneself. It is true that at times, conflict can be disruptive and destructive. But it can also be a source of creativity and constructive action. Some people go to the extent of describing "conflict" as the "mother of creativity". Conflict becomes natural wherever incompatible activities occur and vested interests are involved. In other words, conflict is a situation involving people, or a group of people, with incompatible concerns (Morton, 1973 cited in Campbell, Corbally & Nystrand, 1983; Thomas, 1979 cited in Vecchio, Hearn & Southey, 1992; Maurer, 1991; Donohue & Kolt, 1992; Lussier, 1993).

10.3 Types of Conflict

Analyses of the types of conflict that exist in human society, and more importantly, in organizational settings, reveal four categories. These are:

- Intra-personal Conflict: An individual may sometimes perceive the environment in ways that bring two or more of his or her needs dispositions into conflict. A school principal's desire to develop better educational programmes to improve a school's image and his or her desire to exercise economy to please the systemic authorities is likely to create a conflict within him/her.
- Interpersonal Conflict: Individual to individual conflict, the most common and visible type of conflict in schools, as well as in other organizations, is interpersonal conflict. Potential conflict involving

students, teachers, administrators, parents and community, is a common phenomenon in most schools.

- Individual-Organizational Conflict: Getzels and Guba (1957) formulate the concept of administration as a social process, where personal and organizational dimensions are likely to be in conflict. This concept is helpful in understanding the nature of conflict between individuals and institutions.
- Intra-organizational Conflict: Conflict may also exist among various groups within an organization. For example, a conflict may exist amongst the members of a formal workgroup such as the science department staff at a high school who wants the students to devote more time for academic work and the sports coach who wants them to be involved in more and more practice sessions.
- Inter-organizational Conflict: Conflicts also may arise between two or more organizations or independent units of a large organization or even between two countries. Such inter-organizational conflict most commonly reflects the competition and rivalry that characterize their operations or functioning. Cold War was the result of competition and rivalry between the former Soviet Union and USA, which led very many conflicts around the world. The competition and rivalry between Mitsubishi and Ford Motors could be cited as another example where conflicts can arise relating to market share.

Leaders and/or managers, who wish to deal with conflicts effectively, should not merely know the types of conflict but also should know how to manage and resolve conflicts. Understanding the causes of conflict is the first step towards effective conflict management (Sheanh, 1996). However, as argued by Caudron (2000), from the roots of conflict come the fruits of innovation. The different factors that cause organizational conflicts, identified by various conflict management writers, can be synthesized into four, namely:

- Limited resources;
- Ineffective communication;
- Personal differences in values, beliefs and goals; and
- Complex organizational structures

10.4 The Value of Conflict

Conflict, in the sense of an honest difference of opinions, resulting from different positions on an issue and the possibility of two or more alternative courses of action, is not only unavoidable but also a valuable part of life. According to Langdon and Marshall (1998), constructive conflict brings about productive organizational changes and healthy competition. Caudron (1999, p. 26) captures this idea well and writes that "conflict is a potent source of creativity, especially in troubled times." Conflict provides an opportunity to consider different possibilities, which were not examined earlier. Another advantage in conflict is that the chosen course of action is tested at an early stage, thereby, reducing the risk of an important fault, which may emerge later. Of course, some leaders actively encourage differences of opinion, or conflicting views, as was the case of Alfred Sloan at General Motors.

> Alfred Sloan, a former president of general motors, did always refer for further consideration at the next meeting any proposal on which his board members were unanimous. A large proportion of such proposals were, it appears, eventually rejected (Sloan, 1980 cited in Everard & Morris, 1996, p. 81).

Smith and Piele (1997, pp. 338–339) have considered both the negative and positive effects of conflict. Conflict opens up an issue in a confronting manner, develops clarification of an issue and increases involvement. It also improves problem solving capacity and communication, needed for growth and creativity, and strengthens relationships, once it is creatively resolved. If an organizational conflict is neglected with no attempts to find an amicable solution, it diverts energy from the task at hand, destroys morale, polarizes individuals and groups, deepens differences, obstructs cooperative action, produces irresponsible behaviour, creates suspicion and distrust, and adversely affects productivity. Here, what is important is how the leaders and managers approach conflicting situations. Often, it is advisable to evaluate the situation and intervene when it is necessary to do so, as prolonging a conflict can lead to negative consequences.

10.5 The Danger of Conflict

Conflict becomes a dangerous and disruptive force whenever personal glory is staked on the outcome, and parties become hostile to each other. The further the conflict develops, the more "glory" is staked, the bitter the conflict becomes and the less easy it is to achieve a solution. For example, Saddam Hussain vs. George Bush Sr. during the Gulf War in 1993 resulted in the deaths of thousands of people and the wastage of billions of dollars (Gamage, 1998c).

Owens (2001) enumerates three broad categories of negative effects of organizational conflicts. The first in his list is *psychological*. This may take the form of alienation, apathy and indifference. Langdon and Marchall (1998) state that unrelieved tension, called "stress", is another dysfunctional result of conflict. Moreover, damaged morale and prevalence of suspicion and distrust among employees, are psychological manifestations, identified by Lippit (1983, as cited in Lindelow & Scott, 1989). The second destructive effect is *physical*. This comes in the form of absence, tardiness and turn over among the employees. Lippit (1983, cited in Lindelow & Scott, 1989) has found that once employees resort to physical withdrawal, their energies are diverted from the task, and consequently, their levels of productivity diminish. The third dysfunctional effect is *outright hostility and display of aggressive behaviour* such as property damage, job actions, such as strikes and minor thefts. Blackard (1999) adds sabotage to this list. Lippit (1983) identifies aggressive behaviours as polarization of individuals and groups, obstruction of cooperative action, and manifestation of irresponsible behaviour.

10.6 Philosophies of Conflict Management

According to Smith and Piele (1997, pp. 343–344), the literature refers to three primary philosophies of conflict management.

- Traditional philosophy, which considers all types of conflict as destructive and believes that it is the role of the management, or the leadership, to rid the organization of such conflict. This view prevailed from the late nineteenth century into the 1940s.
- The behavioural philosophy accepts conflict as a normal part of organizational life. But still sees conflict as a negative concept. Accordingly, behaviourists concentrate on resolving conflicts.
- The "interactions" philosophy, advocated by Robbins (1974), recognizes the absolute necessity of conflict in organizational life. This view, explicitly encourages conflict at times, defines conflict management to include stimulation as well as resolution methods. It considers the management of conflicts as a major responsibility of the leadership.

Emphasis on conflict resolution and management recognizes that school systems all over the world are in a state of rapid change, with inevitable conflict situations between stakeholders. Some educational leaders feel the usefulness in stimulating conflict, with a view to being creative and innovative. However, most school leaders are interested in learning how to manage and resolve conflict that already exists within organizations and between individuals and groups.

10.7 Conflict Management Styles

There are many theories and approaches for the management of conflicts between individuals or groups within organizations. However, no particular method would be suitable for all situations, as the people involved, as well as, the organizational cultures could be different (Hoy & Miskel, 2001). In such circumstances, it is important for the leaders and managers to possess a sound knowledge of all possible conflict management techniques, so that s/he can select the particular technique, which would suit the situational factors. Some of the techniques are described below.

10.7.1 Style of Avoiding Conflicts

Robbins (1974) believes that the most natural manner, in which all animals, including humans, prevent conflict, is by avoiding it. Avoidance of conflict includes several different approaches:

- Ignoring differences of opinions or Procrastination;
- Isolation;
- Withholding feelings or beliefs;
- Working with like-minded people.

Even though avoiding conflict in an organizational setting is the right thing to do, it can be considered a short-term alternative. This "lose-leave" style (Filley, 1975), is useful when what is at stake, and often the issue at conflict, may not be of great value. The manager and/or leader either withdraws from the problem or actively suppresses the issue (Lussier, 1993). When the problem is difficult or worsening, this style may not be the answer (Kreithner & Kinicki, 1992). Walking away from conflict or neglect has not produced desired results (Kemp-Longmore, 2000). Blumberg and Greenfield (1980) suggest that most school principals tend to approach conflict in benevolent avoidance.

10.7.1.1 Ignoring/Procrastination

Most people prefer to withdraw from conflict and ignore the situation whenever it is possible. In many instances, events reach their own equilibrium, and intervention becomes either unnecessary or counter-productive. At times, procrastination or "deciding not to decide" becomes a valuable short-term management strategy, until the tempers are cooled. Leaders may need more information or time to understand the situation better, or may allow the situation to become clearer before taking action. Taking a "wait and see" approach could be the best strategy in such instances. On the other hand, it is important to determine whether bringing conflicting parties to a forum will have destructive or constructive consequences. Independent and prior consultation with the parties involved, could be a better way of handling such conflict.

10.7.1.2 Isolation of Conflicting Parties

A leader can avoid unwanted conflicting situations by isolating two potentially explosive individuals or groups, so that they seldom interact with each other. Often, superordinates and subordinates adopt this technique. In cases where a subordinate and a superior do not like each other, or disagree on many issues, but the superior considers that the subordinate's performance is good, while the subordinate feels that finding another job is difficult, both parties are likely to employ the isolation or avoidance technique.

10.7.1.3 Withholding Feelings

In cases where two individuals have different opinions on many issues, but it is not possible to avoid each other, each may withhold expression of feelings and beliefs at forums where both are present. It is true, such withholding conceals differences, but such behaviour avoids unwanted confrontations, which could lead to hostility.

10.7.1.4 Seeking to Work with Like-minded People

Most leaders in selecting their leadership or senior management team prefer to work with like-minded staff. This approach may be appropriate in situations where many complex issues and divergent viewpoints prevail. But it is very important to remember that the leader who adopts this approach shuts out innovation and creativity in an organizational setting, as s/he is likely to select the team on friendship and loyalties, rather than on merit or technical competence.

Smoothing could be considered the process of playing down differences of opinions, while emphasizing the issues on which they tend to agree. The strengths are discussed while weaknesses are avoided. Similarly, praise is given while criticisms are avoided. But the solutions achieved by this technique would be only superficial, as the differences will continue to exist until they are confronted and sorted out.

10.7.2 Accommodating Style

Campbell et al. (1983) believe this sort of "appeasement" approach is common to people who are highly assertive and cooperative. The "friendly helper" administrator complies with the demands of subordinates, since he gives utmost premium to the maintenance of smooth relationships (Filley, 1975). Wertheim, Love, Littlefield, and Peck (1992), believe that the "Giving in" approach plays down differences, while emphasizing common factors or issues. It is also believed that people with a high level of need for affiliation approach conflicts using this style. Similar to avoiding conflict, this is not applicable to complex and worsening problems.

10.7.3 Forcing Style

The "competitive" administrator uses coercive power, or formal authority, to achieve compliance. Campbell et al. (1983) call this "domination", while Filley (1975) uses the term "tough battler". One who uses this style needs to understand that threats and punishments tend to intensify the aggressive staunch of the other party, as it has been obvious in the Middle-East crisis between Israelis and Palestinians. This "fighting" way of handling conflict is not suitable if the leader/manager wishes to maintain an open and participatory climate, as it could breed resentment.

10.7.4 Compromising Style

The leader/manager, using this style, balances cooperation and assertiveness in moderate degrees. Campbell et al. (1983), as well as Owens (2001), state that in terms of this style, the leader and/or manager stresses negotiation, search for the middle ground and encourages tradeoffs to fix mutually acceptable solutions. Kreitner and Kinicki (2001) caution, however, that this approach which can be resorted to when collaboration and competition fails, does not promote creative problem solving.

10.7.5 Collaborating Style

The leader/manager who uses this style encourages high levels of cooperation and assertiveness. In this "integrating" approach, Campbell et al. (1983) view conflicts as challenges. Filley (1975) believes that even though "problem solving" is more time consuming, the integrative solutions that may result make all parties in the making of win-win decisions. Parks (1998) suggests that the parties delve into an issue, and talk about their respective concerns, in finding a mutually satisfying solution. It has also been observed that this style brings a higher degree of satisfaction amongst the members of the group. However, Kreitner and Kinicki (2001) warn that this style might not work well when conflicts are rooted in clashing value systems. Nevertheless, all conflict management gurus strongly recommend this style. Antonioni (1998) suggests that the managers and leaders who are extrovert, conscientious, open and agreeable, tend to use this integrating style.

10.8 Different Approaches to Managing Conflict

It is important to emphasize here that no single approach will work at all times. An intelligent leader needs to assess the issues and the parties involved, including the possible implications and consequences of ignoring or postponing it, bringing the parties together or involving third parties. Some of the approaches are:

- Compartmentalizing or individualizing conflict;
- Setting superordinate goals,
- Creative problem solving,
- Use of third parties,
- Modification of organizational structure, and
- Reconciling or putting the pieces back together.

10.8.1 Compartmentalizing Conflict

There are instances where a particular staff member of an organization may have a genuine grievance, which cannot be sorted out, within the existing rules. In such a situation, a leader needs to examine the issue carefully and find a special solution, so that the issue is individualized, without allowing it to become a common issue. If a conflict arises in one faculty of a school or a university or a section of an organization, a wise leader, with timely intervention, can solve the conflict in such a way that it will not spread to other faculties or sections.

10.8.2 Setting Superordinate Goals

When different types of stakeholders are involved in managing schools, it is likely that different individuals and groups may join the process, with different and conflicting agendas. Gamage (1998c) points out that in such circumstances, it is important for the school leaders to set superordinate goals such as "doing our best for the kids", to direct the energies of all involved. In the recent reforms of governance structures of the aided schools in Hong Kong, the Advisory Committee on SBM, reminds the stakeholders that "giving students' welfare the highest priority" is the paramount principle. This common goal is considered as the only way to resolve conflicts arising between stakeholders such as managers nominated by the school sponsoring body, the principal, teacher managers, parent managers, alumni managers, and independent managers (Pang, 2001b). On occasions when elite groups try to implement their own agendas, rather than allowing a conflict situation to be created, the school leader can consult the school community by conducting a survey and thereby ruling out the issue on the basis of community consensus.

10.8.3 Creative Problem Solving

Mutual problem solving is considered as one of the best means of resolving a social conflict. If conflicting parties can be brought together to discuss the issues and differences involved and if the discussions are properly managed, finding an amicable solution is not difficult. Appropriate structures and processes facilitate effective communication between the parties. Articulating the importance of the resolution of the conflict will improve mutual understanding, leading to more constructive and collaborative action.

10.8.4 Engaging Services of Third Parties

Problem solving can be achieved by bringing the conflicting parties together, through internal processes, or with the intervention of third parties. In this approach, the means of resolving conflict leads to working out a compromise. To avoid a win or lose situation, each party needs to be persuaded to give up something else showing that the final state would be better than the existing state. In accordance with the saying "a bird in the hand is worth two in the bush". In this approach "compromise" is the key factor, where negotiating parties are required to work at their best to reach a settlement to the ongoing conflict. The mediator needs to be a person, or a party, who has earned the respect and trust of both parties, involved in the conflict. In reaching a long-term solution, the compromise reached needs to be a just and equitable one, which is acceptable to both parties, as against a solution that each party accepts under protest.

10.8.5 Modification of Organizational Structures

Conflict management can be successfully achieved by effecting modifications to the organizational structure. A deputy who has been at the centre of a conflict can be assigned different responsibilities. A new grievance procedure and an appellate body can be introduced to enable the staff to challenge the decisions they feel are unjustifiable. The policy making body can be enlarged, with representatives from all relevant groups. A position can be created and a monitoring body established, to review the problems and issues as they arise, promoting improved communication.

10.8.6 Reconciling the Parties

If a conflict between two individuals or two groups is resolved by imposing an arbitrary solution, with the intervention of a higher authority, or the parties agree to a compromise due to the exhaustion of time and resources there can be dissatisfaction on both sides. In such a situation, it is important for the leadership to make a conscious effort to reconcile the conflicting parties and create a cooperative environment in which they can build with mutual trust and confidence.

10.9 Solving Problems of Conflict

Gulbranson (1998) outlines the important steps towards conflict resolution. First, is to realize that conflicts in organizations are not only natural, but also inevitable. Second, is the determination of the causes of conflict. Third, is to emphasize on the benefits that members can gain from the resolution of the conflict, and finally, the adoption of a plan for resolving the conflict.

It is obvious that no parties in a conflict can solve the problem unilaterally. If acrimony has built up, it may be necessary to choose your time well and to spend some time in making it clear that you really do want to solve the conflict. Having set the stage for a meeting for a conflict resolution, Everard and Morris (1996, pp. 85–86) state that it is important to observe the following principles to guide the discussion:

- Parties will talk to each other openly on real issues concerning them;

- Parties state their aims, views and feelings openly but calmly avoiding reiteration;
- Parties should place conflict into the context of superordinate or common goals;
- Parties should listen carefully, and even rephrase other's position, to show understanding. It must be a genuine effort to understand the two positions;
- Parties have to focus on future action rather than on the past;
- Parties should avoid taking offensive or defensive positions;
- Parties should build on each other's ideas;
- Parties should trust each other's good faith and try to act in good faith;
- Parties should plan specific actions to follow the discussion, specifying what, when, how and who will undertake them;
- Parties should set a date and time to review progress and should make a firm commitment to honour it.

10.10 Handling Organizational Conflicts

Conflict and frustration will often centre round the way in which a school, a college or a department is being run. The school review uses a number of useful techniques:

- Gap Theory — asking the parties to state their ideal view and compare it with their actual perceptions. The gap between the two is what has to be bridged.
- Categorizing and quantifying views of formulating a group statement, which does not correspond exactly with any of the alternatives.
- Categorizing statements around examples by stating "for instance."

10.11 Conflict Model

This model is concerned with taking a tough stand towards conflict, rather than taking steps to minimize the differences and harmonize the situation. The parties prefer to deal with the conflicting issues unilaterally, rather than bilaterally, and attempt to sell it to the other party. The key features are that:

1. Parties are concerned only with the protection of their own interests.

2. Parties involved in taking or implementing decisions take up their positions, make their decisions, and possibly try to sell them to other parties and, if necessary, fight it out.

As shown in Figure 10.1, this tough approach to conflict, can lead to a climate that makes the situation worse, and is likely to develop increasing frustration, and destructive behaviour. In the final analysis, these factors can contribute to poor or declining organizational health affecting productivity.

10.12 Harmony Model

This model assumes that conflict is something, which is natural in organizational life, and takes a positive approach, with a view to sorting out the issues leading to the conflict situation. It emphasizes the need for collaborative approaches to controversial and conflicting issues confronting the organization. The key features of this model are:

* Collective responsibility both for the interests of the organization and for the individual interests of the staff.

Figure 10.1 An Ineffective Conflict Response Climate Syndrome

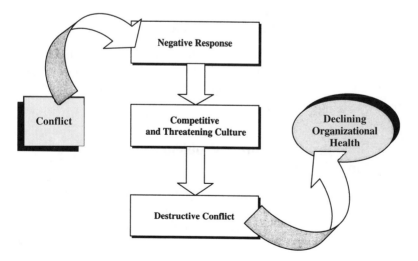

(Source: Adapted from Owens, 2001, p. 309)

Figure 10.2   An Effective Conflict Response Climate Syndrome

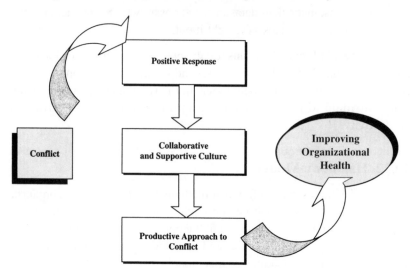

(Source: Adapted from Owens, 2001, p. 310)

- Participatory decision-making in which the views of interested parties are sought out, before coming to a decision. This allows differences of opinion to be handled, before a position is taken up from which retreat means a loss of face.

As shown in Figure 10.2 above, this positive approach results in outcomes that are productive and harmonious. These collaborative and participatory approaches lead to improved organizational health, which in turn improves organizational effectiveness.

10.13 Solving a Generalized Problem before Taking a Specific Case

Usually, it is much easier to engage in productive problem solving to reach an agreement on general policy issues, than on a specific problem, as most people are unlikely to hold a firm view on a general issue. If you are confronted with a difficult, emotion-laden issue, it is better to put off the decision and sort it out by means of creative problem solving.

Whenever a specific issue is taken up, almost inevitably, the interaction is thrown into a win-lose confrontation. All those with vested interests see the solution, which would serve their interest in a most feasible manner and press it to be accepted, making it difficult to find compromises. On the other hand, if the general issues are solved first, those solutions become the guide and the criteria to solving the specific issues, in a more constructive manner, rather than in a win-lose manner. An imaginative and competent leader, or person within a group, can do this task well.

Solving general problems, before the consideration of the specific problem, decreases the influences coming from vested interest groups, which might contribute to group success. Success contributes to the group strength and problem solving capabilities. When a group becomes successful in solving a difficult problem, it develops pride in problem solving capabilities, which in turn improves the morale, group loyalty, as well as, favourable interaction with the group. These attributes enable the group to acquire additional skills in problem solving.

In the early stages of building problem solving groups in order to deal with difficult, conflict-ridden issues, it is important for leaders to advise the group to avoid solution mindedness. Likert and Likert (1976, pp. 157–181) state that very often, when an issue is presented to a meeting or a large group, who feel that they would be benefited, will support it, while others who feel that their interest will be adversely affected, will oppose it, thus, creating a win-lose situation. In such a situation, the leader should help the group to save time and facilitate its work, with the use of sub-committees to collect more information and consult those affected and interested, etc. When such a sub-committee is established, it should have the group's full approval, to come up with a suitable recommendation for the group's consideration. In addition, individual members should also be provided with facilities, in finding solutions.

10.14 The Nature of "Strategic Conflict"

On the basis of an extensive study on power and conflict at the University of New York, Victor Baldridge (1971) states that although a political interpretation of power and conflict is based on conflict theory, it does not mean that the university is torn apart by ceaseless conflict. Conflict itself is often quite healthy, as it may revitalize an otherwise stagnant system. One of the most important lessons that we can learn from Marx (cited in Baldridge, 1971, p. 202) is that "conflict is often necessary and beneficial, it constantly provokes the social system into self-examination and change".

However, it is important to remember that upheavals within the campus contain both the seeds of reform and the seeds of destruction.

Thomas Schelling (1980) in his book *The Strategy of Conflict* argues that conflict is best understood as a complex interaction that is middle ground between complete conflict and complete cooperation. According to him all-out conflict, or the do or die type of strife, is not a realistic interpretation of most social conflicts. On the other hand, he believes that pure cooperation is rarely found in human relations, since all humans are usually motivated by self-interest. He believes that the most realistic interpretation of conflict must be in the middle ground, which includes elements of conflict and cooperation, a relationship that he calls "strategic conflict". The typical form of conflict, then, is strategy and negotiation, in which each party trades favours in order to gain advantages. Conflict in the university is essentially strategic, as interest groups in the academic community are competing with one another, and at the same time, cooperating. Complete antagonism is not the normal kind of conflict in an academic setting. The essence of their conflict is negotiation and exchange of advantages and favours (Baldridge, 1971).

10.15 Guidelines for Handling Conflict

In order to manage or resolve organizational conflicts, a leader/manager should be able to take the following steps:

* Maintain as much communication as possible with any party whose ideas, interests or attitudes appear to be in conflict with your own.
* Refrain from the temptation to talk about the other person behind his/her back.
* If there is interdepartmental conflict, try to establish projects, on either neutral or sensitive subjects, which increases interaction and possibility to work together.
* Try to avoid all the phenomena of the "win-lose" orientation, and above all, try to see all sides of the dispute.
* Try to avoid settling conflict situations through the "reward" structure and, if they are already in the structure then change them. If two are in competition, ensure you recognize results and not flattery or show.

10.16 Conflict Management Skills

In order to manage and resolve organizational conflicts, a leader/manager should improve his/her understanding of the theoretical concepts, relating to the management and resolution of conflicts. Based on such an understanding, the following skills should be developed:

- To confront, and say "no" when a difference of opinion emerges, but be open to reason, logical discussion and problem solving;
- To present ideas and feelings clearly, concisely, calmly and honestly;
- To be a better listener and show the other party that you understand him/her by playing it back;
- To evaluate all aspects of the problem and understand the pressure on either party; and
- To articulate common goals, as against conflicting ones, and a way of looking forward to future achievements, rather than past frictions.

A useful exercise is to think about a conflict where you were a party, and try to understand the position of the other party by asking you questions. Why did s/he behave as s/he did? What were the pressures on the other party? What did s/he wish to achieve? What common goals could have been agreed to? What possibilities were there for a mutually acceptable accord? It would be helpful to discuss your perceptions with a colleague. In improving one's ability to resolve conflict, a leader/manager can resort to:

- Discover the reasons for and meaning of the conflict.
- Listen actively and openly.
- Communicate emotions openly and directly.
- Search for the hidden fears, desires, interests, emotions and intentions of the conflicting parties.
- Do not seek to establish who is right and who is wrong, but create a dialogue between the conflicting parties.
- Develop your own capacity for empathy and perseverance.
- Solve problems creatively and commit to action (Adapted from Goldsmith, 1999, pp. 17–18).

10.16.1 Direct Conflict Management Techniques

Most consultants and scholars agree that true conflict resolution can occur only when the underlying substantive and emotional issues, which led to the conflict, are identified and a solution that allows both parties to reach a "win-win" solution is reached. It is important for the conflict managers to determine when to use the following conflict management techniques:

- Cooperation and problem solving should always be used to gain true conflict resolution, provided that time and other circumstances permit.
- Avoidance may be used when an issue is trivial or more important issues are pressing, or to let the parties cool down and regain perspective.
- Authoritative command may be used when quick and decisive action is vital, or when unpopular actions must be taken.
- Accommodation may be used when conflicting issues are more important to others than oneself, or when a party wants to build "credits or goodwill" to be used in later issues.
- Compromising may be used for temporary settlements to complex issues or to arrive at expedient solutions when the available time is limited (Adapted from Wood, Wallace, & Zeffance, 2001, p. 547).

10.17 Conclusion

Conflicts arising out of differences of opinion, within all human undertakings, should be considered as natural and inevitable. It is not something that is unusual or undesirable. For most leaders and participants, conflict evokes negative feelings, believing that it can lead to destructive ends. But it is important to assume that conflict is only natural and it can be a constructive force, leading to positive and creative outcomes. The art of conflict management needs to maximize constructive conflict and minimize destructive conflict. In order to achieve a mastery of this art, educational leaders/managers need to obtain a comprehensive understanding of the types, sources and dynamics of conflicts, and must become familiar with and develop the skills necessary to use the different techniques and approaches, in resolving and managing conflict. A sound theoretical understanding would enable an educational leader/manager to view organizational conflict with neutrality, and focus on positive aspects, by going to the extent of encouraging constructive criticisms. Such an attitude would enable him/her to be a proactive leader/manager in creating a cooperative and healthy working environment.

10.18 Review Questions

1. Discuss the different philosophies, techniques and approaches available for managing conflict.

2. Examine the theoretical approaches to resolving organizational conflict and how a proactive leader could develop the necessary skills to create a healthy working environment.

PART III

Leading and Managing Educational Organizations

CHAPTER 11

Leaders and the Art of Leading: More Appropriate Styles of Leadership

11.0 Learning Outcomes

Based on a systematic study of this chapter, the readers will:

- Improve knowledge and understanding, to relate to significant developments of theoretical concepts of leadership, and the art of leading in different contexts and situations;
- Comprehend the main theoretical contributions made by scholars and how those concepts can be related in refining one's own practice to adapt to changing needs;
- Have a better understanding of the actual organizational situations and develop the knowledge and skills to function as flexible, pro-active leaders and managers;
- Acquire the necessary knowledge and understanding, and develop the skills and competencies in leading the organization in an efficient and effective manner by playing the roles of artist, architect and commissar.

11.1 Focus

What makes an effective leader? How is the concept of leadership defined and what sort of theoretical concepts will enable us to understand this elusive but fascinating concept? A common assumption in leadership, being that it is the social process of influencing others; it is critical to have a better understanding of human nature. A leader needs to make every endeavour to establish appropriate relationships with staff in leading and managing an organization. The focus of this chapter relates to notions of leadership and management and how these relate to achievement of organizational goals. In this process, emphasis is also placed on entrepreneurship, vision and political acumen, and getting the best out of people in collegial cultures, concluding that a leader needs to be an artist, architect and a commissar.

11.2 The Need to Understand the Concept of Leadership

Leadership continues to be an elusive, but a fascinating topic to students in administration and management. Hoy and Miskel (2001) state that during the last several decades, the number of books and articles devoted to leadership attests to the prominence and collective efforts to improve our understanding of the concept. Leaders are important as they serve as anchors, provide guidance in times of change, and are responsible for the accomplishment of organizational goals. The terms "leaders and administrators" refer to individuals who occupy positions in which they are expected to exert leadership, which is a social influence process. Everyone knows the primary importance of leadership for the success of any organization, including the smallest family unit to the strongest nation in the world. Why do some schools, companies and teams, succeed while others are failing? The credit or blame goes to the principal, manager or the coach.

The critical situational factors of educational leadership are environment, organizational structures or organizational roles, nature and maturity levels of staff, and the characteristics of the organization. It is clear that while innate characteristics influence the capacity to lead, many leadership qualities can be learned or acquired. This fact adds credibility to the study of leadership and the importance of programmes similar to the Graduate Certificate in Leadership & Management and Master of Leadership & Management in Education (MLMEd), offered by the University of Newcastle, Australia.

11.3 The Nature of Leadership

Until now, numerous attempts to search for an accurate definition of leadership have not been successful and it is unlikely to succeed in the near future. Even though some useful insights have been found, no comprehensive theory of leadership has received universal acceptance. Katz and

Kahn (1978) identify three broad categories into which leadership theories can be classified. These are:

- Leadership theories based on attributes of the position;
- Leadership theories based on the characteristic of a person; and
- Leadership theories based on one's behaviour.

A position in an administrative hierarchy provides an opportunity to exercise leadership, but the position itself does not guarantee that the occupant will use that potential. There are schools where persons, other than the one who occupies the principalship, exercises leadership while the principal maintains the status quo. The idea that leadership is derived from the possession of some personal characteristics has not been validated in research. A large number of research projects have produced varying results leading to the conclusion that any particular set of traits does not result in effective leadership in all circumstances. The contingency theory of leadership offers a more accurate explanation of the effects of specific traits. Leadership behaviours and traits largely depend on the prevailing conditions of an organization. However, it is important to note that certain personal characteristics are likely to become more highly valued than others.

Leadership theories, based on particular types of behaviour, have been a more appropriate approach in understanding how to exercise influence within organizations. However, Stogdill (1974) in his studies finds no consistent relationship between behavioural styles and productivity in organizations structured along traditional hierarchical lines. A more useful approach is to consider leadership as a function. According to this view, leadership emerges as a responsibility shared and exercised by an individual or individuals, within an organization who are able and competent to contribute under a specific set of circumstances. This concept is most appropriate in the context of a participatory management mode. This has been made clear in Ouchi's (1981) discussion on Theory Z organizations. In Theory Z organizations there are two key characteristics of management: the sense of collective responsibility and the recognition that leadership is a function performed by the person best qualified to do so. Leadership is the act of deciding, usually by consensus, even though the ultimate responsibility may rest with a particular official. Under these conditions, leadership becomes the exercise of influence; beyond the authority vested in an organizational position. It is the increment of influence that moves members of a group beyond mere compliance, which engenders the fullest commitment for organizational goals.

The approach to leadership has far-reaching implications as to how individuals should define their roles as administrators. Robert Greenleaf (1977) offers one of the most provocative perceptions of leadership, proposing a concept of servant leader. He suggests that the effective leader is first of all a servant with a prior commitment of service to the group and that simple fact becomes the key to his/her greatness. The concept of servant-leadership is in harmony with the Biblical admonition that anyone who wants to be a leader among you must be your servant. Modern day politicians, often repeat that they want to win elections to serve the people, but do not hesitate to betray once elected to office. Leadership and/or administrative positions are bestowed upon individuals, to serve the group, whereas, the group can take away the bestowed leadership or administrative position, if the service is not appropriately rendered.

11.4 The Importance of Understanding Human Nature

Leaders who still believe in Frederick Taylor's (1911) approach to workers are not much different from those who subscribe to Machiavelli's (1938) advocacy than those who inherit positions of power as the privilege of being born into a dominant social class. Similar to Machiavellian advice in using guile and deception some leaders try to manipulate position power to advance personal agendas, with indifference to the concerns of others. This style of leadership closely resembles that of McGregor's (1960) Theory X soft behaviour modified to meet the democratic demands of modern times.

At the turn of the 20th Century, Max Weber (1947), who saw the emergence of huge industrial corporations in the Western world, realizing the inadequacy of the Machiavellian autocratic model, came up with the bureaucratic model. In contrast to autocratic rule, a bureaucratic organization is guided by the written rules and regulations, official standard operating procedures, chain of command, hierarchical authority and superordinate and subordinate relations. The bureaucratic model made the organization rational, logical, impersonal, formal, predictable and systematic. Bureaucratic Theory assumes that people tend to be motivated by Maslow's lower order needs, such as pay and benefits, job security and promotions. Until the 1970s the bureaucratic theory was the most pervasive and credible organizational concept in the world.

But, in 1960, with the introduction of McGregor's Theories X and Y, Theory X came to be identified with a softer Machiavellian approach, while Theory Y came to be identified with a more humanitarian approach of leadership. If a leader believes in Theory Y approach, then s/he needs to create an organizational environment that is likely to elicit and support high motivation and high levels of effort that they find satisfying in their work. Such an environment is growth enhancing and encourages the staff in their personal growth and development, as well as organizational growth, where the staff seeks Maslow's higher order needs.

11.5 Organizational Goals and Staff Motivation

The goals of any organization, point towards a desired state or condition that has not yet been accomplished. Achievement of goals has never been automatic. A major difficulty is the discrepancy between individual needs and goals of the organization. Integration of these generally divergent orientations is the most difficult task. However, it has been revealed that full integration of individual interests and organizational goals are an impossible task. What can be achieved is only a matter of degree rather than a full congruence. Advocacy of leadership by consensus is based on the belief that this approach to organizational problem solving can produce a significantly greater degree of integration of individual and organizational goals. Because of the personality and value differences, some combinations of leadership, by consensus and traditional management methods could produce a better result.

Motivation remains a persistent concern in most organizations. Motivation can be considered as the level of one's incentive to work. It comes from within the individual. If a staff member changes his/her behaviour, perhaps, it is not because that person is motivated, but because his/her perception relating to the organization has changed. The development of an environment conducive to higher motivational behaviour must come from the leader, as individual motivation and organizational climate is significantly influenced by the leadership style of the administrator. Experience has revealed that extrinsic motivation is generally effective in controlling short-term behaviour. However, if we are to sustain long-term motivation, it needs to be intrinsic. Edward Deci (1975) notes that participatory management structures, when appropriately operated, tend to make the staff members intrinsically motivated.

11.6 Power and Authority of Leadership

In organizations, official positions in the hierarchy are vested with authority and it is believed that those who occupy such positions have a legitimate right to command. This vested authority rests on legal power, customarily granted to positions such as Heads of Departments, Deans, Principals etc. As those vested with authority occupy higher positions, in theory at least, subordinates have no alternative but to obey. But in practice, especially in educational organizations, such as in schools or faculties, such absolute power rarely exists. The attempts to use such commands are not only resisted, but also considered as oppression.

On the other hand, followers who accept leaders' influence, voluntarily entrust the power to leaders, and agree to take directions by shared agreements, whether made formally or informally. Usually, leaders do not wield authority vested in office; instead they use entrusted power. Followers entrust power to the leader and/or manager, either because they share the values and beliefs of the leader, or are convinced by the leader's vision and believe that s/he can manage the resources well to achieve the shared goals. It is generally acknowledged that Mahatma Gandhi and Martin Luther King Jr. were some of the most powerful leaders in the 20th Century, yet they had little in the way of legal authority to make their followers do anything. But, they had extraordinary power to influence the behaviour of hundreds of millions of followers and, ultimately, the course of two nations.

11.7 What Are the Kinds of Power Available to Leaders?

First, French and Raven (1968) describe power as the capacity to influence others and refer to five bases or sources of power that a leader can utilize in motivating his/her followers. These are:

- Reward power: ability to persuade others to comply with the leader's wishes by controlling the rewards.
- Coercive power: ability to excise authority to impose sanctions on staff who in turn will try to avoid them by complying with the leader's directions.
- Expert power: Leader having expertise in the core business of the organization, enabling him or her to advice and guide staff. But, every leader is unlikely to possess this power.
- Legitimate power: Leader having legal authority for the position that is recognized by the staff.
- Referent power: Leader having ideas and beliefs and/or charisma that the staff admires and are happy to seek advice and adjudication.

Thus, it is clear that the exercise of power is a reciprocal relationship between the power holder and others. A leader has power not only to control resources that can reward or punish followers, but also, to empower, thus, enabling them to participate in organizational decision-making. There are other leaders who have ideas about the future of the organization that followers find exciting and want to "buy into". Leaders who can draw their power from multiple sources are stronger than those who depend on a single source (Louis, 1986). The principal's coercive power and the ability to command have decreased substantially. Especially, since the organization of teachers' unions and the broadening judicial interpretation of the rights of teachers, the inability of the principals to use coercive power to control teachers has increased the need for leadership. However, teachers recognize the official position occupied by the principal in the school hierarchy. Principals who have a vision for the future, and express it coherently and vividly to inspire enthusiasm and involve others to mould and develop ideas are admired. This enables them to build referent power, which becomes an important source of power, for principals to lead others.

11.8 What Do We Mean by a Situation?

Many scholars agree with Fiedler (1967) that the particular leadership style of the leader and/or manager will depend on the situation. But, most scholars are unable to agree on the important components of a situation. Fiedler describes three elements of a situation i.e. status, leader-member relations, and task structure. Reddin (1970) refers to five elements such as: organizational philosophy, technology or how the work needs to be performed, the superior, the co-worker, and the subordinates. Reddin (1970, p. 12) identifies four possible styles that are combinations of task-oriented and relationship-oriented behaviour:

- Integrated Style emphasizes both relationship and task-oriented behaviour.
- Separated Style is deficient on both task and relationship orientation.
- Related Style emphasizes relationship-oriented behaviour at the expense of task orientation. And
- Dedicated Style emphasizes task, neglecting the relationship orientation.

Reddin (1970) believes that each of these four could be either effective or ineffective, depending on the situation. He develops eight descriptive terms to describe the possible managerial types, embodying the eight effective and ineffective leadership styles. He has pointed out that the "autocrat" *dedicated to* the ineffective implementation of high task and low relationship styles, becomes an ineffective leader. But a "benevolent autocrat", using the same *dedicated style* appropriately, becomes an effective leader. Reddin has described situations where the leader possesses a superior knowledge of the job in comparison to subordinates. When unscheduled events are likely to occur, when directions must be given, or where subordinates' performances are easily measurable; a benevolent autocrat can be an effective leader.

Tannenbaum and Schmidt (1958) have described three "forces" that the leader/manager needs to consider in deciding how to lead an organization or a group. They refer to forces within the leader, forces within the subordinate and forces in the situation. These are as follows:

- Forces within the leader include the values and beliefs of the leader i.e. how does s/he feel about participatory decision-making, his/her confidence in subordinates, his/her inclination towards a particular style, whether s/he is willing to loose control etc.
- Forces within the subordinate include desire for autonomy, willingness to take responsibility, and willingness to tolerate ambiguity.
- Forces in the situation include the type of organization, whether participatory decision-making is appropriate, whether staff can work in teams, whether the issue is complex or simple, and whether adequate time is available.

11.9 Maturity Levels of Followers and Leaders

In a subsequent study, these scholars have pointed out several components of situations. By referring to "follower maturity", they have described maturity as comprising of: (1) a capacity to set high but attainable goals, (2) a willingness and an ability to take responsibility, and (3) the level of education or experience. They have contended that as follower maturity can change over time, leader behaviour also should change over time. Accordingly, when the followers are low in maturity, they need highly task-oriented leaders. But, when the maturity level increases, they prefer relationship-oriented leaders. When the maturity level of the followers is above average even the relationship orientation becomes irrelevant to them.

Blanchard, Zigarmi and Zigarmi (1987) have advocated that a school leader needs to decide on his/her leadership style based on the "developmental level" of the followers. This has to be determined by the degree of competence and commitment to perform a task, without supervision. If a teacher is highly enthusiastic in performing a particular task for which s/he does not have the skills, the leader needs to tell the teacher what to do and how, while monitoring the performance. This approach can be referred to as the *directing style*. In contrast, when a follower is competent and motivated to perform the task, s/he can be given the responsibility without supervision, which can be called *delegating style*. When a follower has some competence, but is not highly motivated, the leader needs to combine direction with praise to raise the level of motivation, which can be called *coaching style*. When a follower is competent, but varies in commitment, the leader needs to listen and support the follower, thereby employing the *supporting style of leadership*.

11.10 Leadership Style and the Need for Flexibility

Hersey and Blanchard (1988) insist that successful leaders adapt their leadership behaviour to meet the needs of the group. They refer to four possible combinations of task-oriented and relationship-oriented behaviour i.e. task-oriented behaviour; relationship-oriented behaviour; both task-oriented and relationship-oriented behaviour; and neither task-oriented nor relationship-oriented behaviour.

Like Reddin, Hersey and Blanchard (1988) believe that any of the four styles can be effective. They believe that some leaders are able to modify their behaviour to fit any of the four styles, while others utilize two or three styles. This shows that some have the ability to be flexible, while others are more rigid. Those who are most flexible are the ones who are most effective in jobs that require a lot of adaptability.

Reddin (1970) also believes that some leaders have the ability to be flexible while some others have very little flexibility. The best leaders have three important abilities i.e. (1) "situational sensitivity", which enables leaders to diagnose situations; (2) "style flexibility", which allows them to match their style to the situation; and (3) "situational management style", which helps them to change the situation to fit their styles.

The model developed by Blanchard et al. (1987) provides for the greatest flexibility of leadership styles. Accordingly, a leader must vary his or her style according to the followers' competence and confidence, which needs to change not only from person to person, but also, with each task assigned to the same person. In assigning each task, a leader must choose between directing, coaching, delegating and supporting styles. They believe that leader behaviour must vary to fit the "maturity" level of followers. As followers become more able to operate on their own, they believe that leaders should be able to change their styles. Similarly, Gates, Blanchard and Hersey (1976) believe that leader behaviour must vary to fit the "maturity level" of the followers. As followers become more able to operate on their own, they believe that leaders should be able to change their leadership styles.

Goleman (2000) argues that the best leaders do not rely on, only one style of leadership. He points out that an effective leader employs six different styles of leadership styles and identifies them as:

- Coercive — demanding immediate compliance;
- Authoritative — mobilizing people towards a vision;
- Affiliative — creating emotional bonds and harmony;
- Democratic — building consensus through participation;
- Pacesetting — expecting excellence and self-direction; and
- Coaching — developing people for the future.

He adds that these styles spring from different components of emotional intelligence. He concludes that leaders who have mastered four or more — especially the authoritative, democratic, affiliative, and coaching styles — have the best climate and [organizational] performance. More importantly, the most effective leaders switch flexibly between the styles, as the context and situation demands.

11.11 Which Is More Appropriate: Task or Relationship Orientation?

Some leaders take a keener interest in the task as against the people with whom they work. There are others who take a keener interest in their relationship with co-workers, rather than focus on the task to be accomplished. Whether one emphasizes task orientation or human relation's orientation, is often considered to be central to the leadership style. Fielder (1967) believes that leaders are able to focus either on task or the relationship, but not on both. He considers task orientation and relationship orientation as the two ends of a continuum and, hence, that it is logically impossible to be at both ends of the continuum.

Later, in his research on "contingency theory", Fiedler (1973) reveals that leaders who describes their "least preferred co-worker" in positive terms are "human relations oriented". Leaders who describes "least liked co-worker" in negative terms are task oriented. He believes that both styles could be effective. What could be most effective is to have the appropriate fit between task orientation and relationship orientation depending on the task, context, the situation and the maturity levels of staff.

11.12 Is There an Ideal Style of Leadership?

The views on leadership styles discussed so far are broad categories. Those that focus on the maturity levels of followers do not fit conveniently into one of these categories. Effective leaders also vary their styles in response to such factors as community expectations, organizational climate and culture and certain aspects of the task such as timeliness and availability of resources. All these views of leadership necessitate a choice. Administrators must choose to make use of the theories that best fit their personalities, experiences, situations, and, not just to depend on intuitive perceptions of themselves and others.

Many leaders and prospective leaders ponder over the question, "which leadership style is most effective?" They want to know the ideal way to approach leadership. They ask themselves whether they need to be subordinate centred or boss centred or whether to base their leadership on Theory X or Theory Y. Whether they should concentrate on task or relationship orientation or whether they need to initiate changes or respond to others. Researchers believe there is no ideal leadership style that will work in all situations. The best view of leadership style is that which varies to fit the particular situation at hand.

When some emphasize the importance of relationship orientation, and others insist on the importance of task orientation, Fielder using his contingency theory, maintains that either one of these could be appropriate, depending on the degree of control that the leader has over the situation. He refers to three components of situational control: (1) status or position power of the leader; (2) quality of relations between the leader and the staff; and (3) the structure of the task. Fielder's extensive research reveals that when a leader is extremely influential or extremely un-influential, the most effective style will be a task-oriented style. Relationship-oriented leaders are more effective in the situations that fall in between.

11.13 Leadership as a Relationship with Followers

Today, whenever a person wants to lead an organization, as the key person who influences the organizational culture, the leader becomes part of the equation of organizational behaviour. In this context, leaders need to be concerned, not only with the leadership styles and techniques that they intend to use, but also with the quality and kinds of relationships with staff. *Leadership is about working with and through people to achieve organizational goals.* As against commanding obedience, an effective leader can empower and energize the followers. Leaders need to relate to staff in ways to arouse their personal commitments and motivate them towards the accomplishment of the shared vision. The leader also needs to create an environment, which facilitates the realization of common goals.

How should a leader set about doing these things? It depends on what s/he thinks what the role of leadership is, thus, defining the character and quality of relationships between him/her and staff. This will depend on his/her assumptions and views on staff and the types of values and cultural beliefs s/he holds. If we reflect on Douglas McGregor's Theories X and Y, a leader who believes in Theory X, will try to issue orders or directives and undertake supervision while providing resources to keep things moving. A leader, who believes in Theory Y assumptions, will share a vision, create enthusiasm for the work to be done, provide help in solving problems, and support and encourage staff.

The key to understanding leadership lies in understanding the leader's own perception of human nature, staff and how s/he relates to them. The clear distinction between how leaders' assumptions become clearer from a statement made by General Schwartzkopf (1991) who commanded the coalition forces against Iraq. According to him, when a competent leader stands before a platoon he sees only a platoon whereas a great leader sees a group of 44 individuals with their own individual interests and aspirations. This statement expresses a very different view of human nature than that expressed by Max Weber in his ideal bureaucracy. It clearly distinguishes between X and Y leadership styles.

11.14 Sergiovanni's Five Forces of Leadership

Sergiovanni (1984) incorporates Fielder's two dimensions of task and relationship orientation of leadership for advancing insights into the theories of leadership. He proposes five forces of leadership, namely, technical, human, educational, symbolic and cultural. He explains that the technical, human and educational forces combine to accomplish the effectiveness in schools. If excellence is the goal to be achieved, then it is necessary to focus on symbolic and cultural forces. Technical and human elements address management competencies, while the educational dimension ensures the effectiveness of teaching and learning in an educational organization. Symbolic and cultural forces take account of the need to go beyond competent management to higher values and beliefs. These dimensions help a school, or any other educational organization, to bring a better state of affairs, through a shared vision and the building of a strong organizational culture. A leader can exercise the five forces as follows:

- Technical: by accomplishing the tasks of the organization, such as planning, organizing, coordinating, encouraging and controlling;
- Human: attending to human factors such as consideration of relationships within the organization, morale and empowerment;
- Educational: getting involved in instructional leadership, such as addressing educational problems, developing and evaluating curriculum, and the professional development of the leader and staff;
- Symbolic: involving himself/herself in creating, communicating, and gaining commitment to the shared vision, by articulating the purpose, values and significance of the future state;
- Cultural: building a strong organizational culture, enabling the staff to share values, beliefs and a strong commitment to the organization (Adapted from Sergiovanni, 1984, p. 6).

The role of Educational Leadership includes diagnosing and solving pedagogical and curricular problems. The role of Symbolic Leadership includes communicating a vision, purpose and values to all followers enabling them to personally commit themselves because they share and support the vision, mission and values of the organization. Cultural Leadership is focused on developing a strong organizational culture. Here, when staff identifies personally with the leader and/or the organization, they pledge their loyalty to the organization. Cultural leaders devote time and energy to attend to customs, traditions, group norms, and daily routines, which exemplify the best that a school has to offer.

A survey conducted in 1994, involving 101 teachers from 14 aided secondary schools in Hong Kong, to analyse the effects of leadership on teachers' feelings about school life suggest that cultural linkage in schools promotes teachers' feelings of commitment, job satisfaction, sense of community, order and discipline, whereas bureaucratic linkage undermines such feelings. An important implication of the study is that school principals should place more emphasis on cultural linkages in leadership as the strategies to bind people together and to give people meanings in their work (Pang, 1996).

Hence, it is important for the contemporary educational leaders to recognize and understand these three forms of leadership, if educational organizations are to be made more successful, or move them to being excellent organizations. *The leaders need to make informed decisions, based on the theoretical foundations and accurate and adequate data.* It is also important to remember that schools are built around an educational philosophy and community values, which empower the leaders to make educationally sound decisions.

11.15 Transformational Leadership

Since the late 1970s, with better insights into human behaviour in organizational settings, new approaches have emerged that invoke inspirational, visionary and symbolic leadership behaviour. Burns (1978) makes a clear distinction between transactional and transformational leadership. This provides a major shift in the thinking behind leadership theory, particularly in connection with the moral dimensions of leadership (Sergiovanni, 1992). Burns points out that under transactional leadership, the individuals within the organization negotiate their individual interests as opposed to group interests, and come to mutual agreements with the leader. Sergiovanni and Staratt (1988) point out that transformational leadership goes beyond exchanging favours in terms of transactional leadership. It seeks common purposes, uniting the group to go beyond individual interests in the pursuit of higher goals.

Today, where we face a challenging and demanding education climate of constant change, it is believed that no single person can have all the answers to the problems confronted by organizations. In such a situation, transformational leadership combines capacities of all those within the organization in order to engage in effective leadership, towards the accomplishment of organizational goals. Louis and Miles (1991) suggest that if implementation of a vision is to be effective, power sharing becomes critical. Further, they have found that leaders of successful schools have been able to support the initiatives of others, without the fear of losing control. They facilitate the formation of teams and working parties, by allocating funds for their initiatives, at the same time keeping in close contact with the groups and monitoring progress.

Research by Gamage, Sipple and Partridge (1995, 1996) in the Australian Capital Territory (ACT) and Victoria, and by Gamage (1996c) in New South Wales and other systems, have confirmed such findings. Their research suggests that the empowerment of a range of stakeholders within a school community (such as teachers, parents, students and local community), provide a combined richness of educational thought and activity, in improving school effectiveness. Achievements within such transformed institutions are superior to any that a principal alone has been able to achieve. That is, leadership at its best, when it is a shared venture, involving as many as possible within a school.

Recently, Cardona (2000) introduces the concept of transcendental leadership, which to him is an authentic transformational leadership. In this form of leadership, the leader provides fair extrinsic rewards, appeals to the intrinsic motivation of the collaborators, and develops a transcendental motivation, in order to promote unity in the organization. He also points out that authentic transformational leaders are engaged in the moral uplifting of their followers, share mutually rewarding visions of success, and empower them to transform those visions into realities.

In an analysis of school leadership, in an empowered environment, in terms of school-based governance, Gamage (1996d) has developed a model with the types of skills that leaders should possess to face new challenges. In another recent research project, Gamage (1998d) reveals that a principal who recorded a written dissent, against the school council's recommendation, but proceeded to implement such a recommendation, realized two years later that it was the best decision under the circumstances, proving the superiority of the combined wisdom. Fullan and Hargreaves (1992) note that with the spread of leadership in the school, the principal is free to take a more constructive role. Transforming the principal from that of a meeting bound bureaucrat to an instructional leader, who can closely work with the staff in developing and implementing educational goals. Telford (1996) points out that being a leader in a school, in particular, and organizations, in general, in modern times is not a picnic. It needs hard work, dedication and a firm desire to do the right things by putting heads together, discussing, challenging, brainstorming and problem solving, through the issues, in a steadfast and resolute manner. It is most likely that a school leader, or any other individual, no matter how much an expert s/he is, may not have the answers to all the questions on how to proceed. The related theory and research, conducted over the last 50 years, and the best practices of the 1990s, confirms this view, by suggesting that no single person has the combined wisdom and capacity to do the job of a leader.

Bolman and Deal (1997) have further advanced Goffman's (1974) frame theory, pointing out how four frames of leadership, enlarge the focus of leader's thinking to organizational practice. The organizational theoretical concepts of cultural, symbolic, educational, human and technical, have been consolidated and reorganized into the structural, human resource, political and symbolic frames. Thus, providing a framework on which to interpret, analyse and understand what is happening in an organization. This approach enables managerial freedom and leadership effectiveness, with opportunities to examine the same situation in four different ways. They encourage the leaders to use a multiplicity of frames, rather than depending on their preferred frame, and state that the ability to move in and out of the four frames brings deeper insights and broadening horizons. Arnold, Arad, Rhoades, and Drasgow (2000) have developed a new scale to measure leader behaviours and identified five indicators of empowering leadership, namely: leading by example, participatory decision-making, coaching, informing, and showing concern/interacting with the team.

11.15.1 Guidelines for Transformational Leadership

Even though much more research needs to be done to gain a clearer understanding of transformational leadership, sufficient research outcomes are there to suggest some tentative guidelines for leaders who seek to inspire and motivate followers. These are:

- Articulate a clear and appealing vision — Transformational leaders need to strengthen the current vision or build a commitment to a new vision. In the final analysis, the vision helps to guide the actions and decisions of each member of the organization, which is especially important when individuals or groups are allowed a high degree of autonomy and discretion in decisions relating to their work.
- Explain how the vision can be attained — A leader should not only articulate an appealing vision but also convince the followers that the vision is feasible. A good leader should not pretend that s/he has all the answers as to how to achieve the vision, but tell the followers that they will have vital roles to play in discovering what specific actions are necessary.
- Act confidently and optimistically — Followers will not have much faith in a vision unless leader himself/herself is convinced that it is

realistic. It is best to emphasize what has been achieved and the positive aspects rather than emphasizing how much more to be done, as well as, the obstacles and dangers that lie ahead.

- Express confidence in followers — The motivating effect of a vision also depends on the extent to which staff is confident about their ability to realize the vision. It is important to foster confidence and optimism when the task is difficult or dangerous or when the group members lack confidence in them.
- Use dramatic, symbolic actions to emphasize key values — A vision is reinforced by the behaviour of the leader that is consistent with it. Dramatic highly visible actions are an effective way to emphasize key values.
- Lead by example — It is said that actions speak louder than words or there is no point in preaching unless you are prepared to practice what you preach. A leader who asks the staff to make sacrifices should set an example by doing the same. The values espoused by a leader should be demonstrated in his or her behaviour and it must be done consistently, not just when convenient.
- Empower people to achieve the vision — Empowerment of the staff is the most important aspect of transformational leadership. This means empowering individual staff members and the teams to set the goals and determine the strategies to achieve them towards the realization of the shared vision. In the final analysis, it is the responsibility of the leader to provide adequate resources to perform the tasks towards the realization of the targets (goals) for which the staff is held accountable (Adapted from Yukl, 2002, pp. 263–266).

11.16 Progression of Transformational Leadership

In an evaluation of the developments of transformational leadership within organizations, the following steps have been noticed:

- At the lowest level, leaders exercise power to exact the compliance of followers, which is not considered as leadership.
- At the entry level, leaders practice transactional leadership. Here, the leaders and the followers bargain with each other to establish a "contract" or understanding to work together.
- At the higher level of practice is the transforming leadership. Here, the leaders and the staff work together for a common cause encouraged by shared values and aspirations.

- At the highest level, there is the moral leadership. Here, based on a shared vision and a sense of mutual purpose, a covenant of shared values gets interwoven with the daily lives and practices of staff. Such an environment inspires new and higher levels of commitment and involvement (Adapted from Owens, 2001, p. 244).

11.17 Moral Leadership

Burns (1978), referring to moral leadership within the concept of transformational leadership, points out that the relationship between the leader and the staff needs to be based on a genuine partnership. It should include a possibility for staff to take informed decisions, regarding the understanding that has to be forged between the leader and the staff, and a commitment by the leader to honour what was negotiated. In this context, moral leadership is not mere preaching, without putting them into practice, or insisting on social conformity. Moral leadership emerges from, and returns to, the fundamental wants, needs, aspirations, and values of the followers.

11.18 Participatory Management

A leader's assumption on values and beliefs about power, and how s/he articulates them, helps to shape the organizational culture. In the past, leaders/managers believed that they should acquire all the powers that can be acquired and protect it vigorously. Leaders, who harbour such primitive beliefs, are likely to relieve themselves of the ability to influence the group. Griffiths (1959) considers power as a function of decision-making. A person could be considered to have power if s/he can make decisions affecting the direction of an organization, and also influence other decisions. In a broader definition, the leader has the capacity to influence decisions, which advances organizational goals by responding to the needs of its members. For instance, consider a situation where a principal uses his/her power to supervise classroom teachers, but teachers conform to the principal's instructions, only when s/he is present in the classroom, and ignore them at all other times. This is a situation where position authority is not transformed into power. Therefore, it is very important for the school leaders to offer their staff wider participation in decisions, which affect their professional practice, in order to motivate them intrinsically.

On the other hand, if a leader institutes structures and procedures, enabling teachers to diagnose the problems, identify the corrective measures and provide the facilities and resources, such a step will energize the teachers in transforming the whole school (Pang & Lam, 2000). This would prove the effectiveness of "expert + servant" power, within the concept of participatory management. In this context, it is important to recognize that the concept of power needs to be understood and exercised in a different light to the traditional belief.

It is important for all types of leaders to pay heed to the concept of power, outlined by Wynn and Guditus (1984), and rethink their own positions. These deeper insights into the concept of power are:

- Power is a form of human energy, a variable sum without limits, rather than a fixed sum commodity. If a leader shares it, s/he creates new power and has more rather than less.
- Power is a means to action rather than an end in itself. Power needs to be used to energize the staff towards the accomplishment of common goals, without considering it as a personal prerogative and a commodity to be hoarded.
- Power has to be exercised through and with people, as well as over people. If a leader seeks to use power to control others, s/he will constrain rather than release others' energies.
- Organizational effectiveness is more a function of organizational power than that of individual leaders/managers. When a leader empowers others to prove their full potential, it increases the power of the leader, as well as, that of the organization.
- Power is inherently, neither good nor bad, it is a neutral concept. Most unwise leaders hoard it, assuming it a precious commodity. There are others who foolishly believe in the elimination of power, thinking that everything would be better off (Adapted from Wynn & Guditus, 1984, pp. 36–38).

11.19 Practical Approaches to Leading and Managing

The task of running a complex operation can be referred to as "administration". It has two dimensions. One dimension, which embraces activities, related to change and dynamism in leadership. The other dimension, which encompasses productive efforts to manage a status quo within which staff can work comfortably, is "management". The basis of conceptualization depends upon a particular situation or context. An administrator evokes or invokes management, by following the existing rules. By alternatively using the Accelerator, the Brakes, and Cruise Control, the administrator guides the dynamic organization.

A good administrator needs to diagnose the context correctly, and should know how much pressure to apply, when to apply and why. A person, who is in charge of a complex social organization, should attend to both leadership tasks and managerial tasks. Successful organizations will not have leaders running in one direction and managers another. A school principal has to run the school as a part of a larger social and political context. The administrator, who exercises leadership skills, helps to establish a shared vision, leading to a mission statement and goals for the organization itself, and for the organization, within a larger context. When the vision is shared, structures and processes are established to guide the accomplishment of common goals.

Administrators, while fulfilling the two roles, must operate in a moral-ethical framework. In the capacity of managers, they need to maintain a productive status quo, by conserving useful and facilitative policies and procedures. But as leaders, they need to change the goals, policies and procedures in response to, or in anticipation of, internal and external concerns, issues and problems. Blumberg (1989) states that a successful principal applies the "craft" of administration by the judicious balancing of the art of leadership, and the science of management, leading to continuous improvement in the school.

Leithwood, Begley, and Cousins (1992) have postulated that a leader, who often takes risks and is goal oriented, is more likely to stress goal accomplishment, competency and higher achievement. A leader, who takes risks and is creative, only infrequently, works to maintain status quo. Leader venture-some-ness has been a strong predictor of an "accomplishment culture." It stresses excellence and when there is peer pressure to do a good job with leader's encouragement to be innovative how the organization could be improved, it leads higher levels of productivity. This in turn, is a strong predictor of strong staff commitment, especially, when they identify themselves with the organization, and have a strong sense of ownership of the organization. Thus, leader venture-some-ness can be considered an important factor in boosting the morale of the organizational members, committing themselves to the accomplishment of organizational goals.

Cuban (1986), as well as Ubben, Hughes and Norris (2001) have argued that political acumen is a characteristic of effective leaders. They have pointed out that such leaders know when to break the rules and when to short-circuit the system. Leaders with appropriate political acumen know when it is more important to risk having to beg forgiveness, as against, asking permission. Leaders should be able to balance the inherent conflict between attention to staff and organizational needs, and system mandates. A key leadership function is the establishment of goals, with the participation of others, enabling them to commit to the process of implementation. Leaders should help everyone to feel that the organization belongs to everyone, and make the achievement of goals, the responsibility of everyone. Such leaders empower others who also have a stake in the organization.

11.20 Is the Leader an Artist, an Architect or a Commissar?

The consideration of numerous situations reveals varying styles of leadership, varying degrees of maturity levels of staff, and availability of required resources. In such circumstances, how can an effective leader function? And what contexts and situations offer the best possibilities for success? In the final analysis, an effective leader needs to have a blend of artist, architect and commissar. Hughes (1994) describes an artist as a creative virtuoso — contemplative and unfettered by constraints of the real world, giving birth to ideas and concepts and the notion of what might be. The very notion of contemplation and reflection are important for leaders. In a complex social organization, fragmented days, numerous meetings (characterized by innumerable interruptions), chance encounters, unanticipated problems, infringe upon time set aside for reflection and contemplative behaviour. But, it is essential that an effective leader be a visionary. The concept of a visionary is suggestive of contemplation and reflection, and not of speculative artistry.

An architect is one who possesses a decisive sense of direction and goal orientation. Is a leader best described by this metaphor? A certain aspects of an architect's job require different kinds of design work. But, can an architect be an effective leader? Yes, to a degree, but little would be realized without a "clerk of the works", an evacuator, an overseer, who follows the plan and sees that others follow the plan. Architects will not be happy to attend to such work. If it is so, why not send a commissar?

The commissar is a person of action. When a commissar is placed in charge of a sloppy operation, s/he gets it sorted out quickly. Good commissars are essential when a lot of tasks need to be accomplished. Commissars need neither prodding nor pushing; indeed, they are the people who do the prodding and pushing.

11.21 Conclusion

In an overview of the concept of leadership, commissars understand and appreciate the ways of other commissars; architects understand and appreciate the ways of other architects; artists understand and appreciate the ways of other artists. Leaders need to understand all three, so she or he is not the artist, architect or commissar, but s/he is a mix of the artist, architect and commissar.

In the final analysis, a leader needs to have a shared vision i.e. a sense of what should be the future state of the organization, an effective network of communication, a well-ordered plan, a design and strategy to get there, and a determination to get there. The leader should also be able to utilize all the available means and resources, efficiently and effectively. She or he needs to be internally driven to achieve the requisite goals, needs to understand the true picture of the organization, including its nature, needs, and limitations of the staff. Students of leadership and management need to understand two basic guidelines. First, it is important to be doing the right things rather than to worry constantly about doing things right. Second, the emphasis should be on being effective as opposed to, being efficient.

11.22 Review Questions

1. Why do you consider it important to have a sound knowledge and understanding of the theoretical concepts and best practices on leadership in improving one's own competence in leading a contemporary school?
2. Discuss the importance of transformational leadership along with the concepts of vision, entrepreneurship and political acumen in leading and managing a modern complex organization.

CHAPTER 12

Leading and Managing Change in Organizations

12.0 Learning Outcomes

Based on a systematic study of this chapter, the readers will:

- Have an improved knowledge and understanding of the theoretical concepts in leading and managing organizational change;
- Comprehend theoretical contributions and best practices developed over the years towards the development of leadership skills needed in playing the key role in the change processes;
- Develop skills and competencies in moving the organization, or the unit that one is leading, towards a continuous cycle of self-renewal and/or organizational development.

12.1 Focus

This topic focuses on the theory and practice of leading and managing organizational change. It attempts to identify the exact role of the school leader in the process of introducing and managing change. The discussions also focus on the processes of organizational renewal through the development of organizational climates and cultures conducive to change. The concept of organizational development (OD) is reviewed where the primary aim is seen as being the development of a work-oriented culture and climate, which draws on the involvement of all staff, in decision-making and goal setting processes. It is further argued that effective leaders are competent in diagnosing situational needs and in implementing appropriate intervention strategies. Finally, an integrated approach to organizational change is presented.

12.2 The Inevitability of Change in Organizations

Leading and managing change is one of the most important and difficult responsibilities of a leader. Sweeny (1980) contends that "change" is the very essence of educational leadership, and that everything else is secondary. Effective leaders need to focus on revitalization of their organizations and adaptation to changing environments. In the modern world, no organization can boast about its stability, as more often than not, it is interpreted as stagnation rather than steadiness. Organizations, which are not in the business of change, are sure to face frightening uncertainties for their survival. Besides, in society, there is certain magic surrounding the word change. Since the days of Franklin D. Roosevelt, the Presidents of the United States are expected to effect major changes within the first one hundred days in office. For many people, "change" seems to provide a well of hope, that somehow people will be better off with changed conditions. For others, the opposite is true, as they fear the change of status quo, uncertain futures, needed for retraining, relocation, or loss of employment.

One of the dominant concepts that have emerged in the contemporary world is that of planned, controlled, and directed social and organizational change. Today, leaders need not react to changing situations as they unfold. Instead, a leader can consciously direct the forces of change to suit predetermined goals and organizational values, based on a well-articulated vision. As "leadership" means to act and move forward, it is imperative that effective leaders be proactive, by planning and directing change for continuous improvement of their organizations. The adoption of new ideas and practices in an educational organization is a big challenge and a heavy obligation of the leader. Thus, the educator is caught in a shooting gallery of conflicting expectations and demands. In a lot of cases all sorts of disorders and challenges plague schools. Sullivan (1999) states that the existence of disorder in educational settings is viewed by the chaos theorists as healthy signs that schools are on their way to improvement. He implores educational leaders/managers to positively ride the crest of such dynamics, making small adjustments on the way, and eventually achieving a renewed and improved system of education.

12.3 Changing Times: Its Impact on Societal Contexts

Innovations and adaptation strategies are needed to cope with the impact of technological advancement, globalization and information technology, which have changed the lifestyles of most people in the world. Many futurists believe that society is moving from the industrial or technological revolution, into the information era. If we consider the impact of computer technology, which is now the basis of automation, it has resulted in the displacement of millions of workers, while creating jobs in newer areas. In fact, Bill Clinton, the President of the United States from 1993–2000, in his final address to the Congress on 31 January 2000, boasted about the creation of 20 million jobs during his tenure of office and having a booming economy as never before. Changes in information processing, within the last two decades, have revolutionized the marketplace and are greatly impacting on the education systems and educational administration. It is true that there have been some noticeable changes in schools, but none that compares with the impact of technology on the administration of many corporations. Numerous scholars have warned educators, that public schools should keep pace with societal changes and expectations, in order to survive in such a changing environment. Now, almost daily, educators are confronted with demands from the society to reform the educational process.

Consider the technological advancement, resulting in innovations of the washing machine, microwave oven, and vacuum cleaner. These items have reduced physical labour, making life easier for many people. The prevailing attitude seems to be that change is good and leads to a better life. Manufacturers of products have found that the term "new" on the label increases sales. Similarly, parents expect change in schools, and most of them, equate it with goodness. This sort of community expectation for change has placed great pressure on school leaders to promote changes in schools. Since the 1960s, because of this community interest, the question of determining the type of educational reform has shifted from the hands of the educational professionals to the politicians. The school leader's competency to function as a change agent is becoming increasingly crucial in improving the status of education in the system. Economists have pointed out that other countries, such as Brazil, have more natural resources than the USA, and have singled out America's economic success to her educational system. According to Kimbrough and Buerkett (1990), recently, a group of businessmen, who studied the future of the economy, conclude that the growth of the economy in the USA would depend on the quality of the education system, pointing out that there is a need for change.

Beer and Nohria (2000) state that the organizational change theories are categorized into two, namely: Theory E and Theory O. According to them, Theory E changes are aimed at maximizing shareholder values, and are managed from the top down. It emphasizes structures and systems, motivates through financial incentives, and involves the processes of planning and establishing programmes. On the other hand, Theory O changes, aim to develop organizational capabilities, encourage participation from the bottom up, focus on the building up of a corporate culture, motivate through commitment, and make use of the processes of experimentation and involvement. They suggest that a hybrid of these theories is likely to produce better results in organizations.

12.4 School Leader as a Change Agent

Even though some people are critical of the lack of innovation in schools, in particular, and in education systems, in general, educators are not entirely to be blamed. Because of the plurality of the categories of stakeholders and the diversity of their views and opinions, even an ideal set of reforms are likely to be opposed by some. As a result, the school leader and the teachers might become embroiled in a conflict with the community. Often, the difficulty in reconciling the views and expectations of different categories of stakeholders leads to complications and conflicts. However, if the strategies used are well planned, developed and administered, the change process might not create great problems.

If the educational administrator functions as a change agent, taking the staff with him/her, such a programme will give the leader and the teachers more, not less, control of the school programmes. If the principal and the teachers change the school practices to improve the school's effectiveness, new practices may even be more demanding, making life more difficult for the staff. It could be much easier to maintain the status quo. But in a competitive market, when parents find out that their children have been deprived of educational excellence, they are likely to take their children to a better school. In a system like the USA, where the local community is responsible for the education dollar, or in systems, which operate under school-based management (SBM), parents will endeavour to change the situation by changing the school leader. As professional ethics require them to provide the best possible education for the children in their charge, school leaders are forced to be innovative to survive. The choice lies with planned change.

Schools in Hong Kong are confronting with more or less the same challenges, as in other countries, brought by the huge information flow and vigorous innovative moves owing to globalization. It necessitates schools to transform into learning communities so as to meet the expectations of their stakeholders (Pang & Cheung, in press). If a school has to become a learning community, it needs to enhance its own learning capacity in a way that the whole school seeks organizational improvement in a continuous process. School leaders have to submit to a paradigm shift from hierarchal, supervisory and controlling roles to facilitative and supportive roles with careful planning.

12.5 Organizing Planned Change

Self-renewal, or organizational development (OD), approaches to managing change in schools can be built upon: (1) clear and appropriate diagnosis of the school as an organization, and (2) the role of administration in it. Experience in research and practice has shown that if such reforms are to succeed, approaches need the active support of the principal. The principal needs to be an active advocate of self-renewal, and be prepared to articulate a suitable vision for the school. OD cannot be copied and imposed from outside. The leader needs to understand the current situation, including strengths and weaknesses, opportunities and threats (SWOT) to the organization, determine the goals to be attained within the next 1–3 years, and develop the strategies to pursue in order to achieve them. S/he needs to understand all the crucial elements involved, and to be committed to the goals and the process. The key elements that a leader needs to address are:

- Take a Theory Y approach to staff and tasks.
- Adopt different macro change strategies, involving humanistic approaches, synthesizing and integrating the elements of all relevant strategies.
- Understand that change results from helping individual staff members and teams to identify and solve organizational problems. The leader needs to create the organizational structures, procedures and processes to facilitate staff involvement in problem solving, with open communication.
- Understand the interdependent nature of the task, technology,

structure, and people, by avoiding partial, limited or piece-meal solutions.

12.6 Prerequisites for Change

The leader needs to: (1) acquire appropriate knowledge and understanding to develop the necessary skills and attitudes towards change; (2) think through his/her role as a guide to action; and (3) clarify for himself/herself the strategic elements that are essential for an effective implementation plan. Then, s/he should examine the types of knowledge, kinds of skills and the attitudes need to be developed for successful implementation of organizational change. According to Owens and Steinhorf (1976), the research outcomes at the Oregon School Study Council (1974), suggest that high school principals will have to perform roles, such as (1) instructional leader, (2) systems specialist, (3) planner, (4) coordinator, and (5) change agent. The special competencies projected are (a) skills in developing evaluative criteria, (b) interpersonal skills, (c) conflict management, (d) community involvement, and (e) the ability to bring about instructional change. The 1985 Committee of the National Conference of Professors of Educational Administration also has agreed with these findings.

In managing change effectively, the leadership must be capable of implementing appropriate strategies and tactics of organizational change. Some of these can be selected from the ones advocated by Havelock and Havelock (1973), Chin and Benne (1985) and Katz and Kahn (1966). The best approach in selecting and implementing change strategies and techniques will undoubtedly be morphogenic in nature, emphasizing the need for self-renewal. It should be combined with a planned approach to improving organizational health, featuring adaptive organizational problem solving. Another approach is the integration of work-group training, in such skills as communication and problem solving, with the normal functioning of the school. The main outcome of such training is a self-renewing system that is intrinsically motivated to monitor their own functioning, and a change environment, flexible enough to modify the school's own organizational form and functioning to meet its needs effectively.

In meeting the challenges faced by the leader, s/he needs to consider whether s/he should play the role of mentor, i.e., all-knowing teacher of teachers, or whether s/he also should become a learner. In this context s/he needs to consider how well s/he has developed his/her own knowledge and skills and how much time can be spared to organize the necessary training and staff development sessions, as well as, to encourage professional development of the staff. For this purpose, s/he also needs to determine how much specialist assistance has to be obtained.

12.7 Leader's Role in Changing the Organizational Culture and Climate

The main concern for OD is the human social system of the organization, rather than task, technology or structural dimension. In a social organization, it is the role of an effective leader to work with and through individual staff members and groups, towards achieving the goals of the organization. Involving staff in identifying organizational problems is a complex task. First, the leader needs to create an appropriate climate, where trust and confidence prevails, interpersonal relations are cordial and superordinate and subordinate relations are substituted by collegial relations. In preparing the ground for change, threat and fear need to be removed; communication should be made more effective, by increasing lateral communication, by encouraging staff to express their ideas and opinions frankly.

Wherever needed, the leader should organize the necessary training, enlisting specialist help, thereby, enabling the staff to feel competent in implementing change. The leader, if competent, should undertake the training of staff by himself/herself, or organize an outside specialist to do so. In this role, more emphasis needs to be placed on being a facilitator, rather than a leader. Even in instances where the leader is highly skilled, it can be more appropriate to work with a consultant, who can take a neutral approach towards the staff and the organization in sorting out difficult and complex problems. Owens and Steinhort (1976) point out that those who oppose change also contribute to the shaping and molding of decisions, and in the process are subject to their views being shaped and modified. To obtain this type of effective participation by all staff, the leadership needs to create a developmental, or growth-enhancing, organizational climate and culture. The resulting climate is likely to have following features:

- Intellectually, politically, and aesthetically stimulating to staff;
- Emphasis on individual and group achievement;
- Importance being placed on the personal dignity of individual staff members;
- Encourage differences of opinions in a non-judgmental way; and
- A commitment towards problem solving, as against win-lose situations, based on intra-organizational skirmishes.

In taking a problem solving approach, the leader should not believe that engaging the services of a consultant is an admission of weakness. A leader, who identifies the strengths and weaknesses of an organization and engages the services of outside specialists, is creating opportunities for him/her to exercise more powerful leadership behaviours. A good example in illustrating the importance of this concept can be taken from the medical profession. A family physician, who refers a patient to a specialist for help in diagnosing, is considered to be exercising his/her professional judgement in the best interest of the patient. No one looks down upon such a decision, as an admission of weakness or lack of knowledge. Sharing of power and authority with the staff, the provision of real opportunities for the staff to participate in decision-making, and the provision of adequate staff development, can make the difference in the process of implementation and institutionalization of change. All these are opportunities to exercise leadership behaviour.

In these times of rapid changes, personal resilience is an important trait for the educational leader/manager. According to Richer and Stopper (1999), personal resilience enables a competent individual to stay at the top of his or her craft, even as it changes. They characterize resilient people as positive, focused, flexible, organized, and proactive.

- Positive people make the best use of opportunities, in the midst of turbulent situations, feeling confident to succeed.
- Focused people have a clear vision of what they want to accomplish.
- Flexible people, employ internal and external resources in developing creative, strategies in responding to change.
- Organized people plan and structure approaches to coordinating and implementing strategies effectively.
- Proactive people take calculated risks in facing uncertainty.

Clarke (1999) also endorses the importance of human resources in educational reform, with the conclusion that human energy is the key to school reform. Focused human energy is what school change requires. It is the flow of human energy that links small initiatives to a larger purpose, bringing a flexible shape to the whole.

12.8 Taking a Socio-technical Approach to Reforms

Traditionally, schools have concentrated on staff development for the purpose of effecting reforms. This approach involves in-service training, to improve knowledge and understanding, as well as, developing the skills, leading to detailed and close supervision, to check on appropriate practices. Planned organizational change does not discard traditional approaches in skills and knowledge enhancement, but introduces another dimension of developing the organizational skills of staff. This step facilitates the productive involvement of staff, in all processes, such as training in skills required for effective functioning within teams, effective communication, interpersonal and inter-group functioning, and group problem solving. The administrative thrust of organizational development requires the development of staff skills in organizational participation, so as to enhance the functioning of the school as an organization. In the absence of such a thrust, teachers take a narrow fragmented piece-meal approach. Emphasis should be placed on problem solving, towards the realization of organizational goals.

When a leader needs to move the organization, to take a more organic self-renewing direction, with active involvement of the staff, it does not mean abandoning system's orderly procedures and controls. What happens is the replacement of hierarchical rigid structures with new structures and procedures, which are flexible and adaptable to change, thereby, enhancing staff participation and organizational development. This approach facilitates a more functional basis for task analysis, structural arrangements, selection and use of technology, and the selection and professional development of individuals and groups within the organization. A socio-technical approach becomes more apparent when we believe that technology and innovations will play key roles in schools of the future. This necessitates the leader to develop structures, which are amenable and adaptable, to coordinate the efforts towards goal achievement. These should ensure the integration of people, technology, tasks, and structures, in a dynamic problem solving fashion.

12.9 Planning for Action

Force-field analysis provides a good approach for a better understanding of organizational situations, in addressing the problems and issues confronting an organization. This approach sees organizational status quo as a state of equilibrium, where the staff forces, who are opposed, and the staff forces who support the proposed changes, are equally powerful, enabling the continuation of status quo. Here, those who support change can be named driving-forces and those who oppose termed as restraining-forces. When one of those forces are either removed or weakened, equilibrium gets disturbed and change occurs. This can be effected by the introduction of new techniques, and the acquisition of required skills by participants. But, as organizations are essentially stable entities, after the change is effected, another state of equilibrium will be achieved with the realignment of organizational forces. This approach can be a very complex one when applied to large organizations.

Kurt Lewin (1943) develops this force-field analysis into a three-step strategy, which has become more appealing to planned change. Accordingly, in introducing change, first, it is necessary to disturb the balance i.e. organization must be unfrozen. Once that is done it is possible to introduce the planned change and move the organization to a new level of equilibrium. Then, to prevent the organization slipping back to the old level, the leader needs to take concrete steps to refreeze the organization at that level, by establishing a new status quo. This is a step needed to protect the reforms by institutionalizing them. Lewin (1951) also feels that an appropriate level of flexibility could be built in by establishing an organizational structure, which is equivalent to a stable circular causal process.

The success of such a plan will depend, to a large measure, upon the clarity of analysis of the likely consequences of the planned reforms. Out of the four major sub-systems, i.e., task, technology, structure, and human — only the human sub-system has the capacity to react differently to different conditions. However, if the leader uses his power and authority to push staff to get behind the change efforts, it can lead to a strong reaction against the changes. This might be, especially in the context of a school, where the leader's coercive power is limited. Such a cause of action may not break the force-field equilibrium. Once the pressure is relaxed, it is likely that the teachers will get back to the old ways of doing things. It would be more advisable for the leader to create a climate and forums for the opposing forces to discuss issues, concerns and fears in the open, rather than secretly. Then, addressing the issues of concern, and articulating the desired goals, the leader needs to minimize resistance and convince the staff, as to how the advantages of the change process will flow on to create a more effective organization.

Garrett (1997) refers to micro-political mapping as another diagnostic tool for raising the awareness of the managers and others, to the existing barriers to change. Micro-political mapping is focused more on people and their behaviour. This process enables a leader/manager to identify the influence, concerns, and support for the proposed changes by the individual

Figure 12.1 Micro-political Mapping

High	Powerful but Unsupportive	Powerful and Enthusiastic
Power/ Influence	Uninfluential and Unsupportive	Uninfluential and Enthusiastic
Low		**High**

Concern/Support

(Source: Adapted from Garrett, 1997, p. 110)

members of the organization. This map, which makes use of a grid (Figure 12.1), provides a clear picture of the winners and losers, as well as, how the power will be redistributed as a consequence of the proposed change.

12.10 Organizational Development or Self-renewal

The focus of OD is primarily upon improving the functioning of the organization itself. Improving organizational productivity and effectiveness is seen as largely dependent upon developing opportunities for making better decisions on a range of issues. These decisions need to relate to its structure, its use of technology, staff and its goals. Gamage (1992) emphasizes that the primary aim of OD is to develop a work-oriented culture and climate, that will maximize the involvement of its staff in more effective decision-making on issues that affect and interest them, including goal setting and developing the strategies to accomplish them. Even though the technology of OD is sufficiently developed and diverse, to enable the use of a variety of interventions and training techniques, there is a well-developed orderly process. It contains several identifiable stages (i.e. problem recognition, organizational diagnosis, feedback, development of a changed strategy, interventions, and measurement and evaluation), which needs to be fully implemented, in a sequential order. Thus, this schema is useful to a leader in coordinating and controlling the organization. It needs to be emphasized that the leader should have a good understanding of what the concept of OD or self-renewal process is. Its major elements and the sequence of events should be:

- Problem recognition: Organization becomes aware of the existence of a problem that needs to be fixed. The leader either recognizes or confronts it, or ignores it.
- Organizational Diagnosis: On the basis of data collected, through a questionnaire, observations or interviews, from those affected, clarify and define the problem.
- Feedback: Staff should be briefed on diagnostic data and involved in developing strategies to solve the problem, providing opportunities for staff training on group dynamics, communication techniques, and goal setting.
- Development of a Change Strategy: An attempt should be made to fix the gap between current situation and what should have happened. A consultant or an expert can help in determining; what steps should be taken? by whom? when? and how? Implementation should be monitored to fix any arising difficulties.
- Interventions: Efforts should be made to build trust and confidence, improve communications, team building, skills in problem solving, develop cooperation between and amongst different sub-systems of the organization.
- Measurement and evaluation: Final stage should involve both implementation and evaluation. Again, data should be collected through a questionnaire, observations and interviews, to ascertain whether the problem has been fixed or still exists. Feedback should be provided to staff as a completion of the OD cycle. A new cycle needs to be initiated to institutionalize OD as a continuous process of innovation and change.

12.11 Central Role of the Leader

Leadership is a highly dynamic relationship between an individual and other members of the group, in a specific environment. What counts, is not so much the traits that the leader may or may not possess, is the kinds of things s/he does. What is important is the process in which the leader exercises his/her influence over others, towards achieving organizational goals. It is through an analysis of leader behaviour that one can hope to identify the elements of leadership that could be studied, learned and practiced. The key elements are (1) the behaviour of the leader, (2) the behaviour of the followers, and (3) the environment of the situation.

Even if outside experts are engaged in the OD process, unless the organizational leader is directly involved as a central figure in making decisions, diagnosing problems, and launching a new process, they will not be very effective. Organizationally, s/he is in a predominant position to function as the change agent. Few efforts will ever succeed in the face of his/her opposition or indifference. The leader's active support in the change process involving — clarifying issues, selecting alternative solutions, making decisions, committing resources, and coordinating the necessary activities — are essential for the success of OD.

According to Owens (2001), the validity of the central role of the leader was revealed in a comparative study of two elementary schools, in which one school consistently outperformed the other in reading achievement tests. The only clearly discernible difference between the two was the leader behaviour of the two principals. In the high achieving school, reading was identified as the major problem, the teachers knew this, and supported the clearly defined plan developed by the principal and the assistant principals to fix it. The leadership team provided leadership and support to classroom teachers, and teachers felt that it was helpful, and finally the climate of the school became supportive to the reform. The main cause for the difference between the performances of the two schools was that the low achieving school principal was guided by classical/mechanistic views, whereas, the high achieving principal applied an appropriate balance of concern for the task and for people. Thus, leadership style became the driving force in achieving better results. Leadership style, evidenced by a specific leader, is a combination between task-oriented behaviour and people-oriented behaviour. Some leaders are extremely task oriented or authoritarian, whereas, others are much more democratic. Effective leaders apply an appropriate balance between the two, depending on the particular situation and the maturity level of the followers.

12.12 Approaches to Different Intervention Strategies

Planned organization change necessitates that organization members should diagnose their situation and initiate appropriate action. OD specialists have developed a comprehensive schema, which enables the leadership to understand the relationships between three factors: (1) the mode of OD intervention, (2) the human group upon which the intervention is focused, and (3) the diagnosis of the organizational problems. The OD Cube, developed by Schmuck and Miles (1971), is a useful guide to intervention techniques and their application to special conditions (Figure 12.2). The interventions are based on the assumption that organizations have to be changed by organization members, themselves, often with the help of outside experts. OD interventions need to be based, not only on how to solve current problems, but also on how to help build skills within the organization in order to identify and solve other problems, as well as, to continue the self-renewal process. The OD Cube, developed by Schmuck and Miles, have three intervention strategies.

12.12.1 Finding an Organizational Theory Frame of Reference

This approach of OD planning requires the leadership to take time to re-examine their concept of organizational behaviour to determine whether it conforms to his/her management practice. It is important for the leadership to undertake serious discussions on organizational theory, organizational

Figure 12.2   A Scheme for Classifying OD Interventions

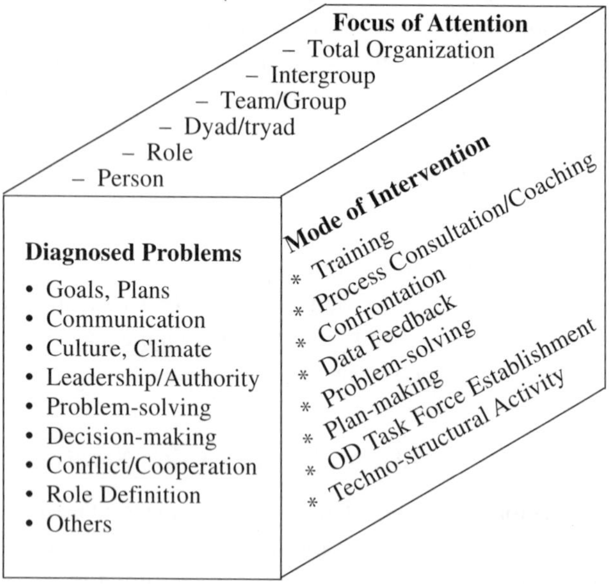

Focus of Attention
- Total Organization
- Intergroup
- Team/Group
- Dyad/tryad
- Role
- Person

Diagnosed Problems
- Goals, Plans
- Communication
- Culture, Climate
- Leadership/Authority
- Problem-solving
- Decision-making
- Conflict/Cooperation
- Role Definition
- Others

Mode of Intervention
* Training
* Process Consultation/Coaching
* Confrontation
* Data Feedback
* Problem-solving
* Plan-making
* OD Task Force Establishment
* Techno-structural Activity

(Source: Adapted from Schmuck and Miles, 1971, p. 8)

values, and philosophy of administration. An examination of differences between theory and practice, in terms of McGregor's Theory X and Theory Y, or Herzberg's motivation and hygiene factors or Blake's Managerial Grid concepts, can be useful. Such findings can lead to (a) help close the gap between professed belief and action and (b) a search for ways of actually fixing the problem.

12.12.2 Confronting the Organization's Problems

This general approach assumes that OD depends on a better diagnosis and analysis of the problems confronted. The thrust is to identify all significant problems and go with the basic solutions, and implement the preferred solutions. This enables open communication between individuals and groups to identify and diagnose problems. Existing or newly established committees and ad-hoc work groups can be utilized creatively to open up communication on problem identification and solving. In schools, whole staff meetings can establish sub-committees or working parties, with appropriate empowerment for problem identification and working out alternative solutions to be reported back to the whole staff meeting, for final decisions.

12.12.3 Exploring the Systemic Nature of the Organizational Structure

This approach suggests the examination of the organizational structure and the interrelationship of the sub-systems. This requires the creation of task forces and work groups to link the organization with the sub-systems. In this process, it is important to study and relate to the organizational sub-systems, such as school leader, school executive, teachers, students, parents and local community, as well as, inter-organizational sub-systems such as other schools, school district, state system, and national system. These activities and interactions can increase not only the variety and range of human resources utilized in problem identification and solving, but also the development of new organizational forms and structures, better suited to the realization of organizational goals (Owens, 2001).

12.13 An Integrated Approach to Change

Jackson (1997) suggests that most traditional approaches have failed in effecting organizational change, and suggests a different approach. He emphasizes that leadership of an organization is about creating an environment in which people perform their individual best, and where leadership is encouraged and practiced, right across the organization, to drive adaptation. Similar to an architect, who focuses on creating an environment suited to the purpose of a building, the leader should also be concerned about details such as the materials and methods of construction. In an organizational setting, a leader needs to focus on — (1) developing a shared vision, (2) shaping a core culture, and (3) developing appropriate processes of management. Accordingly, the values and vision of an organization should be compatible with each other. The managerial processes help shape the organizational culture, which in turn, help the pursuit of its vision. As it is difficult to act on a single front, it needs an integrated agenda for change.

12.13.1 Developing a Shared Vision

There needs to be a sense of direction that is felt across the organization. It should not be a blind allegiance, or one person's view of the future, even though, the leader may have initiated it. Some organizations may use a mission statement, strategic intent or purpose to mean the same thing. What is important is that staff should be able to understand what it means to them and their work, and be prepared to translate it into action. This commitment will come only if they have opportunities to participate in shaping the shared vision. A good vision must focus on something that is dynamic, such as needs and aspirations of the staff. It should relate to some higher values, that the organization subscribes to, and it should be imprecise, leaving room for interpretation, discussion and diversity. Most importantly, it should convey the same meaning and intent, despite the method of description employed. The secret is that people should be able to talk about the vision in general conversations.

12.13.2 Culture and Values

A vision, projects the future state of the organization, values manifested in the culture, creates the boundaries of acceptable behaviour. Most of us have experienced the power of organizational cultures. But, so much of how an organization behaves is unwritten; who are the winners; who are respected; how priorities are set; how communication works and; how rules are set and followed. These unwritten rules are more powerful than any procedure manual. Most organizations fail to recognize the pervasive nature of culture and values. Managerial processes are reflections of an organization's culture. A culture that lacks trust and openness reflects a system where control is paramount and information is available on a need-to-know basis. Culture also reflects the type of people that the organization hires. The culture includes, the basic values that the organization is committed to, the beliefs, structure and systems, symbols, rituals, competencies and heroes. Efforts to change the organizational culture should be well planned and implemented, through a gradual process. The journey for changing the culture can be undertaken by someone who practices what is being preached. Saying something and doing something else, is a recipe for failure.

Gamage (1999) discusses how the school cultures have changed over a quarter century of Australian experience in implementing school-based management, supported by the participation of the representatives of relevant categories of stakeholders. Attention is drawn to how the schools have become more open than closed, more receptive to appropriate changes that are conducive to improved teaching and learning environments. Gamage (2000c), referring to the creation of a unified national system of higher education in Australia, discusses the difficult task of institutionalization of change within universities. He refers to the processes of, sometimes, painful mergers between traditional universities and colleges of advanced education. He describes how the systems recognized the necessity of establishing accommodating structures and processes to build healthy working environments, working together to modify the organizational cultures, resulting in a smaller number of more effective, larger institutions.

12.13.3 Focus on Evaluation of Progress

The mechanisms, by which an organization translates its vision and values into reality, are the ones which determine the long-term health of an organization. These involve delivering change, competency development, reward, recognition and evaluation.

- Delivering Reforms or Change: This stage should address key issues to prepare the system — What is happening? What do we do? How do we do it? And how do we keep it going? In this process, developing the skills of leadership, facilitation, team dynamics, systemic restructuring and learning skills of organizational members, need to be given priority.
- Competency Management and Development of the organizational members needs to be adopted as a continuous process. Developing

skills, knowledge and behaviours should form the basis of a comprehensive competency framework.

- Reward and Recognition: Achievements should be celebrated and/ or appreciated, but the system needs to be just, fair and equitable. Recognition and acknowledgement of achievements motivates staff to proceed with the process.
- Measurement: Progress should be evaluated against performance and outcomes, to ascertain the current situation, adopting an integrated approach to change.

12.14 Overcoming Resistance

Hargreaves and Fink (2000) identify various problems that cause the failure of schools to sustain innovations. According to them, leadership succession, staff recruitment and retention, school size, district and policy context, and community support, are crucial in sustaining a school's innovative character. To sustain innovations, they recommend that schools approach change along the three dimensions of reform, namely: *depth*, which refers to high-performance learning for understanding; *length*, which means that how long the change can last; and *breadth*, which means that change can, likewise, have an impact on the surrounding environments of the school. Three-dimensional school reform happens when educational leaders/managers focus on deeper learning, not just on superficial performance results, use model schools to reculture, not just restructure the system; and treat the wider policy context as integral to the school and the systemic reform efforts.

Pang (1998d) suggests a two-pronged approach to organizational change in pursuit of a quality culture in schools: a Kaizen (improvement) approach and an innovative approach. Both quality and culture are subtle, intangible concepts, which take time to develop in schools. The pursuit of quality school education and self-renewal requires the change of the school practitioners' beliefs, values and norms. Schools should be given more autonomy, time and resources to develop their own. Thus when organiza-tional change at the school or classroom level, a Kaizen approach with major uses of rational-empirical strategies and normative–re-educative strategies is recommended. However, those factors, which hinder the development of a quality culture in schools, should be eliminated as quickly as possible. For example, those schools with unclear goals and missions, with improper appraisal systems, with poor quality school management committees should be mandated to change as early as possible. In such cases, an innovative approach with the use of power-coercive strategies in effecting changes is suggested.

Moffett (2000), likewise, recommends several strategies in sustaining reform at the school level. She notes that it is important to develop a reform-support infrastructure, nurture professional communities, reduce turnover, and use facilitators to build capacity. Developing a reform-support infrastructure entails restructuring policies, practices, communication mechanisms, support structures, norms, and incentives, as well as, redeploying resources. Nurturing professional communities involves changing the professional culture. Reducing turnover increases the likelihood that the changes being implemented will be sustained. Finally, using facilitators provides the school undertaking change with support, technical assistance, and clarity about the change project.

Teller (1995) cautions change managers not to assume that all organizational members will be excited about a new idea. She encourages leaders/managers to demonstrate commitment to the proposed change, by investing resources. Likewise, leaders/managers should evaluate the extent of the people's commitment to the proposed change and find out reasons for their resistance. Moreover, she claims that it is possible to overcome resistance when there is adequate information available about the change. Finally, involving people in the change planning process draws greater commitment from them.

Grasmick (2000) shows how communication can be handled to ensure the success of educational change. She notes that the following communication practices hasten the acceptance of educational change initiatives. Hence, she suggests that leaders/managers should keep providing information; take advantage of technology; adapt processes as the project evolves; make engagement meaningful; and show evidence that feedback [from the subordinates] influences policy.

Then, it is important for the educational leaders/managers to cultivate a culture, which makes teachers highly receptive to new ideas for change. Considering the variables that influence the receptivity of teachers to system-wide educational change, Moroz and Waugh (2000) recommend that educational leaders/managers should try to improve the non-monetary cost benefits that the change may offer to teachers. Make an effort to alleviate the fears and concerns of the teachers, relative to the change being initiated, provide for other forms of support in the schools, and publicize the advantages of the change in comparison to the previous system. Waugh's (2000) model of teacher receptivity to planned system-wide education change provides insights, and draws the attention of educational leaders/ managers to particular aspects, in managing educational change. According to the model, teacher receptivity is composed of four aspects: characteristics of change; managing the change at school; value for the teacher; and perceived value for students.

Sullivan (1999) encourages educational leaders/managers to master the art of creative suspension, which he defines as the art of being able to intuitively feel the simple and small changes within the education system and being able to apply gentle, creative action in the appropriate places. Likewise, in implementing change, Sullivan (1999), encourages educational leaders/managers to study the self-renewing and the self-transcending dynamics operating on a particular aspect of the organization. In educational settings, he argues that the strategy is to lessen the self-renewing dynamics, in order to create a natural space in which the desired change will grow. Bush and Gamage (2001) evaluate the models of self-governance in Australia and the United Kingdom, for revitalizing schools, with the participation of school communities in school governance. They conclude that the success of the widespread adoption of reforms in self-governance depends on the development of workable models, which enables professionals and lay governors to work together in the best interests of the students.

12.15 Conclusion

Leading an organization involves much more than managing. Leaders need to have a vision and should possess good interpersonal and group skills, and should be able to be creative and innovative in leading organizational members towards the accomplishment of organizational goals. An effective leader plays the central role in placing the organizational development, or self-renewal, on a development cycle of continuous improvement. The leadership role should be based on a clear understanding of schools as socio-technical systems, and what the role of a leader in such a system is. The leader needs to pay sufficient attention to the organizational culture and organizational behaviour, and how these elements impact on the management and organizational members. In other words, the leader needs to be aware of, how the problems need to be identified with the involvement of staff and what needs to be done to improve the organizational culture and behaviour.

The essential principle in OD is to convert the organization into a community of learners. The central purpose of OD is to improve the knowledge and skills of organizational members to diagnose and solve problems on an everyday basis. The main focus should be on developing skills for solving interpersonal and group problems. It is a process of acquiring skills in dealing with on-the-job problems. A multiplier effect is built into the organizational development concept. The experience gained from solving one problem should be utilized to tract down other problems and, when they arise in the organizational context, should follow a similar process in solving them. Because individuals are linked to other groups, the OD concept tends to spread to the whole organization and encourages them to get involved in a cycle of continuous improvement or self-renewal.

12.16 Review Questions

1. Examine the role of the leader in the process of leading and managing organizational change.
2. Undertake a critical evaluation of different approaches to organizational development or self-renewal.

CHAPTER 13

Leading and Managing Professionally Staffed Organizations

13.0 Learning Outcomes

Based on a systematic study of this chapter, the readers will:

- Gain an understanding of the key characteristics of professionals and their relevance to educational organizations;
- Understand the inevitable conflicts that could arise between professionals and bureaucratic structures and develop the skills to manage them;
- Gain a better understanding of the types of authority, and bases of power, enjoyed by an educational leader and how to make the best use of them; and
- Develop the skills necessary to play both the roles of leading professional and the chief executive officer in the most effective manner.

13.1 Focus

Leading a professionally staffed organization, particularly within bureaucratic contexts, can prove a difficult task. This chapter examines the nature of leadership within professional groups, and proposes an understanding of management and professional behaviours that, firstly, will help to avert potential conflicts and, secondly, help promote frameworks of action, which will result in more positive outcomes for all. The dual roles of professional and administrator are discussed and the notions of empowerment and teacher participation in decision-making processes are advanced as providing a source of worthy practices to follow.

13.2 Working with Professionals: A Different Leadership Challenge

In the contemporary world, leadership and professionals are terms, which have a wide variety of interpretations. Leadership and professionals in organizational settings have specific relevance to educational institutions, as all educational organizations are staffed with professionally qualified staff. For this discussion, irrespective of surrounding controversies as to whether they fall within the professional category, teachers are considered as professionals. Since the 1890s, the concept of leadership has been studied from a variety of perspectives. Most studies, particularly those of industrial psychologists, have concentrated on improving the selection process of leadership behaviour, but not much attention has been paid to the contemporary challenges to traditional concepts of leadership within professional areas. However, a fair number of these studies have been conducted, specifically in educational contexts. Hoy and Miskel (2001, p. 176), who analysed these studies, describes leadership as an elusive but a fascinating topic of continuing interest among students of administration. Everard (1984) has emphasized that leadership qualities are indispensable to an effective manager, as s/he is the person responsible for motivating staff within his/her organization. Whatever the title employed: chairperson, coordinator, representative, organizer, dean, principal; the person in charge is performing a leadership role, with attention primarily focused on situational factors and maturity levels of the followers. In this context, leadership in organizations staffed with professionals, needs to adopt different approaches.

13.3 What Are the Key Characteristics of a Profession?

Similar to leadership, the term "profession" has produced a wide variety of meanings and interpretations. Millerson (1964, p. 5) notes 23 distinct traits in defining the term. Goode (1957, pp. 194–209) has referred to a sense of identity associated with shared values; an agreed role definition; a common technical language; and recognition that a professional group has power over its members. In 1960, he pointed out that most of these characteristics are derivative, and identified two as: (1) a lengthy period of training in a body of abstract knowledge and (2) a strong service orientation, as the key characteristics. Eraut (in 1994 in Bredeson & Scribner, 2000) points out most professionals as constant learners to enrich their knowledge base through unique occurrences in professional development undertakings and special experiences. As opposed to the traits approach, Goode (1960) and Barbar (1963, p. 672) adopt a functional approach, and identify the following characteristics:

- A degree of systematic knowledge;
- Orientation to community interest;
- Control through a code of ethics, emanating from a voluntary association; and
- A system of rewards in the form of a set of symbols of work achievement.

The Task Force on Teaching as a Profession (1986) characterizes a professional as having the following attributes: "expertise; judgment; a high degree of autonomy, as a result of this expertise and judgment; and, collegiality, rather than supervisor control" (cited in Gratch, 2000, p. 47). Even though, several definitions have been advanced, in an examination of these propositions, a number of common characteristics have emerged.

- Need to base professional decisions on technical expertise acquired through a long period of education, training and practice;
- Subordination of professional's own interests to those of clients, by avoiding emotional involvement;
- Peer group orientation and professional loyalty to the profession and to the service of clients;
- A strong desire for autonomy in exercising their special competence; and
- A code of ethics that guides their activities and standards through peer review (Martin & Shell, 1988; Hoy & Miskel, 2001).

Later, Barbar (1978) and Wirt (1981) point out instances where the clients have challenged the structures and procedures adopted by professional bodies, to ensure professional autonomy. Wirt (1981) has provided a developmental model of political conflict between professionals and non-professionals. He refers to the following five phases of this conflict:

- Quiescence, which entails professional dominance;

- Issue emergence, including a growing number of individual complaints by clients;
- Turbulence, characterized by strong challenges and militant pressure groups, and in some "inside agitators" within the professional ranks;
- Government gets involved in mediation or adjudication in resolving debates and/or conflicts between the professional and non-professional groups; and
- Closure, because of compromises or legal constraints resulting in redefinition of professional services (Adapted from Wirt, 1981, cited in Hughes, Ribbins, & Thomas, 1985, p. 270).

But, in the face of practical politics between the professionals and non-professionals, Wirt's last two categories of resolution and closure raise questions as to whether they have been fully accomplished.

13.4 Conflicts in Organizations Staffed with Professionals

Professionals employed in organizations are likely to have difficulties from time to time in their relationships. This occurs not only with their clients, or the public at large, but also with those in authority within their employing organizations. They display similar patterns of conflict between the occupational group and organizational requirements. The real issue is that these conflicts result not only in strains between professionals and organizations, but also between professional organizations and non-professional institutions. On a number of occasions, the areas of conflict have been comprehensively reviewed. Etzioni (1975) has suggested that teachers, social workers and nurses be regarded as semi-professionals, on the assumptions that they are more amenable than other professionals to bureaucratization and that a higher proportion of them are women. However, this view has been challenged.

The main factors that are conducive to political conflict and modification of leadership behaviour are the professional's claim to autonomy, and the professional's external orientation. Until recently, the conventional wisdom of most researchers and writers seems to suggest that the school is best described and analysed within the classical bureaucratic framework. This is evident from the hierarchy of authority (principal, deputy principal, assistant principal, faculty head, year coordinator, classroom teacher, student etc.) and the concentration of authority in the position of principal. The rules prescribing expected and prohibited behaviour; division of labour (non-teaching executives, teachers, subject specialists etc); and prescribed criteria to enter the profession, are further proof of this conflict. But, Talcott Parsons (1960) and Alwin Gouldner (1959) stress that the classical approach has failed to recognize the effects of professionalism on the process of governance, in professionally staffed organizations.

13.5 Professionals' Claim for Autonomy

On the basis of long periods of specialized training, professionals expect a large measure of discretion in professional practice within their fields of expertise. It is argued that it is by exercising their well-trained professional judgements that they can best serve the interests of the employing organization. When professionals are employed in highly structured rigid bureaucratic institutions, it is almost impossible to prevent some conflicts arising.

A comprehensive study, undertaken by Hall (1986), relating to doctors, lawyers, nurses, social workers, accountants and teachers, revealed that most conflicts were due to the high value attached to professional autonomy. In their service to the public and the need for autonomous operation, professionals had responded negatively to all five dimensions (i.e. hierarchy of authority, division of labour, rules, procedures and impersonality) of bureaucratic orientation. Hall concluded that very often, strong professional drive for autonomy come into conflict with organizational jobs requirements. Professionals are reluctant to accept the legitimacy of the hierarchy of authority. However, professional resistance to the hierarchy of authority varies with circumstances and situations. Establishment of structures, procedures and processes for consultation, and appeals, usually, take the heat out of such resistance. On the other hand, organizational orientations and practices towards professionals also make a difference. Professionals welcome opportunities for peer review, with senior colleagues playing supervisory roles for the purpose of providing guidance to refine their practice. This view has contributed to the appointment of professionals as heads of most institutions staffed by professionals.

13.6 External Orientation of the Professionals

The second basic factor, which tends to create problems, is that the ideal stereotype of a professional establishes him or her as an incorrigible cosmopolitan. Reissman (1959) finds that there is a tendency for professionals to look away from the bureaucratic structures of the organization. Because of the accelerating increase of knowledge in all specializations, the external aspect of professionalism has steadily increased in importance. The need for familiarity with current professional literature and contact with colleagues across organizational boundaries, have become essential for maintaining standards and further development of expertise. These orientations have helped to renew and retain professional credibility, but at the expense of immediate organizational tasks (Hughes et al., 1985). If the organizations are to retain the credibility of a professional's expertise, a cosmopolitan outward looking stance is an essential element in the role orientations of professionals within organizations. However, similar to that of autonomy, the professionals' tendency for external orientation is likely to give rise to tensions and problems in organizations, which employ professionals.

13.7 The Professional as Leader/Manager

In almost all professionally staffed organizations, a tradition has developed where the institutional head has to be a person with a strong professional background in the relevant area of expertise. Such appointments are regarded as coopting devices, designed to defuse tensions between practicing professionals and their leaders/managers. Moore (1970) has pointed out that the leader/manager, who has a good background in understanding the problems intrinsic to the professional role and its organizational setting, is likely to elicit somewhat greater confidence than would be accorded to a mere lay-person. He also has observed that there is a representative, as well as, an internal coordinating function to be performed by a leader/ manager. Here again, professionals prefer one amongst them to represent them rather than an outsider. In this context, the professional-as-administrator (administrative head of a professional organization) can be considered in structural-functional terms, as the ultimate accommodating technique, which legitimizes the hierarchy. This mode of operation ensures that bureaucratic formalization does not restrict professional autonomy and provides external representation, through the head, who expresses a professional standpoint. Of course, this depends on the leadership style adopted by the head, as it needs to elicit the cooperation of the professional group.

Usually, it is a difficult transition when a professional is promoted from a doer to a leader, planner and organizer. Very often, this transition is a difficult one for a professional. A professional, who has a large personal investment in specialized training, is likely to see the application of those acquired skills as the most vital part of his/her life. On promotion, when placed in a hierarchical position, most professionals feel that their greatest contribution can still be made through the application of their specialized training. Because of this assumption, most of their time is spent to perform professional functions away from the leadership and/or managerial role within the organization. Generally, when a leader/manager does this, the organization suffers. Organizational effectiveness is usually increased as more time is spent on the leadership and managerial functions of planning, organizing, and facilitating the work of others. Newly installed leaders need to shift their focus away from the operational and technical activities, towards the development and application of leadership and managerial skills.

In an educational organization, the leader's behaviour has a significant impact on what goes on within that organization. Because of their acknowledged wisdom, as educational experts in their particular field, they are able to exert influence both internally and externally which is beneficial to the continuous development of the institution. Those with leadership responsibilities in a primary or secondary school or in a university, aspire to achieve professional authority, as well as, functional authority as organizational leaders/managers. Nowadays, the professional-administrator is an ever-present phenomenon in educational systems, in each sector and each level. But, the strain involved in the occupancy of such positions is not always fully recognized. External accommodation is often achieved at the expense of internal conflict.

13.8 Operation of the Dual Roles of Leading Professional and CEO

Generally, those who have the managerial responsibility in educational organizations such as schools would claim to be educational professionals. So far the practice has been to appoint a well-experienced classroom teacher, either on seniority or on merit, to the position of principal. Here again, very often, classroom teachers are first promoted as a head-teacher or an assistant principal and deputy principal, before being appointed to the position of a principal. When professionals are appointed to leadership/managerial positions, they give rise to ambiguities, as well as, opportunities. A professional turned administrator has to accommodate strains and tensions both in relation to him/her as an individual and those of the organization.

Usually, most teachers and academics have both managerial and academic responsibilities. This is clear from the position of the head of an educational organization, who automatically becomes the chief executive officer (CEO) and leading professional (LP) (Dubin, 1991). In the British context, the position becomes clearer as the head of the school is designated, head-teacher, making that key link obvious, while it is the same in Australian and Hong Kong high school faculties, where the principal teacher is designated head-teacher. Thus, the dual role of heads of professionally staffed organizations as CEO and LP is a very appropriate description. An essential element in this model, is the close interdependency of the two roles.

The simultaneous activation of the two sub-roles i.e. LP and the CEO are a special phenomenon in professionally staffed organizations. As a tentative first approximation, one can then visualize the two sub-roles as distinct entities. This involves differentiating between activities which are prima facie professional and those which are prima facie managerial, while explicitly recognizing that there are internal and external aspects to both role conceptions.

According to research, conducted by Hughes (1976), involving 72 heads of schools and a stratified sample of teachers and governors, significant interrelationships between internal and external aspects of each of the two sub-roles have been revealed (see Figure 13.1). Within the LP sub-role, heads who were strong in their external orientation, tended to, and were expected by the staff to take an innovative stance in their internal professional role. They encouraged their colleagues to try out new ideas and media. Within the CEO sub-role, heads who granted recognition and autonomy by external authority, were the ones who took the initiatives themselves in executive matters in delegating authority to other members of staff. Thus, within both sub-roles, internal and external aspects were interrelated.

Research has identified areas in which LP and CEO sub-roles were supportive, those in which they appeared not to relate, and those in which there was potential conflict. There were two aspects of the CEO role for a head and the claim to be the leading professional appeared particularly relevant. These were (1) allocation of resources; and (2) presenting and interpreting the data relating to a school's academic achievements, to the governing body and the system. The research had confirmed a substantial inter-penetration of the two sub-roles. It seems that a professional-administrator does not act in some matters as the LP and in others as the

Figure 13.1 The Dual Role Model

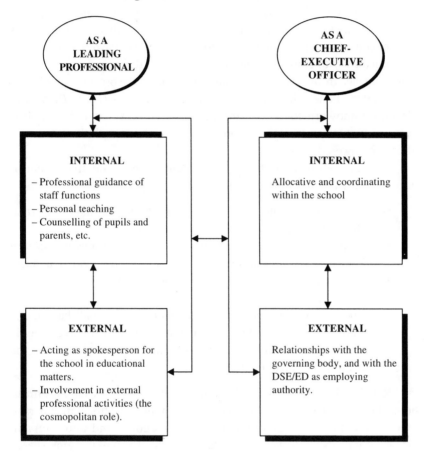

(Source: Adapted from Hughes et al., 1985, p. 279)

CEO. Instead, professional knowledge, skills and attitudes are likely to have a profound effect on the whole range of tasks undertaken by the head of a professionally staffed organization.

13.9 Concepts of Power and Empowerment

From a traditional point of view, control comes from power. Power is a positive force, without which little would be accomplished. Dunham (1984, p. 116) defines power as "the need to control other persons, to influence their behaviors and to be responsible for others". People satisfy their need for power by either personalized or socialized means. Personalized power seekers attempt to dominate others, whereas, the socialized power seekers are concerned with achieving group goals. It is this socialized power which is connected with empowerment. Hanson (1985) defines autonomy as the independence from the control of other sub-units in the organization. Power is the ability of one unit to impose its will on another. *The Oxford Dictionary* defines empowerment as "giving authority or power to others". How effectively this power is used to produce results determines the efficacy of those empowered.

Bennis (1990) refers to empowerment as the collective effect of leadership, which has four strands:

- Empowered people, who believe that they can make a critical difference, are significant and have meaning.
- Learning and competency do matter. Leaders who value mastery and mistakes enable staff to gain experience and provide feedback.
- Empowered people feel a sense of community, e.g. a sports team and the family.
- Working in an empowered environment is exciting and challenging. Empowerment by leadership is magnetic, in that it moves people towards the mission and energizes them to act individually, in the pursuit of organizational goals.

Rapport (1987 in Klecker & Loadman, 1998) claims that empowerment joins the personal competencies and abilities of organizational members to environments that offer opportunities for choice and autonomy in demonstrating these competencies. Maeroff (1988) believes that empowered teachers have a sense of authority over what they do and are perceived as experts.

> Empowerment can mean running the show, but many teachers say they do not want responsibility for all the decisions in their schools. What they desire is that their voices be heard and heeded. They yearn for dignity. They want their needs and opinions reflected in the policies of the schools and the district (p. 475).

Short and Rinehart (1992 in Klecker & Loadman, 1998) develop a scale that measures teacher empowerment on six dimensions, namely: decision-making, professional growth, status, self-efficacy, autonomy, and impact. Empowerment in decision-making enables teacher to take part in making decisions on matters that affect their work. Empowerment in professional growth provides teachers with adequate opportunities to learn continuously. Empowerment in status imbues teachers with the feeling of being respected. Empowerment in self-efficacy makes teachers feel confident that they can help students learn. Empowerment vests teachers with the freedom to make pedagogical decisions. Finally, empowerment enables the teachers to have a positive influence on school life. Among these dimensions, Klecker and Loadman (1998) discover that teachers feel more empowered in their status, professional growth and self-efficacy.

Empowerment and autonomy assume that teachers will have the opportunity to participate, actively, in the process of decision-making, implementation and evaluation. As a result of teacher participation, the structure gets modified, the perception of professional role changes, ensuring that teachers take more responsibility along with accountability. Schools with transformational leadership enables the authorities to tap the untapped human resources to be successful. In most organizations, success retards because of the isolation of talented human resources. Empowerment presumes that the staff member does not have power to act and, therefore, s/he needs to be given authority to act. Efficacy means the power to produce the intended results. The concepts of power and empowerment centre on the link between power, control and action.

13.10 How Does Empowerment Benefit the Organization?

Power and control affect organizational structure. Structuring schools around professionals, rather than bureaucratic models, alters roles, role relationships, the focus and locus of decisions, and expectations for professional accountability. An empowering organization assumes that:

- Teachers will contribute to the professional operation of the school consistently through their individual expertise.
- Ethical standards for practice are stipulated and followed.
- Accountability for student outcomes and instruction will depend on individual teachers and not on the bureaucracy.
- Teachers will have more time to reflect on educational practice.
- Teachers will have an effective role in setting professional standards, employment procedures and evaluation processes.
- Once empowered, teachers will have the authority and autonomy, with concomitant responsibility, for competent performance.

- Teacher autonomy, a cherished commodity, is affiliated with professional accountability, as in other professions (Adapted from Goens & Clover, 1991, p. 233).

Louis and Marks (1998) believe that professional teachers, working in collaboration with their colleagues to improve their practice, will become more effective in making their students learn. Collaborating with colleagues is a manifestation of a strong professional community, which Lee and Smith (1996) note as having a great impact in developing a sense of collective responsibility for the students' learning. This sense of responsibility relates positively to higher levels of student achievements. A strong professional community is likely to emerge in a school with a high level of empowerment. This concept of professional community is similar to what Lieberman and Grolnick (1997 in Webber and Robertson, 1998) call professional networks. According to Webber and Robertson, professional networks provide professionals with venues for applying their personal practical knowledge in solving their common problems.

Empowering teachers also has implications for leadership. In organizations with empowered professionals, the leadership roles change. It focuses on values, missions, and purposes, rallying staff to reach significant goals and objectives. The implications for transforming leaders in empowering organizations are:

- Authority for leadership comes from the ability to develop a shared vision, ability to fuse individual needs with organizational goals and to motivate people to improve their practice and performance.
- Vision and mission motivates and attracts staff, as opposed to being pushed by the leader.
- Ethical leadership, leads by example, while ethical standards and core-values are adhered to.
- Participatory style of leadership empowers staff, leading to ownership, commitment and effectiveness.
- Transformational leadership, with empowerment, creates leadership density.

Usually, teacher organizations wield a great deal of power and influence on educational agenda and structures, through negotiations and political pressure. With teacher empowerment, the teacher organization's ability to influence teacher behaviour gets affected. In an empowered school, teachers are free to make decisions on policy and practice, outside union politics. Teacher unions should encourage teachers to act as professionals.

Knowledge, skills, competence and performance supercede seniority. As teacher roles differ, depending on whether they are operating at a kindergarten, primary, secondary, or physical education environment, they should exercise professional autonomy.

However, effecting changes needed in professional expectations, accountability and leadership, as well as, changing the roles and approaches of teacher organizations, are tough issues needing careful attention.

13.11 Advantages of Teacher Participation in Policy Formulation

Participation is beneficial to the self-esteem of individuals and helps to improve productivity of organizations. However, as noted by Gracth (2000), most school improvement measures fail because the teaching professionals, who are held responsible for the success of school reform, are not allowed to take part in the conceptualization and planning. It should, likewise, be noted that most innovative organizations implement changes through participation. Kanter (1984) points out that participation creates the excitement of being involved and having an impact, but it needs to be managed. It has been observed that highly specialized and centralized organizations can make decisions faster and have a shorter "learning curve". On the other hand, participatory organizations, while slower to get started and get used to the new way of doing things, eventually respond faster. This view has been confirmed by a large number of stakeholders in Victorian and Australian Capital Territory schools, where school councils are taking effective decisions that are based on sub-committee recommendations. It has been revealed that participation can enhance motivation, commitment to change, cooperation, and the quality of decisions. When we consider that participation means "joint decision-making", it improves the quality of information, as it needs to be shared to make effective decisions. In the field of education, participation by professionals is positively correlated to job satisfaction and morale, and building trust and confidence in leadership (Gamage, 1996b; 1996e).

On the other hand, leaders/managers need to be aware of the dilemmas of participatory decision-making. Issues can arise relating to: how to plan the involvement, participation in what issues, the structure for participation, developing teamwork and, what the procedure for evaluation should be. First, if participation relies on volunteers, it does not become representative. If it is mandatory, the staff can perceive it as coercive. From an organizational point of view, the team needs to possess the right knowledge and skills for effective participation. A second dilemma is the need to determine the issues on which participation is sought. Issues that affect the interest of the staff are the ones that are likely to create effective participation. Staff is unlikely to be interested in complex organizational issues that have little relevance to them, most staff is happy to leave them to the leadership. Third, "Too much talk and too little action" will discourage staff. What is needed is to create a structure which enables people to operate creatively, autonomously and responsibly, within well-demarcated boundaries. Fourth, it is important to avoid participation falling into bureaucratic traps. If committees become rigid and operate with the higher status executives dominating, staff may feel threatened making the participation ineffective. Finally, participation should not be viewed as a means of magically solving all problems. Usually, participation can lead to increased satisfaction, because of empowerment and the possibility available to harness all potential resources and talents, leading to better overall results.

In the final analysis, clearly defined management structures, tasks, with clear boundaries and time frames, including procedures for rendering accountability and reporting, need to be introduced. The creation of appropriate structures, procedures and processes to minimize conflicting situations, enabling maximum results, along with effective means to improving the knowledge and skills of the staff to perform the tasks, are needed. A rewards structure improves the morale (Kanter, 1984).

13.12 Reconciling to Bureaucratic-Professional Conflicts

Pang (1998e, 2000) in his studies of excellent schools in Hong Kong succeeded in identifying two distinctive organizational cultures in the excellent schools: a "professional" culture (a P-culture) and a "bureaucratic-professional" culture (a BP-culture). These schools were excellent because parents preferred them to the other schools and teachers themselves had a high degree of acceptance of the organizational values. These schools had an exceptionally strong organizational culture in the sense that the perceived organizational values of the schools were extensively shared.

In a school which was regarded as excellent in Hong Kong, a professional culture was identified, where teachers were treated as professionals having self-control and norm-driven. Teachers enjoyed a great deal of freedom and discretion in their teaching and administrative functions. There was a high degree of flexibility and tolerance to enable the teachers to execute daily duties at their own discretion to enhance their creativity in achieving goals. In that sense, the school's adherence to hierarchical structures, rules and regulations were kept to a minimum. This school had an exceptionally strong organizational culture where autonomy and professionalism were the main organizational values extensively shared.

On the other hand, in the two other schools which were regarded as excellent schools in Hong Kong, a bureaucratic-professional culture was identified. That is, organizational bureaucracy and teaching professionals were found to be compatible in the two schools. These two schools were strong in both bureaucratic linkage and cultural linkage (Firestone & Wilson, 1985; Pang, 1996) and they were both tightly coupled and loosely coupled (Sergiovanni, 1984; Peters & Waterman, 1981). While in these schools there were strategies in the hierarchical and organizational structures built to facilitate and enhance the achievement of school goals (bureaucratic linkage), there were strategies that facilitated the development of a school culture which bind people to the core values (cultural linkage). There were effective ways by which the school administrators bind people to the goals, visions and philosophy; create coherence of efforts; and reinforce appropriate behaviour of their members towards the accomplishment and success (tight coupling). Similarly, there were aspects of flexibility and tolerance to allow teachers to execute daily duties at their own discretion (loose coupling). Teachers in these schools had a high degree of sharing of these organizational values with the schools in the use of these administrative strategies. They agreed with the schools that there should be strong emphases on bureaucratic linkage, cultural linkage, tight coupling and loose coupling in the daily administrative and managerial practices (Pang, 1998a).

The above findings are antitheses to the evidence in the literature. Some researchers (Scott, 1981; Corwin & Borman, 1988; Hoy & Miskel, 2001) have claimed that there exists in schools a basic conflict between professional values and bureaucratic expectations. Scott (1981) argues that it is a conflict between the teaching profession and the school organization arising from the incompatibility between professional expertise and autonomy, and bureaucratic discipline and control. Corwin and Borman (1988) refer to it as the dilemma of control and autonomy in the school management. Teachers usually resent interference and directives from the administration and call for shared governance in schools (Hoy & Miskel, 2001). Pang's studies (1998e, 2000) show that in Hong Kong's excellent schools, there exists a professional culture in which teachers have minimal tie but maximum discretion and a bureaucratic-professional culture in which both professionals and bureaucrats work together harmoniously. That is, the interaction between the school administrators (bureaucrats) and the teachers (professionals) in these schools were not constrained. The school administrators in the three identified excellent schools in Hong Kong succeeded in accommodating the bureaucratic-professional conflicts by strengthening the schools' organizational cultures. It suggests that the characteristics of bureaucratic organization are compatible with a professional work group when strong organizational cultures exist in schools.

13.13 Conclusion

Most professionals desire to participate, in a meaningful way, in the organizations in which they are employed. It should be in the interests of the leadership to encourage participation, as the intent is to increase morale and job satisfaction, enabling ownership and greater commitment to the organizational policies, thus, fostering adaptation to change. More opportunities for teacher involvement, in planning and policy formulation, will facilitate and commit the teachers to their effective implementation and evaluation. Such involvement increases consensus on goals and priorities and breaks the narrow perception that many teachers may have when they are isolated in their classrooms. Seeing the broader picture and understanding their role in the overall organizational perspective, will influence classroom decisions towards the creation of more effective learning organizations.

The professional form of occupational life and the bureaucratic form of administration are the two organizational patterns that are prevalent in modern educational organizations. Unless the leadership is aware of the professional desire for autonomy, external orientation and involvement, conflicts with the bureaucratic administration could be more marked, resulting in less effective organizations. In this context, it is highly desirable for organizations to provide facilities and encourage the staff to undertake professional development, in the areas of leadership and management. To maintain a strong and stable cadre of professional teachers and administrators, the organizations and systems should develop career opportunities and assist them as they move into their new positions of leadership. This can be done by providing systemic incentives for teachers and principals to undertake professional studies, as is being done in England and Wales, with the introduction of local management of schools (Bush & Gamage, 2001).

To reconcile the bureaucratic-professional conflicts in schools, strengthening the organizational cultures is an effective way. It requires school leaders to shape, direct and manage organizational cultures of the schools and to steer the sharing of organizational values between teachers and administrators. If professional commitment in a bureaucratic workplace such as a school is to be enhanced, it should be done through (1) strengthening the organizational culture, (2) allowing teacher discretion and autonomy, and (3) empowering teachers. All these call for a cultural leadership in managing the contemporary professionally staffed organizations.

13.14 Review Questions

1. Examine the key characteristics of a professional and whether an educator/teacher needs to be considered as a professional in the context of a school organization.
2. Examine the difference between leading a professionally staffed organization and a normal business or industrial organization.

CHAPTER 14

Leading and Managing Human Resources

14.0 Learning Outcomes

Based on a systematic study of this chapter, the readers will:

- Have a better understanding of the concepts of personnel management and/or human resources management and its significance;
- Improve the knowledge and understanding, and develop the skills to tap the full potential of the staff as the most valuable resource of the organization;
- Develop the skills in the selection, training and development of staff to match the roles they need to play, and energize and motivate them to accomplish the creation of an effective institution.

14.1 Focus

This chapter draws the attention of educational administrators to the significance of staff, as the most valuable resource entrusted to them, which has ability to transform and shape the other resources. It focuses on the distinction between personnel management and human resources management, and how leaders and managers look upon staff as a resource to be empowered and tapped. Discussions also include the policies relating to personnel, recruitment and selection, induction, as well as, training and development, to get the best out of them. With the implementation of school-based management, in most school systems, the necessity for school leaders to acquire the competencies in recruiting, developing and energizing human resources is given special attention. Discussions on industrial relations and performance appraisal are also included.

14.2 Significance of Human Resources

The general aim of educational administration is to ensure that the institutions and systems function properly, in accordance with the preconceived purposes and plans of action. Administrators are required to convert a variety of resources, such as financial, physical and human, into an effective enterprise, capable of achieving the institutional and/or system's mission. Administrators are the activating element in the transformation process. From the major plans that the administrators develop for the operation of an educational institution (such as organizational structure, educational programmes, logistics, human resources, and external relations), none is as critical to the success of the undertaking as that affecting the people responsible for their implementation. In short, human resources can be considered as the lifeblood of the organization. They help to conceive the type of service that the institution renders, to develop and implement plans and strategies needed to achieve the goals, and make adjustments between plans and reality.

In an education system, it is the human resources, which consume the most investment and most other resources. In many ways, we have to treat people as any other resource, selecting the best for the purpose we wish to accomplish, managing and developing, as one would build a piece of equipment to ensure that it meets the organizational needs. However, there is one significant difference, people have brains, whether we like it or not, they decide jointly with their managers and colleagues, how their time, energy, knowledge and skills will be used. French (1998) points out that it is the human resources' efforts, talents and skills, in using other resources that result in the creation of useful products and services. In fact, the true human resource is the effort, which is jointly managed by the individual and the management of the institution, in which s/he works. Hoeflich (1999) states that these efforts are optimized when employees are satisfied and highly motivated. Employee satisfaction is hastened in an organization where communication is open, fairness is the rule, best performers are appreciated by the leaders/managers, and appropriate tools and training are available.

Usually, capital is thought of in terms of tangible assets such as, cash, raw material, real estate, machinery and equipment, as well as, intellectual property such as ideas, inventions and creations. But, economists refer to the knowledge and skills that people have, and their attitudes and social skills, as assets to any human enterprise and label them as human capital. Applied to societies, this concept helps to explain why some societies, which are rich in natural resources (e.g., Brazil, Nigeria, Congo, etc.), such as, minerals, water and land, are less productive, whereas, others with hardly any natural resources (e.g. Japan, Singapore) are much more productive. Societies where people have high levels of education, well developed work skills and social traditions that place high value on hard work and productivity tend to become wealthier nations, because of the very significant contributions made by human capital. On the other hand it is obvious, that other resources such as lands, buildings and funds take shape only as the people commit them to different uses.

Organizations that take care of their human capital reap better productivity levels. As Dobbs, Gordon, Kiser, and Stamps (2000) argue, recruiting skilled workers, having clear incentive plans and offering flexible arrangements are management strategies that yield better productivity.

14.3 Personnel Management or Human Resources Management

In recent years, there has been an increasing tendency to use the term, "human resources management", in place of "personnel management". In an attempt to distinguish between the two terms, Guest (1987) points out that human resources management (HRM) is concerned with long-term perspective, the psychological contract based on commitment, self-control, a utilitarian perspective, an organic structure, integration with management, and maximum utilization. The above propositions contrast with the short-term perspective, compliance, external controls, pluralist perspective, bureaucratic structure, specialist roles and cost-minimization, expected with the concept of personnel management. Torrington and Hall (1991) argue the differences between personnel management and HRM, as largely matters of opinion, rather than fact, where the similarities are greater than the differences.

According to a critical analysis undertaken by Legge (1992, pp. 27–28), the following three general differences have been detected:

- Personnel Management (PM), is often seen as a management activity, aimed at non-managers, whereas, HRM emphasizes not only the importance of employee development, but also the development of a managerial team.

- In PM the role of line management is an expression of "all managers manage people", while specialist personnel work, still continues under management. In terms of HRM, direction of all resources, including personnel policies, is an integral part of management strategy.
- PM is not fully integrated with organizational development (OD), as it is generally separated from formal organization. HRM emphasizes the management of organizational culture, as the central activity of senior management and more closely associated with organizational values and strategy.

However, Legge (1992) has emphasized that these differences are largely in meaning rather than in substance. Considerable thought, planning time and efforts of all administrative personnel are needed to maintain system stability and viability, with proper management and development of human resources.

The general intent of the human resources function is to recruit, train and develop, and maintain a highly motivated and effective workforce. Most modern institutions accept the fact that the human resources function is an essential activity. The concerns of personnel administrators are twofold:

- How to cope with the human resources problems emerging in organizations? and
- How to incorporate them into the personnel function and how to utilize the most promising ideas from the rising stream of conceptual developments, to resolve personnel problems more effectively?

The main function of a school, in particular, and educational institutions, in general, is "instruction", which is a line function. Supporting functions such as logistics, planning, personnel management, and industrial relations are staff functions. There is considerable agreement, in both theory and practice, as to the underlying assumptions involved in organizing the personnel division.

14.4 Structuring the Human Resources Function

Whether an organization calls its relevant department or section, personnel administration, staff branch or human resources branch, all refer to the activities devoted to identifying the institution's needs for people and the management of those in its employ. Plans for decisions, relating to personnel, flow from the purpose and objectives of an organization. Positions evolve from purposes, resulting in the organizational structure. Personnel decisions, including the quality and quantity of human resources needed, recruitment, selection, induction, performance appraisal, industrial-relations, compensation, training and development, employment security, retirement or termination of employment, all have significant impact on the budget, as well as, on the attainment of institutional goals. In this context, the human resources function of resources planning, recruitment, selection, compensation, induction, appraisal, training and development, security, performance appraisal, industrial relations and information, become responsibilities of specialist divisions, or officers responsible to top management.

Personnel, is both a responsibility and a function of the entire organization, and a special department or a division, within the central administration. In an educational institution, staff function is usually concerned with activities auxiliary to or supportive to the main function of instruction. However, research has revealed that, often, most educational leaders spend more time on the personnel function, even though, it is not the number one priority.

Another approach in analysing, the personnel function is to separate it into decision-making and decision implementing activities. Personnel decision-making, such as those involving basic courses of action, affecting structuring of the function, or broad personnel plans, affecting the system's budget, can be the responsibility of the region or the district office in consultation with heads of schools. Recruitment can be a centralized function at head-office, or district level, while the selection can be a function at school level. Even under school-based management, most school leaders are reluctant to take over recruitment, because of the heavy volume of work involved, but are happy to be involved in the selection of staff.

Resolution of complex problems on industrial relations is of such crucial importance that most modern organizations usually include an administrator primarily responsible for the personnel area. Larger organizations also employ a lawyer or a legal division to deal with industrial issues.

In keeping with the demands of the times, human resources management professionals are expected to perform new roles. Johnson (1996) suggests that human resource officers should become partners in the operations of the organization, leading and facilitating organizational change. They should establish networks of strategic partners, in pursuing global best practices, facilitate and lead in the adoption of new technology, and develop employee potential to create competitive advantages.

14.5 Human Resources Policies and Activities

Whatever the nature of an organization, a manager achieves results through the performances of other people. Policies on recognition of the needs and wants of staff and approaches to their grievances, depend on how the administrators perceive the nature of human beings. The efficiency of staff, their commitment to organizational mission and goals, the skills and attitudes they bring to bear on the quality of service offered, is fostered by good human relationships. Success in this field depends on human resources policies and practices in effecting personnel function.

The formulation of personnel policies, practices and procedures is usually based on underlying philosophies of managerial behaviour, industrial climate and the relationship with the relevant trade unions. Such philosophies embrace:

- The recognition of peoples' needs and expectations at work;
- Respect for the individual;
- Justice and fair-play in treatment and equitable reward systems;
- Job security;
- Good working environments and conditions of service;
- Opportunities for personal development and career progression;
- Democratic functioning of the organization; and
- Full observance of state/provincial and federal statutes, relating to employment.

Overall, personnel policies are designed to embrace:

- Designing an effective organizational structure;
- Staffing the structure with suitable people;
- Defining work roles and relationships; and
- Securing optimum working arrangements.

The purpose of personnel policies is to improve the morale of the staff to evoke willing cooperation, towards the attainment of optimum operational performance. The personnel activities may be considered within the framework of the following broad headings:

- Manpower planning and employment.

- Salary and wage administration, including related reward systems.
- Organizational design.
- Education, training and development.
- Employee relations.
- Staff services, welfare, health and safety.

14.6 Job Design

French (1998) has conceptualized that job design involves the specification of the tasks to be performed by individuals and groups within the organization, and the rules, schedules and working conditions under which people perform their tasks. Johnson (1996) believes that grouping tasks around processes, rather than functions, is the emerging trend in job design. According to Bateman and Zeithaml (1990), an enriched job has five core dimensions, namely:

- Skill variety — different job activities that involve several skills and talents;
- Task identity — completion of a whole, identifiable piece of work;
- Task significance — the job having an important and positive impact on the lives of others;
- Autonomy — independence and discretion in making decisions; and
- Feedback information — on job performance, productivity charts, etc.

When jobs are designed, it is important that the duties and functions of the position holder discharges is interesting and challenging. It should also create intrinsic motivation, which leads to productive performance. If the job involves only routine type of work, it can lead to boredom, not motivation. In a study undertaken by Nankervis, Compton, and McCarthy (1999), the following strategies are suggested to energize the position holder, by making the job more interesting and challenging:

- Job enlargement or horizontal loading, which increases the number and variety of tasks to a job, thereby, offering additional variety to the jobholder.
- Job rotation, which enables employees to do entirely different jobs on a rotating schedule.
- Job enrichment, which involves any effort that makes the work more rewarding or satisfying by adding more meaningful tasks to an employee's job.

14.7 Staff Recruitment

The process of finding qualified people, encouraging them to apply and selecting the most suitable applicants and persuading them to work with the organization is called recruitment (French, 1998). Matching the right people for the right jobs is an important responsibility of a recruitment manager. Recruitment can be either internal or external. Internal recruitment can be advantageous because the candidates can be evaluated on the basis of their work history and the opportunity for internal mobility, motivating employees to stay in the organization. However, in a competitive environment, if the internal applicants are inferior to those in similar organizations and to those who could be recruited externally, it can be detrimental to the organization (Bateman & Zeithaml, 1990). In such a situation, it is better to resort to external recruitment as it brings people with new ideas into the organization. It also provides the organization with wider choices of candidates, enabling the selection of an applicant with the best possible credentials. Standard elements considered in the process of recruitment of staff are:

- The job description;
- Advertisement and attracting suitable candidates;
- Consideration of the personal profile;
- Referee reports; and
- Short listing or culling the applicants to select the most suitable to be called for interviews;
- Establishment of an interview panel, preferably, including the head of the division, where the vacancy exists as a member of the panel.

It is very desirable for the person under whose direction the new recruit is expected to work, be a key person in the process of selection of the candidate. However, in most traditional school systems, heads of schools are not provided with such opportunities. But, in systems, which have embraced school-based management, heads of schools enjoy the privilege of being involved in the process of selection of his/her executives, teachers and non-teaching staff.

14.7.1 The Job Description

The occurrence of a vacancy is an opportunity to rethink roles, as the changing needs of the times and organization may demand change. Once a job description is developed, it should be open to revision after appointing a candidate to the position. This is necessary because of the possibility of having a candidate with unforeseen talents that the institution wishes to exploit. Usually, a job description includes: (1) job title, (2) brief description of the purpose of the job, (3) reporting relationships, (4) description of duties, (5) competence required, and (6) criteria for effectiveness or how performance is evaluated. In the case of the latter, a candidate can be asked "how do you propose to improve the performance of the job", and so forth, to check whether the person has taken a real interest in considering the job situation seriously and whether the applicant has any plans to make it work for the organization and for himself or herself. If an applicant has not made an effort to find out more about the organization in which s/he proposes to work and the challenges involved, it is unlikely that such a person will take the job seriously and perform well. However, in practice, there are many applicants who attend interviews for job vacancies without making that effort to learn more about the job and the organization.

14.7.2 Personal Profile

It is important to define the characteristics of the person whom you are seeking to recruit, and make provision for candidates to provide answers in the application form, including the essential and desirable characteristics. It is pertinent to raise the following issues:

- Educational qualifications, date of birth, nationality, permanent address and language skills;
- Employment record, achievements, awards etc.;
- Competencies, abilities, aptitudes, skills;
- Motivation for the type of job advertised, social and intellectual drive;
- Personality, leadership, interpersonal skills and emotional stability, and so forth.

14.7.3 Attracting Suitable Candidates

Attracting a suitable person for the job is a question of supply and demand. But, the advertisement calling for applications can be designed in such a way as to either, increase or decrease the numbers. The essential and desirable characteristics required in the personal profile can be varied to suit the job design. The number of candidates can also be increased or decreased, by the number of media, in which the advertisement is published. Varying the number of years of experience required, as well as, projecting a good image of the work environment and the type of facilities and fringe benefits that the recruits will enjoy can also vary target group.

14.7.4 Referees

Calling for the names, addresses and contact numbers of 2–3 referees is a standard practice. Again, the type of referees can be clarified, whether academic or employment related, or both. The usual practice is to call for referee reports for those applicants who are short-listed, to be called for an interview. As most referees are reluctant to include the deficiencies of candidates in writing, nowadays, many employers resort to the practice of carefully analysing the application and looking for gaps, before talking to the referees over the phone to seek clarifications. This approach provides more accurate and frank opinions.

14.7.5 Interview and Selection Panel

Short-listed applicants are summoned before a properly constituted panel for an interview. Before the formal interview, the applicants are usually welcomed by a specially assigned person, perhaps the head of the department or division, and shown around the work environment. This is done to interact, to check-on and familiarize with the person. Now, most academic institutions invite the short-listed applicant to conduct a seminar for the faculty members, providing them an opportunity to judge, for themselves, the abilities and competencies of the prospective colleagues. This procedure provides opportunities for the faculty members to interact with the prospective colleagues, before and after their presentations.

It is important to structure the procedure of the interview, providing required paperwork to all members of the panel. How and who is to welcome the candidate and put him/her at ease, who will lead the panel and what will be the areas covered by each panel member, including time allocations, have to be agreed upon before the candidate is summoned. The type of questions to be asked should also be agreed, before the interview commences. It is better to start with "open questions", enabling the candidate to express himself or herself, to demonstrate knowledge and experience, and perhaps what is not found in the application. Carefully crafted questions can be asked for probing further into gaps if any, as well as, to seek clarifications and additional information. The following can be raised: "Tell me about your experience at ... What was your role in ...? What were your achievements ...? How would you tackle a problem like ...?"

If a candidate is nervous, it is better to make him or her comfortable by acknowledging previous achievements, smiling and making reassuring noises. It is better to listen carefully, ask tactful questions, avoid repetitions and revisit areas that a candidate tries to avoid. Get the candidate's views on the job and how s/he would project himself or herself in that position, while observing behaviour. Provide an opportunity for the candidate to ask questions about the job, whether s/he is still interested and whether s/he has any reservations. Avoid prejudices and record your overall impressions of the candidate, before you invite the next candidate (Everard & Morris, 1996).

Once all candidates are interviewed, the panel members should compare their notes and impressions, and finalize the selection by consensus (Law & Wong, 1997). In the selection process, the equity and affirmative action legislative provisions, of both the Federal and State/Provincial Governments, need to be observed. The recommendation of the panel needs to be presented to the relevant officer, to organize the necessary approval and the issue of the letter of appointment. The letter of appointment should contain all relevant terms and conditions, including salary, period of notice required to leave or terminate employment, leave entitlements and grievance procedures. When the candidate reports for duty on the due date, organizing a proper induction programme is a very important step in the right direction. It makes the person feel welcomed and comfortable with the job.

The induction is the process aimed at acquainting new employees with the organization (Rebore, 1998). Nankervis et al. (1999) suggest that inducting new employees promotes lower turnover, increased productivity, improved employee morale, lower recruitment and training costs. It also facilitates learning, provides an opportunity to get an overview of the group with whom he or she has to work, develop working relations, and reduce new employee's anxiety. The more time and effort spent in helping new employees feel welcome, the more likely it is that they will become loyal and better adjusted to the working environment. One of the most important aspects of induction is to brief and familiarize the new employee with the organizational culture and work practices.

14.8 Training and Development

Staff being the most expensive and crucial resource to sustain the economic viability and the effectiveness of an organization, an employer needs to work towards the optimization of employee contributions. On this basis, most employers agree on the importance of the training and development of staff for the success of an organization. According to Drucker (1977), the leading expert in modern management, one contribution that a manager is uniquely expected to make is to give others a vision and ability to perform. A primary function of a manager is to develop, motivate, encourage and train the staff working with him or her. With the rapid advancement of technology and the changing societal demands, it is essential for all organizations to take all possible steps to update their staff, by providing training and development, as well as, encouraging professional development on an individual basis. Training is necessary to ensure an adequate supply of staff who is technically and socially competent and capable for career advancement into specialist and managerial positions. Training needs to be viewed as an integral part of the process of total quality management. Nankervis et al. (1999), claim, that training is any procedure initiated by an organization to promote learning amongst its members.

Training helps to improve the knowledge, understanding and skills, as well as, to improve interpersonal relations, group dynamics and changes in attitudes. These can bring many benefits, both to the individuals themselves and the organization. Some of these could be:

- Increased confidence, motivation and commitment of staff;
- Enhanced recognition, responsibility and the possibility of increased pay;
- Provide a feeling of personal satisfaction and achievement, with broader opportunities for career progression or advancement; and
- Help to improve the quality and availability of staff.

According to Armstrong (1991), training increases the level of individual and organizational competence, while helping to reconcile the gap between what should happen, relating to desired targets and standards of performance and actual work performance. In securing the full benefits of successful training, a planned systematic approach to the effective management can be based on the following criteria:

- A clear commitment to training, in all levels of the organization;
- An objective assessment of training needs;
- A clear set of objectives and a defined policy for training;
- Provide opportunities for staff involvement, making them partners in the training process;

- A carefully planned training programme;
- A choice in selecting the most appropriate method for the selection of staff members; and
- An effective system of review and evaluation of plans for training.

To ensure that training contributes optimally to the goal of improving employee performance, Fox, Byrne, and Rouault (1999) suggest that career development activities should be relevant and cost-effective. They likewise, discourage organizations from offering generic training that does not cater to specific individual employee needs. Moreover, Antonacopoulou (2000) notes that training is likely to be effective when the individuals regard such training as a learning opportunity.

It is better to establish a staff development committee, with appropriate representation, for the purpose of identifying and providing training and staff development needs of the organizational members.

It is also important to note that training does not mean only attending training programmes, workshops, seminars and in-service, but, there are many job embedded opportunities that can provide real world experiences, enabling the employees to develop skills and competencies. Chairing staff meetings can be rotated amongst staff, depending on potential, staff members can be invited to head working parties and sub-committees. During temporary absences of the heads of faculties could be used to rotate the acting head-ship. Similarly, in cases of temporary absences of the deputy head, can be rotated amongst the members of the school executive body. For example, instead of appointing the same head-teacher to act as the deputy principal, the opportunity could be offered to all head-teachers, to provide them organizational wide experience.

14.9 Industrial Relations

Kalleberg and Moody (1994) refer to industrial relations as the relationships between managers and workers and union-management relations. These relations are crucial to industrial harmony and higher levels of performance and job satisfaction. Australia, Hong Kong, and most other developed countries, have enacted legislation for the purpose of governing workplace relations and resolution of disputes. Award systems and industrial tribunals have been established for the purpose of settling complex issues and disputes. The usual practice in Australia is for the relevant trade unions and the employer organizations to resort to collective bargaining and sign collective industrial agreements between the parties, covering wages and other employee benefits, as well as the benefits of increased productivity for the employer. Until recently, these agreements are negotiated at the national and state levels, but in many instances, the current practice is to negotiate such agreements at the institutional level.

Australian Council of Trade Unions (ACTU) has taken an increasing interest in industrial matters relating to education. This interest has arisen with the affiliation of several education unions, such as Teacher Unions including NSW Teachers' Federation (NSWTF) and National Tertiary Education Union (NTEU) to the ACTU. This interest is likely to increase further with the election of NSWTF's president to the position of President of the ACTU, commencing from 2000. A paper on "Labour Market Reforms and Industrial Relations Agenda", released with the 1998/99 national budget, outlined the government's intention to restructure awards in order to provide incentives for skill formation and more flexible forms of work organization. But, with the election of the Liberal National Coalition Government at the Federal level, the philosophy on industrial relations has taken a different turn, straining the relations between the trade unions of the employees and the employer organizations, as well as the government. Accordingly, the current trends seem to discourage the trade unions representing workers' rights, while encouraging direct negotiations by workers with the employer, resulting in individual contracts. In 2000, this approach has strained the industrial relations, even in the big Australian — Broken Hill Private Ltd. (BHP), which was considered the best model employer on the Australian scene.

In Hong Kong, the biggest trade union in education, among others, is the Hong Kong Professional Teacher's Union (HKPTU). The HKPTU was established in 1973, just after a full-scale strike to force the government to withdraw its proposal of cutting 15% of the salaries of the Certificate Masters/Mistresses due to the economic recession. At present, the HKPTU unites more than 90% of Hong Kong's teachers and consists of 60,000 teaching staff from universities, secondary schools, primary schools, kindergartens and other educational institutes. Its main objectives are: (1) to maintain and extend teachers' rights, as well as, the provision of many welfare services; (2) to promote Hong Kong's education, teachers' professional spirit and teaching techniques; and (3) to participate in all kinds of social campaigns to promote human rights, social justice and democracy in Hong Kong and the mainland. For example, in 2000, the union launched a large-scale strike, to force the Secretary/Manpower and

Education Bureau to suspend the benchmarking language policy for a half year for further consultations and consideration.

The increasing tendency for the devolution of authority to school level and the community participation in school governance has necessitated the school leaders to be familiar with industrial relations. In systems such as New Zealand, England and Wales, the school leaders have already taken such responsibilities. In an environment, where all eight Australian and Hong Kong school systems have embraced the concept of school-based management, with different approaches, it is high time for the educational leaders and managers to acquire a comprehensive knowledge and understanding of issues relating to personnel. Increasing incursions of the laws relating to industrial relations, as well as, the care and safety issues that come within the purview of educational administrators and classroom practitioners necessitate a better understanding of the implications. As the increased responsibility comes with accountability, both to the authorities and the community, the educational leaders may not be able to plead ignorance of the legal obligations.

14.10 Performance Appraisal

Performance appraisal is an approach to reviewing performances and potential of staff. It is important for the members of the organization to know what is expected of them and how their performances are measured. A formalized and regular systematic system of appraisal enables the assessment of individual performance as well as his or her potential and the needs for training and development. It helps improve future performance, review the financial rewards, and career progression. A comprehensive appraisal system can guide the managerial decisions on allocation of duties and responsibilities, salary, levels of supervision required, delegation, promotion, as well as, the training and development needs.

Nowadays, in England and Wales, New Zealand, some of the Australian school systems, as well as, Hong Kong, the appraisal of staff performance has become a common practice. With the devolution of authority to the school level, appraisal is being adopted to ensure accountability. Mullins (1999) has identified the following benefits of performance appraisal to the individuals and the institutions:

- It can identify an individual's strengths and weaknesses and how such strengths may best be utilized, and weaknesses overcome.

- It may help to reveal problems, that may be restricting progress and causing inefficient work practices.
- It can develop a greater degree of consistency, through regular feedback on performance and discussions about potential, encouraging better performance from staff.
- It can provide information for manpower planning, to assist succession planning, to determine suitability for promotion and for particular types of employment training.
- It can improve communications, by giving staff the opportunity to talk about their ideas and expectations, and how well they are progressing.
- It can also lead to a better quality of working life and improved organizational health, arising out of the mutual understanding between the management and the staff.

There are several essential features, which contribute to constructive and mutually beneficial appraisal systems:

- Objectivity — The basis for a constructive system is a prior agreement on the criteria for effectiveness. A job description with criteria and clear objectives can be the foundation, to focus on the results to be achieved against the criteria and objectives.
- Willingness to listen — Rather than telling the staff what is right and wrong, the manager can seek the staff member's views first. Most appraisal models require the employee to fill in the forms, with his or her own answers before the discussion.
- Openness to criticism — Both parties, the manager and the worker, should be prepared to listen to criticism and use it for improvement, as silencing criticism is a demonstration of insecurity.
- Counselling not judgement — Advice that can be tendered to improve the productivity.
- Action planning — Development of new objectives and plans to be carried forward, progressed and reviewed systematically, at the next round of appraisal.

Recruitment, training and appraisal are three activities, which should not be seen in isolation from each other, but, as a part of a comprehensive approach to developing a competent, motivated and effective staff, leading to the accomplishment of institutional goals.

14.11 Conclusion

There is an increasing tendency to devolve authority to the institutional level, similar to that of the systems, for example, England and Wales, New Zealand, Australia (especially in Victoria and the Australian Capital Territory), most states in USA and Hong Kong. This has necessitated the school leaders to gain a better knowledge and understanding and acquire the competencies in leading and managing staff. Unlike in the past, now they are also facing the challenges of recruitment and selection, as well as, induction, training and development. These responsibilities require some understanding of the laws governing industrial relations and care and safety issues. The above discussions focused on the distinction between the concepts of personnel management and human resources management, and the significance of staff, as the most valuable resource, in transforming the other resources to take the required shape. The importance of matching the employee to the job has been emphasized in the recruitment and selection process. Similarly, the importance of the formulation of personnel policies, regarding how to approach issues on training and development more effectively, and the need to undertake staff appraisal to energize and navigate the troops to accomplish the institutional goals, have been emphasized.

14.12 Review Questions

1. Discuss the procedure and processes that are involved in the creation of a position of a deputy head (deputy principal, deputy manager, etc.) and selection of a person to match the role.
2. What are the three major areas of human resources management? Discuss each of these areas with a view to getting the best out of them towards the accomplishment of institutional goals.

CHAPTER 15

Leading and Managing Meetings

15.0 Learning Outcomes

Based on a systematic study of this chapter, the readers will:

- Gain a better knowledge and understanding of the usefulness and the purposes for which meetings need to be called;
- Gain the ability to plan effective meetings and organize appropriate preliminary work; and
- Develop the skills and competencies to plan, lead and manage the meetings as effective instruments of communication and decision-making.

15.1 Focus

This topic focuses on the importance, usefulness and the inescapable nature of meetings. The purpose for which meetings need to be held and how to plan and organize effective meetings are also discussed in detail. Attention is drawn to considerations in organizing and limiting the agenda, background papers, participants, structure, time management and providing fair opportunities for staff input. Attention is also given to organizing, chairing, minute taking, follow-up action and the evaluation of the effectiveness of meetings. Finally, checklists on organizing, notices to be issued, as well as, checking the effectiveness of leading, managing and evaluating meetings are presented.

15.2 Why Have the Meetings?

In any social organization, and more specifically, in a school, all channels of communication are useful, but meetings are singularly important. Hunt, Tourish, and Hargie (2000) reveal that 63 percent of interpersonal communication in educational settings occur at meetings. A meeting provides a setting and a forum in which organizational members can communicate and coordinate information about problems and decisions. According to Hardin (2000), meetings produce many of the organizational decisions affecting how jobs are done and what opportunities will be available for the members in the future. More importantly, at the same time, it satisfies the emotional need for activity, achievement, affiliation and power. It provides participation, not found in memoranda, newsletters, telephone calls, intercom announcements and the like. Meetings enable the participants to notice others' reactions to statements that are made by the speakers, as well as, one's own utterances. If managed effectively, high levels of satisfaction and productivity can be gained through the means of meetings, as the principal channel for staff motivation and common understanding.

Schmuck and Runkel (1994) suggest that meetings provide opportunities for participation not found in memos, newsletters, loudspeakers and announcements. Meetings enable participants to immediately check the reactions to a speaker's contribution, and if managed properly, a meeting can encourage the staff to cooperate with each other on common goals and be highly productive.

Most teachers spend one or more of their afternoons a week, after school at meetings. If the meetings are useful, they become extremely valuable as an effective means of direct communication, a method of in-service training and shared decision-making as well as for planning. If meetings are not felt to be productive or interesting, then the participants are likely to see them as an unnecessary encroachment on their time that can otherwise be more profitably spent. Whether meetings are valued as useful, or resented as useless, is largely in the control of the leader/manager, who usually chairs most of the organizational level meetings.

Many different meetings take place in educational institutions, ranging from the fairly informal working parties, where the brief is straightforward, to departmental or faculty meetings, pastoral team meetings, executive meetings, to the formal full staff meetings. Meetings are of critical importance in coordinating efforts and effecting change. A very important part of the administrator's role is to ensure that meetings are employed as vehicles for communication and decision-making, rather than making them forums for confusion and frustration. For the purpose of achieving this goal, the meeting organizers should ask the question, what is the meeting aimed at achieving? With an awareness of the behavioural process at work, the meetings should be structured in such a way as to channel the energies of those involved in a positive manner. Maidment and Bullock (1985) point out efficiency does not necessarily yield effective outcomes. What is needed is to ensure both efficiency and effectiveness, that is, observe the time lines, provide everyone who wants to participate a just and fair opportunity, leading to effective decisions with a high degree of consensus.

15.3 Types and Purposes of Meetings

Meetings also can have many different functions, and these can determine the style of chairing required in a particular meeting. Usually, meetings are required to define, approve or promote organizational policies, decide on various lines of action, explore the feelings of members and transfer information. Any organization that values consultation will have long, detailed and controversial meetings, at all levels within the organization. Meetings can make people feel more involved and responsible for their institution. Further, the meetings can help to develop people, make them better informed and knowledgeable, and train them for higher positions, as well as benefiting from different approaches and staff expertise.

Most of us tend to think of a meeting as a formal gathering at a prearranged venue on a given date and time. But, many meetings, especially in school settings take place on a casual basis, considering the progress of many issues, consisting of four, three or even two people involved. Some times, these casual meetings become more significant and productive, depending on who attends them. Meetings can take different shapes and sizes. Some of these meetings can be highly formalized, where members speak to each other through the chair while observing a rigid agenda such as the Parliament or a Legislative Council meeting. There are also meetings where there is no formal agenda or a person to preside over the meeting. However, it is likely that they may have legitimate purposes, but very often such meetings may wander aimlessly without being productive. There are instances, where some people who do not have any interest in the topics discussed, are required to attend some meetings, which amount to wastage of their valuable time.

In a school, there are many different types of formal meetings, such as:

school council meetings, whole staff meetings, executive meetings, faculty meetings, year coordinators meetings, student councillors meetings, student council meetings, teachers union meetings, parents and citizens association meetings, parent teacher night meetings, etc.

Some of the reasons for holding a meeting may be as follows:

- To take decisions. For example, a whole staff meeting to consider the recommendations made by a working party or a Parents' and Citizens Association (P&CA) conducted to address an important issue, affecting the school.
- To consult staff, collect information and suggestions in order to enable an informal decision to be taken by the leadership. For example, submission of a memorandum on a special project.
- To brief the staff on a new policy document.
- To exchange information.
- To generate ideas by the use of "brainstorm", "spider-gram", or other creative methods, for self-renewal or moving the organization forward.
- To inquire into the nature and causes of a problem, such as the behaviour of a particular person or a group.
- To express feelings. For example to bid farewell to a departing staff member or commemorate the death of an important personality or a staff member.
- To find solutions to a complex issue or prepare a new programme (Adapted from Everard & Morris, 1996, p. 53).

Smith and Piele (1997, p. 351) state that most meetings are held for one or more of the following reasons:

- To exchange information;
- To make a decision together;
- To define, analyse and solve a problem;
- To reconcile conflicts; and
- To express feelings.

In most schools, a common complaint is that they have too many meetings. Some school heads believe in having "information giving" meetings, which are neither efficient nor effective. The most important purposes of any meeting should be those of stimulating, engaging, exchanging information and opinions, and obtaining commitments for action. Whenever, the objectives of a meeting are set, consider the context, and how the proposed agenda relates to the organizational goals, and whether the resulting decisions make the organization more effective.

15.4 How to Plan for Meetings?

Conducting a meeting without a proper plan is similar to building a house without a building plan. Of course, it can be done, but it can lead to a lot of frustration and time wastage, resulting in disappointments. One hour spent on planning a meeting is likely to reduce one hour of meeting time (involving 10–15 people). Ask yourself "what is the purpose of the meeting?" State the purpose clearly in the notice calling for the meeting. For example, "to decide how the teachers share lunch hour and playground supervision". Then, a decision on who will be involved, in the preparation of a duty roaster? The administrator should ask, "what is likely to happen from the beginning to the end of the meeting", including barriers that could impede progress? The purpose of the meeting is likely to give an idea as to who should attend the meeting and what might transpire.

Maude (1975) suggests that the necessary background information should be distributed to participants before the meeting, providing time for careful consideration of agenda items, but not too long before a meeting. Attempts should be made to avoid pooling of ignorance, by supplying accurate and adequate information to make high quality decisions. Then the stakes that the participants have in the matters under discussion, and the impact of their personalities and positions on the decision-making process, should be given due consideration. Methods of reaching compromises should be determined prior to the meeting in anticipation of arising conflicts. Blanchard (1987) suggests that it is better to follow the four steps proposed by Ray Ross. These are: (1) Define and limit the problem; (2) Determine the nature and cause of the problem; (3) Establish and rank the criteria for a solution; and (4) Evaluate and select a solution from the available alternatives. Other important factors in planning a meeting include, who should attend, date and time, agenda, venue and time allocations for each item in the agenda.

15.5 Agenda and Allocation of Time

The agenda is the blueprint of a meeting. Its purpose is to make sure that all relevant topics are covered and the meeting moves from one point to the other, accomplishing the set goals, unless otherwise determined by the meeting. It is better to prepare the agenda well in advance of the meeting in consultation with the participants. This can be achieved by circulating a simple note from the leadership inviting staff input. In the case of special and new issues, it is better to ask the relevant parties to submit a one-page document, setting out the issues involved and possible solutions, to be circulated with the agenda. It is also important to circulate the agenda and relevant papers at least three days before the meeting enabling the participants to come prepared. Jebb (1999) points out that circulating key documents to all relevant people, in advance, makes the discussions informed and intelligent, rather than vague and unfocused. However, when meetings are called, with little notice, to consider urgent issues, circulation of an agenda may not be possible. Unavailability of background information leads to a pooling of ignorance through discussions and wasting valuable meeting time, whereas, a brief and concise background paper enables the participants to ask relevant questions and make contributions in order to find a better solution.

The agenda should indicate definite starting and ending times, enabling the participants to plan for other commitments, as it is common courtesy to indicate when the meeting will be over. The order of the agenda items is an important aspect of a meeting design. Listing urgent items first, while items for information and formal approval are listed separately, thus, enabling the meeting to dispose of them quickly. If the agenda is a long one, it is better to give an opportunity for the participants to determine the order of priority as well as items they need to address. This procedure will enable the participants to devote more time and energy on important complex issues to arrive at the best possible solutions. The process can be made easier by: (1) the definition and limitations of the problem; (2) determination of the nature of the problem, and possible cause[s]; and (3) alternative-solutions, with some evaluation of the proposed solutions.

Meetings should not be conducted over a longer period of time. A meeting after two hours can become boring and unproductive. The ideal time for a meeting seems to be from an hour to an hour and a half, if it takes longer, it is better to provide tea and/or coffee and fresh air breaks. Participant involvement in agenda setting gives the impression that you value their views, information and problem solving talents. Even though, timeliness needs to be observed, a bit of flexibility, when needed, is a good thing.

To make more economical use of meeting time, Charney (1995) suggests that leaders/managers should ask themselves, why do they want to hold the meeting, and if it is not essential, more efficient ways of attaining the same purpose should be found. Likewise, leaders/managers should be clear about the goals of the meeting, otherwise, the meeting will drift aimlessly. Moreover, it is important to find out whether the people concerned are available on the planned meeting schedule, if not, it is better to reschedule the meeting. Finally, the participants should be informed about the objectives and agenda in advance, to enable them to prepare for their participation.

Jay (1976) points out that the early part of the meeting tends to be more lively and creative than towards the end, and suggests that the agenda items needing mental energy, creative ideas and clear-heads, should be listed high on the agenda. Similarly, items of great interest and concern, to the majority of participants, should be scheduled towards the end of the meeting, thus, enabling other useful business to be dealt with, promptly and quickly.

15.6 How to Lead a Meeting Efficiently and Effectively?

Leading and guiding a meeting to achieve the set goals is an important responsibility of a leader. Tapsell (1999) points out that organizing and focusing meetings well and conducting them within the framework of stated goals contribute to the making of productive meetings. Equally important is to provide opportunities for all those who wish to make a contribution to the issues before the meeting. Domination, by the leader or a few individuals, needs to be avoided if the meeting is to be useful and interesting to those present at the meeting. Whenever feasible, arriving at decisions by consensus or majority vote is also important. More importantly, the individuals or groups who are responsible for the implementation of each decision need to be clearly specified. It is the responsibility of the leader to monitor the implementation process in order to see whether it actually occurs. If these preliminary steps are observed, the staff will not only be interested in attending meetings, but also, will do their best to make use of the opportunity to make a contribution to the effectiveness of the organization. However, the research findings, as well as, discussions with staff of most institutions, reveal that what happens in practice is quite different. Some comments that we hear are: "Our meetings are so boring, most of the staff members don't take any interest." "It is the same group of people who do the talking and make the decisions, and no one else gets involved." "Very often, the principal says she wants us to be involved, but it seems that she has always worked out things in her own way." "Why should we bother, when most of our decisions are never implemented".

On the other hand, well-run meetings can ease the burden of responsibility and loneliness of the leadership. Working together enables the leader to tap the full potential of the staff in sorting out complex issues confronting the organization. Naturally, groups produce more ideas, providing a wider range of alternatives to choose from, stimulate more creative thought, and develop more realistic forecasts of the consequences of decisions. It helps to produce bolder and effective plans, than the average individual working alone. Shared decisions at meetings can satisfy the need for ownership; recognition and affiliation, which engender a sense of collaboration, based on common understandings.

Properly conducted meetings can rejuvenate an organization, leading to a keener interest in teamwork, improved communication and morale, at many levels. What prevents getting this magical synergy up and running is the lack of organizational skills in human relations on the part of the leaders. Yet, most of these are not difficult to acquire. Leaders need to develop an agenda, with staff input, and stick to it at meetings and prevent domination of proceedings by particular individuals. They should ensure that everyone gets a fair chance to express his/her views, accurate records are kept and responsibilities assigned, with target dates to achieve the desired ends. It is important to understand that efficiency and effectiveness mean two different things. Ensuring efficiency at meetings does not mean that the other will follow automatically. Leaders need to work hard to ensure both efficiency and effectiveness. Well-run effective meetings can satisfy the personal and emotional needs of individual members, especially those of participation, belonging, achievement and power. Participants interact, develop roles, and share their experiences, problems and successes. Finally, well-conducted meetings play an important role in building the cohesiveness of an organization.

The leader needs to pay careful attention to planning and preparation and effectively manage the human energy during the meeting. In the past, it was believed that the leader should function as the master and controller of the meeting, similar to the captain of a ship. Now, a leader's role has changed to that of a facilitator, whose primary function is to foster a democratic and cooperative group process among the participants. The leader should strive to mitigate the effects of the major communication problems, in the case of traditional meetings. According to Vecchio, Hearn, and Southey (1996), the sequential nature of turn taking by the leadership group, leaves many participants uninvolved, and the more powerful participants tend to dominate and press others to conform to their views.

Kay (1995) proposes the use of electronic brainstorming as one way of promoting efficient and productive meetings. This strategy employs computer-mediated electronic communication, in place of verbal communications. Combined in this organizational communication approach are the features of traditional brainstorming and the nominal group technique, since it enables meeting participants to share ideas with one another and enables the organization to generate ideas by choice. Ideas are generated anonymously. Anonymity provides a freer exchange of ideas, as participants do not worry about how the others will judge their proposals. Huber (1988 in Kay, 1995) reports that apart from significantly improving the quality of communication in organizational settings, this brainstorming approach generates more ideas than the verbal mode.

15.7 Managing Meetings

Morley (1994) states that the word, "facilitate", means to enable the process of participation, by the individual members of the group, in process of discussion easier. As a meeting leader, the chairperson's role is to facilitate participation in the meeting, enabling the achievement of desired outcomes. However, many of us have observed how some chairpersons abuse the authority vested in them by having his or her agendas while dominating the meetings. Half of the facilitator's job is planning and preparation, whereas, the other half is directed towards successfully managing human energy in order to achieve the set goals. In a meeting situation, three sets of activities take place. The first set, is the "task" or content activities of the group, i.e. what the group is doing. The second set, is called "maintenance" or process activities, i.e. how the group is doing it. The third set, is the "team building" activities, i.e. how the group is improving its cohesiveness and increasing its effectiveness.

Task activities relate to set goals of the meeting. These include, goal setting, prioritizing, using background and history, evaluating the consequences, linking with other issues, setting small group assignments and agreeing on time limits.

Maintenance activities relate to unstated goals of participants, such as, to feel acceptance and affiliation, to achieve and to have power. Some typical process activities involve providing opportunities for all to voice their opinions, reconciling disagreements and sensing group mood in moving towards the set goals. Mood can include body language, relevance of input, emotional expressions, such as: anger, irritation, resentment, apathy, boredom, warmth, appreciation and satisfaction. If emotions start surfacing, the meeting leader needs to restore calm in the group and then guide the group into task related activities.

Team building activities are designed to strengthen a group's capacity to act in the future. It involves motivating, training and celebrating, to enhance the cohesiveness of the group, as well as, to increase individual abilities and effectiveness. When team commitment becomes stronger, expertise and dedication of participants become a powerful force for success, enabling the leader to facilitate the process towards the set goals (Smith & Piele, 1997).

Charney (1995) offers techniques in dealing with participants who tend to affect the success of meetings. In dealing with *quiet and withdrawn people*, she encourages meeting leaders to maintain eye contact and direct questions at them periodically. The questions should be within the competency of the person. Make quiet people feel useful. Make an effort to collect ideas and canvass their views, on a one-on-one basis, outside of the meeting and express their ideas to the group during the meeting. In dealing with *aggressive behaviour*, she suggests that meeting leaders should remain calm. Attempt to find out the cause of the aggressive behaviour. Avoid debating with people presenting ridiculous ideas, but, let the others present decide on the merits of such proposals. Adopt ways to discourage people from using the meeting as a forum for advancing political agendas irrelevant to the meeting's purpose.

15.8 Who Should Attend a Meeting?

Once the desired goals of a meeting are determined, it becomes clear who should participate. Then, it is necessary to identify who are the most affected by the issues to be discussed, who needs to receive information, and whose presence is desirable at the decision-making process. It has been observed that meeting participants should be chosen from the organizational level most appropriate to deal with an issue. When long-term policy is being discussed, the upper level, experienced executives should be involved, as they have an overall view, experience and an understanding of the financial implications. Similarly, middle-level and operational level decisions should be made at the appropriate level. It has been pointed out that one secret of making decisions more efficient, is to push decision-making to the lowest level, where the staff is competent to handle the problem. For creative problem solving, it is important to involve a range of people from different levels and backgrounds, including outsiders, to facilitate the process.

Once the people who are likely to make a contribution or gain something out of it are identified, it is important to invite only those people whose presence is necessary. If too many are present, including those who are least interested, then a meeting becomes ineffective; hence, larger meetings are less productive. Whitehead (1984) suggests that four to seven participants are generally ideal, 10 are tolerable and 12 are the outside limit. If a meeting is likely to involve a large number of participants, it is desirable to create committees or sub-groups to deal with particular topics. If an important issue affects a large number of staff, it is always advisable to establish a working party, or refer to the relevant sub-committee, if any, to consider the issues involved and come up with appropriate recommendations for the whole staff meeting to take a decision. The ideal size for a working party needs to be large enough to provide the required expertise to solve the problem, but, small enough for effective communication and control.

15.9 Provision of Accurate and Adequate Information

In any organizational setting, the provision of accurate and adequate information is of primary importance for effective decision-making. It also indicates the extent to which the leadership is committed to the participatory process of decision-making. However, for participatory decision-making to be effective, leadership and the other participants need to build a high degree of mutual trust and confidence. In the Victorian system in Australia, which has been implementing school-based management since 1976, a high degree of success has been achieved in employing school council meetings as effective instruments of provision of information and of decision-making. In a survey of 965 school council members, belonging to 66 schools, conducted by Gamage, Sipple & Partridge; with a response rate of 53%, 465 respondents (91.2%) were fully satisfied with the accuracy and adequacy of information provided. When further clarifications were sought, a high school teacher stated:

> Information is supplied to members in the written form before any discussion is started. Each council meeting is supplied with full details, whether it is with newspaper cuttings, documents from other schools, views of individuals, views of parents, students and teachers. I think the school council has an

excellent opportunity to read through these, well before hand and talk to other people, with the students, teachers, and parents, before the actual decision is made (Cited in Gamage, 1996b, p. 84).

A primary school principal, referring to what was being done in his school, has stated that they have a weekly newsletter, with input from the principal, school council, teachers and sporting groups. An agenda, accompanied with important correspondence, financial reports and sub-committee reports, is circulated to the school council members, well before the meeting. Whenever, a concern is raised relating to insufficient information, such an issue is referred to the relevant sub-committee for further research and consultations with relevant stakeholders to come up with sufficient information and alternative recommendations to the following meeting (Gamage, 1996b).

In a professional organization such as a school, the natural tendency is for the principal and teachers to dominate the decision-making process, especially when the other members are parents, students and local community representatives. However, both in the empirical survey and at interviews in Victorian schools, the decision-making process was considered effective, as everyone was given a fair chance, and the contributions were valued. In the empirical survey, 93% of those who responded ranked this process as either good, very good or excellent. A primary school council president, commenting on the atmosphere that prevailed at meetings, and the smooth functioning of decision-making stated:

> There are people who have very good ideas, very carefully thought out, but have difficulty in expressing them. So it really comes back to the skill of the chairpersons for those policy meetings, being able to have all those opinions heard and having the meeker people express their opinions and having them discussed properly. Over the last five years or so, we have developed an excellent group atmosphere and most people are very good participants. They understand that there are different opinions and those need to be heard and considered (Cited in Gamage, 1996b, p. 88).

A principal of another school pointed out that having a variety of people on the council was a big advantage. The presence of parents, local community and students, ensures that bias and narrow-mindedness do not influence the policy decisions. Parents provide the feedback that the schools so badly needed, and sometimes they are brutally honest about their opinions on what is happening. This particular principal encouraged such honesty as it provided a clear understanding of their viewpoint on the functioning of the school (Gamage, 1996b).

15.10 The Role of the Participants

The success of a meeting depends not only on the leader, but also on the participants. The first responsibility of the participants is to come prepared. It is important to read the agenda, reflect on the topics to be discussed so as to make sure that you understand them. Review the background information provided with the agenda, formulate your own opinions, and try to visualize what other points of view might be. If you are expected to make a presentation, it is better to prepare yourself fully. It is better to prepare an outline, organize any visual aids and rehearse your presentation, before the meeting. If you are proposing to present controversial issues, it is better to discuss them with key people, before the meeting.

Rotating the position of chairperson is a good idea, to generate interest and preparedness of the participants. Once the meeting starts, use good manners by paying attention, without shuffling papers around or engaging in conversations. Be objective and realistic on your own contributions and give due consideration to others' contributions and, whenever feasible, build on other peoples' ideas. Raise questions to seek clarifications, speak up whenever you have views or ideas to share, but remember not to dominate the proceedings, as you are only one of many participants. If you want to be an effective participant, it is better to avoid interrupting another person's point of view, try to stick to the agenda and time stipulations. It is important to evaluate and criticize ideas, not the people, while being open-minded enough to work out compromises when conflicts arise.

15.11 Minutes of Meetings and Follow-up Action

An important principle of making meetings effective is to prepare accurate records of the proceedings. Prompt recording of minutes including decisions, required actions and person[s] responsible for implementation, would avoid delays and confusions. If there is no official who functions as secretary, at the commencement of the meeting or beforehand, one of the participants, who is unlikely to be involved in controversies, should be nominated as the minutes-taker. If it is difficult to find a suitable participant, it is advisable to hire a minutes-taker. Once a decision is arrived at, it should be recorded and immediately read over for confirmation by the group. After the meeting, with the least possible delay, the draft minutes should be prepared and, with the approval of the chairperson of the meeting, it should be finalized as a formal document to be circulated to participants.

It is a key responsibility of the leader/manager to take follow-up action on the minutes, by referring the relevant sections to those responsible for implementation. Monitor the progress and report the progress made at the very next meeting. Implementation of the decisions made, is a very important part of having successful meetings. If decisions are not implemented as desired at the meeting, participants will be frustrated and lose interest in the process, going to the extent of avoiding attendance at meetings, considering it a waste of valuable time.

From the end of 1980 to mid 1982, when the first author (Gamage) was functioning as the Secretary and Registrar of the Open University of Sri Lanka, the university council meetings were held on the third Friday of the month. The meetings started at 3:00 p.m. and went on until 7:00 to 7:30 p.m., with breaks for tea and coffee. Even though, Saturday was a normal university holiday, he used to go to office and dictate the minutes to his secretary, from 9:00–11:00 a.m. The typed draft-minutes were ready by 1:00 p.m. and the Vice-Chancellor used to call over, around 2:00 p.m., and collect the draft. When the approved draft was returned to the Registrar, on Monday morning, he used to address letters to the relevant executive officers, with the extracts of the minutes relating to their areas of responsibility, to take appropriate action. Thus, the process of implementation of council decisions taken on Friday night, starts on the following Monday. Such prompt action on the implementation of decisions can be referred to as a good practice. Thus, enabling the chair to report the progress made on council decisions, when the business arising from the minutes were taken up at the following meeting.

15.12 Checklists for Leading and Managing Meetings

In order to lead and manage a meeting effectively, efficiently and successfully, the following checklists are provided for the guidance of meeting organizers.

15.12.1 An Organizer's Checklist in Planning a Meeting

- Purpose of the meeting;
- Main agenda, items with the possibility for additions;

- Essential and desirable participants for the whole meeting;
- Participants for particular agenda items, by invitation;
- Date and time for the meeting, with due consideration to:
  - Availability of essential and desirable participants;
  - The degree of urgency;
  - Need for the preparation of background papers on agenda items.
- The venue.

15.12.2 Notification and Circulation of the Agenda

- Date, time and place of the meeting;
- Purpose of the meeting;
- Proposed agenda, with relevant documents;
- Procedure for adding other items to the agenda;
- Identification of those who are expected to attend the full meeting, particular agenda items only, and those informed but not expected to attend.

15.12.3 Preliminary Work

- What are the items on the agenda that the chairperson would like to contribute?
- Are there any hidden agendas for which s/he should be prepared?
- Does s/he wish to introduce any topics and if so how?
- In the light of expected discussions at the meeting:
  - What information should be studied, prepared to present, have handouts ready for distribution?
  - Is it necessary to provide any facilities such as an overhead projector, videos or power-point presentations?
  - Is it necessary to speak to anyone before the meeting with a view to gathering information or lobbying support?
  - Who will chair the meeting and who will take the minutes?

15.12.4 Checklist for Evaluation of the Success of a Meeting

- Did the outcome of the meeting justify the time spent on it?
- Could there have been a better outcome for the same involvement?
- Has the follow-up action been taken to implement the decisions?

In order to analyse whether or not these criteria have been met, the following questions can also be raised.

- Was the purpose of the meeting clear to all those attended?
- Was everyone who needed to be present in attendance?
- Who else should have been there and who was not really needed?
- Were the participants adequately prepared for the meeting?
- Was the time well spent?
- How high was the commitment of the participants?
- Did the meeting achieve its purpose?
- What was the quality of the outcome?
- Was there a clear definition of:
  - Action to be taken following the meeting?
  - Responsibility for taking action?
  - A mechanism for review of the action?

15.13 Conclusion

This chapter considered the significance of meetings, in the context of the management of institutions and units, as a forum for effective communication with staff and relevant parties and for decision-making. Participants are reminded that holding a meeting is a regular feature of most educational organizations, and more specifically in schools. What is important is to develop the skills needed to lead and manage meetings effectively in order to energize and motivate others. Time spent in planning and preparation of a meeting can lead to prevent the time wastage of many others. Giving due consideration to the inclusion of agenda items, background papers on complex issues, focusing on issues under discussion, time management, provision of fair and equal opportunity for participation should receive careful attention from the administrators. More importantly, meeting organizers are reminded of the importance of minute taking, follow-up action and the prompt implementation of the decisions arrived at the meeting.

15.14 Review Questions

1. Undertake a critical examination of the procedures currently adopted in your working organization in conducting meetings and consider ways and means of improving meeting procedures to make them effective forums of communication and decision-making.
2. If you are given the opportunity to organize the monthly staff meeting, discuss how you would do the job to make it a more effective forum for communication and decision-making.

References

Advisory Committee on School-based Management. (2000). *Transforming schools into dynamic and accountable professional learning communities: School-based management consultation document.* Hong Kong: The Government Printer.

Allison, D. G. (1997). Coping with stress in the principalship. *Journal of Educational Administration, 35*(1), 39–55.

American Association of School Administrators (AASA). (1955). *Staff relations in school administration.* Washington, DC: AMA.

Anderson, C. S. (1982). The search for school climate: A review of the research. *Review of Educational Research, 52,* 368–420.

Antonacopóulou, E. P. (2000). Reconnecting education, development and training through learning: A holographic perspective. *Education and Training, 42* (4/5), 255–263.

Antonioni, D. (1998). The relationship between the big five personality factors and conflict management styles. *International Journal of Conflict Management, 9*(4), 336–355.

Argyris, C. (1957). *Personality and organization.* New York: Harper and Row.

———. (1964). *Integrating the individual and the organization.* New York: John Wiley and Sons.

Armstrong, M. A. (1991). *A handbook of personnel management practice* (4th ed.). London: Kogan Page.

Arnold, J. S., Arad, S., Rhoades, J. A., & Drasgow, F. (2000). The empowering leadership questionnaire: The construction and validation of a new scale for measuring leader behaviors. *Journal of Organizational Behavior, 21*(3), 249–269.

Bailey, A., & Johnson, G. (1997). How strategies develop in organizations. In M. Preedy, R. Glatter & R. Levacic (Eds.), *Educational management: Strategy, quality and resources* (pp. 183–193). Buckingham: Open University Press.

Baldridge, V. J. (1971). *Power and conflict in the university.* New York: John Wiley and Sons.

Bandrowski, J. F. (1990). *Corporate imagination plus.* New York: The Free Press.

Banghart, F. W., & Trull, A. (1973). *Educational planning.* New York: Macmillan.

Bangs, D. (1996). *The Australian business-planning guide.* Warriewood, NSW: Woodslane Pty Ltd.

Barbar, B. (1963). Some problems in the sociology of professions. *Daedalus, 92,* 669–688.

———. (1978). Control and responsibility in powerful professions. *Political Science Quarterly, 93,* 599–615.

Barley, S. R. (1983). Semiotics and the study of occupational and organizational cultures. *Administrative Science Quarterly, 28,* 393–413.

Barnard, C. I. (1938). *Functions of the executive.* Cambridge, MA: Harvard University Press.

Bateman, T. S., & Zeithaml, C. P. (1990). *Management: Function and strategy.* Boston: Richard D. Irwin

Beer, M., & Nohria, N. (2000). Cracking the code of change. *Harvard Business Review, May–June,* 133–141.

Belisle, J., & Sargent, R. (1957). The concept of administration. In R. F. Campbell & R. T. Gregg (Eds.), *Administrative behavior in education* (pp. 82–119). New York: Harper and Row Publishers.

Bennis, W. (1990). *Why leaders can't lead.* San Francisco: Jossey Bass.

———, & Nanus, B. (1985). *Leaders: The strategies for taking charge.* New York: Harper & Row Publishers.

Bezzina, C. (1998). The Maltese primary school principal. *Educational Management and Administration, 26*(3), 243–256.

Black, J. S., & Gregersen, H. B. (1997). Participative decision-making: An integration of multiple dimensions. *Human Relations, 50*(7), 859–878.

Blackard, K. (1999). How to make the most of the employment ADR process. *Dispute Resolution Journal, 54*(2), 71–77.

Blackburn, R. S. (1982). Dimensions of structure: A review and reappraisal. *Academy of Management Review, 7*(1), 59–66.

Blanchard, K. (1987). Meetings that work. *Today's Office, 22*(1), 9–11.

———, Zigarmi, D., & Zigarmi, P. (1987). Situational leaderships: Different strokes for different folks. *Principal, 66*(4), 12–16.

Blasé, J., & Blasé, J. (1999). Interpretation of shared governance for instructional improvement: Principals' perspective. *Journal of Educational Administration, 37*(5), 476–500.

Blumberg, A. (1989). *Administration as craft.* Boston: Allyn and Bacon.

———, & Greenfield, W. (1980). *The effective principal: Perspectives on school leadership.* Boston: Allyn and Bacon.

Bolman, L. G., & Deal, T. E. (1984). *Modern approaches to understanding and managing organizations.* San Francisco: Jossey-Bass.

——— (1997). *Reframing organizations: Artistry, choice and leadership* (2nd ed.). San Francisco: Jossey-Bass.

Booher, D. (1999). The power of small talk. *Credit Union Management, 22*(9), p. 8.

Boone, L. E., & Kurtz, D. L. (1987). *Management* (3rd ed.). New York: Random House.

Boyd, W. L. (1999). Environmental pressures, management imperatives, and competing paradigms in educational administration. *Educational Management and Administration, 27*(3), 283–297.

Bredeson, P. V. & Scribner J. P. (2000). A statewide professional development conference: useful strategy for learning or inefficient use of resources? *Educational Policy Analysis Archives, 8*(13), 1–14.

Brookover, W. B., Brady, N. V., & Warfield, M. (1981). *Educational policies and equitable education: A report of studies of two desegregated school systems.* East Lansing: Michigan State University, College of Urban Development, Center for Urban Affairs.

Brown, R. V., Kahr, A. S., & Peterson, C. (1974). *Decision analysis for the manager.* New York: Holt, Rinehart and Winston.

Brown, R., & Brown, M. (1994). *Empowered! A guide to leadership in the liberated organization.* London: Nicholas Brealey Publishing.

Bryson, J. M. (1990). A strategic planning process for public and non-profit organizations. In D. Boyle (Ed.), *Strategic service management* (pp. 111–120). Oxford: Pergamon Press.

Burke, F. (1999). Ethical decision-making: Global concerns, frameworks and approaches. *Public Personnel Management, 28*(4), 529–540.

Burke, L. A., & Miller, M. K. (1999). Taking the mystery out of intuitive decision-making. *Academy of Management Journal, 13*(4), 91–99.

Burns, J. M. (1978). *Leadership.* New York: Harper and Row.

Burton, J. (1990). *Conflict: Resolution and prevention.* London: The MacMillan Press LTD.

Bush, T., & Gamage, D. T. (2001). Models of self-governance in schools: Australia and the United Kingdom. *The International Journal of Educational Management, 15*(1), 39–44.

Caldwell, B. J., & Spinks, J. M. (1988). *The self-managing school.* London: The Falmer Press.

Callahan, R. E. (1962). *Education and the cult of efficiency.* Chicago: The University of Chicago Press.

Campbell, R. F., Corbally, J. E., & Nystrand, R. O. (1983). *Introduction to educational administration* (6th ed). Boston: Allyn and Bacon.

Cardona, P. (2000). Transcendental leadership. *Leadership and Organization Development Journal, 21*(4), 201–207.

Carlson, R., (1998). Barriers to change public schools. In Carlson et al. (Eds.), *Change processes in public schools.* Eugene: Center for Advanced Study of Educational Administration, the University of Oregon.

Caudron, S. (1999). Productive conflict has value. *Workforce, 78*(2), 25–27.

———. (2000). Keeping team conflict alive. *Public Management, 82*(2), 5–10.

Charney, C. (1995). Communicating: Managing the grapevine. *The instant manager: Practical ideas about the 100 most important tasks facing managers today*. London: Kogan Page.

Cheng, Y. C. (1989). Organizational culture: Development of a theoretical framework for organization research. *Education Journal, 17*(2), 128–147.

———. (1996). A school-based management mechanism for school effectiveness and development. *School Effective and School Improvement, 7*(1), 35–61.

———. (1999). The pursuit of school effectiveness and educational quality in Hong Kong. *School Effectiveness and School Improvement: An International Journal of Research, Policy, and Practice, 10*(1), 3–9.

———, & Cheung, W. M. (1995). A framework for the analysis of educational policies. *International Journal of Educational Management, 9*(6), 10–21.

Child, J. (1984). *Organization: A guide to problems and practice* (2ⁿᵈ ed.). London: Harper and Row.

Chin, R., & Benne, K. (1985). General strategies for effecting changes in human systems. In W. G. Bennis, K. D. Benne & R. Chin (Eds.) (4ᵗʰ ed.), *The planning of change* (pp. 22–45). New York: Holt Rinehart and Winston.

Clark, K. E. & Clark, M. B. (1992). Introduction. In K. E. Clark, M. B. Clark & D. P. Campbell (Eds.), *Impact of leadership* (pp. 1–10). Greensbora: Centre for Creative Leadership.

Clarke, J. H. (1999). Growing high school reform: Planting the seeds of systemic change. *NASSP Bulletin, 83*(606), 1–9.

Cohen, M. D., & March, J. G. (1974). *Leadership and ambiguity*. New York: McGraw Hill.

Cohen, M. D., March, J. G., & Oslen, J. P. (1972). Garbage can model of organizational choice. *Administrative Science Quarterly, 17*, 1–25.

Corwin, R. G. & Borman, K. M. (1988). School as workplace: Structural constraints on administration. In J. B. Norman (Ed.). *Handbook of research on educational administration, a project of the American Educational Research Association* (pp. 209–237). New York: Longman.

Coursen, D., Irmsher, K., & Thomas, J. (1997). Communicating. In S. C. Smith & P. K. Piele (Eds.), *School leadership: Handbook for excellence* (3ʳᵈ ed.) (pp. 304–326). Oregon: ERIC Clearinghouse on Educational Management.

Croll, P., & Moses, D. (2000). Continuity and change in special school provision: Some perspectives on local education authority policy making. *British Educational Research Journal, 26*(2), 177–190.

Cuban, L. (1986). Principaling images and roles. *Peabody Journal of Education, 63*(1), 107–119.

Culbertson, J. (1983). Theory in educational administration: Echoes from critical thinkers. *Educational Researcher, 12*(10), 15–22.

Dance, F. E. X. (1970). The concept of communication. *Journal of Communication, 20*, 201–210.

Davies, B., & Ellison, L. (1998). Futures and strategic perspectives in school planning. *International Journal of Educational Management, 12*(3), 133–140.

Deal, T. E., & Kennedy, A. A. (1982). *Corporate cultures: The rites and rituals of corporate life.* Reading, Mass.: Addison-Wesley Pub. Co.

Deal, T. E., & Peterson, K. D. (1990). *The principal's role in shaping school culture: Programs for the improvement of practice by the office of educational research and improvement.* Washington, DC: U.S. Government Printing Office. [ERIC Document, ED 325 914].

Deci, E. L. (1975). *Intrinsic motivation.* New York: Plenum.

Dobbs, K., Gordon, J., Kiser, K., & Stamps, D. (2000). Human capital and the bottom line. *Training, 37*(1), 20–21.

Donohue, W. A., & Kolt, R. (1992). *Managing interpersonal conflict.* Newbury Park, California: Sage Publications.

Drake, T. L., & Roe, W. H. (1999). *The principalship* (5th ed.). New Jersey: Prentice-Hall.

Drost, W. H. (1971). Educational administration history. In L. C. Deighton (Ed.), *The encyclopedia of education, 1,* 68–77. New York: Macmillan.

Drucker, P. F. (1954). *The practice of management.* New York: Harper and Row.

———. (1966). *The effective executive.* New York: Harper and Row.

———. (1977). *People and performance: The best of Peter Drucker on management.* New York: Harper's College Press.

———. (1989). *The practice of management.* London: Heinemann Professional.

Dubin, A. E. (Eds.). (1991). *The principal as chief executive officer.* London: The Falmer Press.

DuBrin, A. J. (1994). *Contemporary applied management.* Bur Ridge: Irwin.

Dunford, R. W. (1992). *Organisational behaviour: An organisational analysis perspective.* Sydney: Addison-Wesley.

Dunham, R. B. (1984). *Organizational behavior: People and process in management.* Homewood: Richard D. Irwin.

Dyer, W. G. (1985). The cycle of cultural evolution in organizations. In R. H. Kilmann, M. J. Saxton & R. Serpa, et al. (Eds.), *Gaining control of the corporate culture.* San Francisco: Jossey-Bass.

Education & Manpower Bureau (1998). *Review of the Education Department: Consultation Document.* Hong Kong: The Government Printer.

Ellis, T. I. (1988). School climate. *Research Round-up, 4*(2), p. 1.

Erickson, F. (1987). Concepts of school culture: An overview. *Educational Administration Quarterly, 23*(4), 11–24.

Etzioni, A. (1975). *Comparative analysis of complex organizations.* New York: Free Press.

———. (1989). Humble decision-making. *Harvard Business Review, 67,* 122–126.

Everard, K. B. (1984). *Management in comprehensive schools — What can be learned from industry*. Northampton: Centre for the Study of Comprehensive Schools, University of Leicester.

———, & Morris, G. (1996). *Effective school management* (3rd ed.). London: Paul Chapman.

Fayol, H. (1949). *General and industrial management* (C. Storrs, Trans.). London: Pitman. (Original work published in French in 1916)

Feldman, M. S., & March J. G. (1981). Information in organization as signal and symbol. *Administrative Science Quarterly, 26*, 171–186.

Fiedler, F. E. (1967). *A theory of leadership effectiveness*. New York: McGraw Hill.

———. (1973). The contingency model and dynamics of the leadership process. *Advances in Experimental Social Psychology, 11*, 60–112.

Filley, A. C. (1975). *Interpersonal conflict resolution*. Glenview, Illinois: Scott, Foresman and Co.

Firestone, W. A. & Wilson, B. L. (1985). Using bureaucratic and cultural linkages to improve instruction: The principal's contribution. *Educational Administration Quarterly, 21*(2), 7–30.

Fish, A., & Wood, J. (1997). Cross cultural management competence in Australian business enterprises. *Asia Pacific Journal of Human Resources, 35*(1), 37–52.

Flavel, R., & Williams, J. (1996). *Strategic management: A practical approach*. Sydney: Prentice Hall.

Follett, M. P. (1942). *Dynamic administration*. New York: Harper.

Fox, D., Byrne, V., & Rouault, F. (1999). Performance improvement: What to keep in mind. *Training and Development, 58*(8), 38–40.

Francesco, A. M., & Gold, B. A. (1998). *International organizational behavior: Text, readings, cases and skills*. Upper Saddle River, N.J.: Prentice Hall.

Freeston, K. R., & Costa Sr, J. P. (1998). Making time for valuable work. *Educational Leadership, 55*(7), 50–52.

Freiberg, J. H. (1998). Measuring school climate: Let me count the ways. *Educational Leadership, 56*(1), 22–26.

French, J., & Raven, B. (1968). Bases of social power. In D. Cartwright & A. Zander (Eds.), *Group dynamics: Research and theory* (3rd ed.) (pp. 259–269). New York: Harper and Row.

French, W. L. (1998). *Human resources management* (4th ed.). Boston: Houghton Mifflin Co.

Fullan, M. G., & Hargreaves, A. (1992). *Understanding teacher development*. London: Cassell.

Gamage, D. T. (1973). *The organization and management of public enterprises in Sri Lanka from 1956–1972*. An unpublished dissertation for M.A. in Economics Degree, the Faculty of Arts of the Colombo of the University of Ceylon.

———. (1992). Organizational change and development: An Australian case study. *Higher Education Research and Development, 2*(2), 173–190.

————. (1993). A review of community participation in school governance: An emerging culture in Australian education. *British Journal of Educational Studies, 41*(2), 134–149.

————. (1996a). *Evolution of universities and changing patterns of governance and administration.* Colombo: Karunaratne and Sons.

————. (1996b). *School-based management: Theory, research and practice.* Colombo: Karunaratne and Sons.

————. (1996c). Community participation in school governance: The Australian and world perspectives. *Education Research and Perspectives, 23*(1), 46–60.

————. (1996d). The impact of school-based management and new challenges to school leaders. *Perspectives in Education, 12*(2), 63–74.

————. (1996e). An Australian alternative in creating more effective schools. *The Educational Forum, 60*(4), 361–368.

————. (1996f). Research on school-based management in Victoria. *Journal of Educational Administration, 34*(1), 27–43.

————. (1998a). How community participation promotes efficiency, effectiveness and quality. *Journal of Educational Planning and Administration, 12*(3), 313–323.

————. (1998b). Teaching principals, their problems and concerns. *The Practising Administrator, 20*(2), 38–43.

————. (1998c). Managing and resolving conflicts in organizational settings. In P. M. Buch & J. P. Dave (Eds.), *Contemporary thoughts in education* (pp. 131–144). Baroda: Society for Educational Research and Development.

————. (1998d). The plight of Australia's teaching principals. *Management in Education, 12*(3), 18–21.

————. (1999). School-based management: An Australian experience. *Research on Education — Tsingua University, 3*, 41–48.

————. (2000a). Local management of schools in England — 1989–1999: A case study from Leicester. *Perspectives in Education, 16*(4), 209–223.

————. (2000b). *Models of school-based management: International trends.* A paper presented at a Public Seminar at the Chinese University of Hong Kong, on 12th December 2000, pp. 1–24.

————. (2000c). The Australian system of higher education: Impact of reforms, current issues and policy directions. *Studies in International Relations, 21*(3), 1–23.

————, Sipple, P., & Partridge, P. (1995). Effectiveness of school boards in the Australian Capital Territory. *Leading & Managing, 1*(4), 277–291.

Garn, G. A. (1999). Solving the policy implementation problem: The case of Arizona Charter schools. *Education Policy Analysis Archives, 7*(26), 1–15.

Garrett, V. (1997). Managing change. In B. Davis & L. Ellison (Eds.), *School leadership for the 21ˢᵗ century: A competency and knowledge approach* (pp. 95–117). London: Routlege.

Gates, P. E., Blanchard, K., & Hersey, P. (1976). Diagnosing educational leadership problems: A situational approach. *Educational Leadership, 46*(6), 22–29.

Geertz, C. (1973). *The interpretation of cultures.* New York: Basic Books Inc.

George, C. S., Jr. (1972). *The history of management.* Englewood Cliffs: Prentice-Hall, Inc.

Getzels, J. W., & Guba, E. G. (1957). Social behavior and the administrative process. *School Review, 65*, 423–441.

Getzels, J. W., Lipham, J. M., & Campbell, R. F. (1968). *Educational administration as a social process: Theory, research and practice.* New York: Harper & Row.

Goens, G. A., & Clover, S. I. R. (1991). *Mastering school reform.* Boston: Allyn and Bacon.

Goffman, E. (1959). *The presentation of self in everyday life.* New York: Doubleday & Co., Anchor Books.

———. (1974). *Frame analysis: An essay on the organization of experience.* Cambridge: Harvard University Press.

Goldsmith, M. (1999). Conflict resolution. *Executive Excellence, 16*(10), 17–18.

Goldthorpe, J. H., Lockwood, D., Bechhofer, F., & Platt, J. (1968). *The affluent worker: Industrial attitude and behaviour.* Cambridge: Cambridge University Press.

Goleman, D. (2000). Leadership that gets results. *Harvard Business Review, 78* (2), 78–90.

Goode, W. J. (1957). Community within a community: The profession. *American Sociological Review, 22*(2), 194–200.

———. (1960). Encroachment, charlatanism and the emerging professions: Psychology, sociology and medicine. *American Sociological Review, 25*(6), 902–913.

Gouldner, A. (1959). Organizational analysis. In R. K. Merton, L. Broom, J. Leonard & L. S. Cottrell, Jr. (Eds.), *Sociology today: Problems and prospects* (pp. 400–428). New York: Basic Books.

Grasmick, N. S. (2000). How Maryland communicates change. *Educational Leadership, 57*(7), 44–47.

Gratch, A. (2000). Teacher voice, teacher education, teaching professionals. *High School Journal, 83*(3), 43–57.

Green R. L., & Etheridge, C. P. (1999). Building collaborative relationships for instructional improvement. *Education, 120*(2), 388–392.

Greenleaf, R. (1977). *Servant leadership: A journey into the nature of legitimate power and greatness.* New York: Paulist Press.

Griffiths, D. E. (1959). *Administrative theory.* New York: Appleton-Century Crofts.

Guest, D. E. (1987). Human resource management and industrial relations. *Journal of Management Studies, 24*(5), 503–521.

Gulbranson, J. E. (1998). The ground rules of conflict resolution. *Industrial Management, 40*(3), 4–11.

Gulick, L. (1937). Notes on the theory of organization. In L. Gulick & L. Urwick (Eds.), *Papers on the science of administration* (pp. 1–46). New York: Columbia University Press.

—— & Urwick, L. (Eds.) (1937). *Papers on the science of administration*. New York: Institute of Public Administration, Columbia University.

Hackman, B. I. C. (1994). Re-conceptualising managerial delegation behaviour. *Asia Pacific Journal of Human Resources, 32*(3), 33–52.

Hall, R. H. (1986). *Dimensions of work*. Beverly Hills: Sage.

Halpin, A. (1958). *Administrative theory in education*. Chicago: Midwest Administration Center, University of Chicago.

——, & Croft, D. B. (1962). *The organizational climate of schools*. Washington, DC: U.S. Office of Education, Research Project.

Handy, C. B. (1986). *Understanding schools as organizations*. London: Penguine.

Hanson, M. E. (1985). *Educational administration and organizational behavior*. Boston: Allyn and Bacon.

Hardin, D. (2000). Speak effectively at meetings. *Los Angeles Business Journal*, June 26.

Hargie, O, Dickson, D., & Tourish, D. (1999). *Communication in management*. Grower: Aldershot.

Hargreaves, A., & Fink D. (2000). The three dimensions of reform. *Educational Leadership, 57*(7), 30–34.

Harrison, M. I. (1994). *Diagnosing organizations: Methods, models and processes* (2nd ed.). Thousand Oaks, Calif.: Sage Publications.

Havelock, R. G., & Havelock, M. C. (1973). *Training for Change Agents*. Michigan: The University of Michigan.

Hellriegel, D., & Slocum, J. W., Jr. (1974). Organization climate: Measure, research and contingencies. *Academy of Management Journal, 17*(2), 255–280.

Herbert, T. T. (1999). Multinational strategic planning: Matching central expectations to local realities. *Long Range Planning, 32*(1), 81–87.

Hersey, P., & Blanchard, K. H. (1988). *Management of organizational behavior: Utilizing human resources* (5th ed.). Englewood Cliffs: Prentice Hall.

Hirokawa, R. Y., & Poole, M. S. (1986). *Communication and group decision-making*. Beverly Hills: Sage Publications.

Hoeflich, H. I. (1999). *Making staff strategic partners in success*. Association Management, 51(9), 14.

Hofstede, G. (1993). Cultural constraints in management theories. *Academy of Management Executive, 7*, 81–94.

Holmes, M., & Wynne, E. A. (1989). *Making the school an effective community*. New York: The Falmer Press.

Hoy, W. K., & Feldman, J. (1987). Organizational health: The concept and its measure. *Journal of Research and Development in Education, 20*, 30–38.

Hoy, W. K., & Miskel, C. G. (2001). *Educational administration: Theory, research and practice* (6th ed.). Singapore: McGraw-Hill.

Hoy, W. K., & Tarter, C. J. (1995). *Administrator solving the problems of practice: Decision-making concepts, cases and consequences.* Boston: Allyn and Bacon.

Hughes, L. W. (1983). Time management problems of instructional supervisors. *Catalyst for Change, 13*(1), 21–25.

———. (Ed.). (1994). *The principal as leader.* New York: Maxwell Macmillan International.

Hughes, M. G. (1976). The professional-as-administrator: The case of the secondary school head. In R. S. Peters (Ed.). *The role of the head* (pp. 50–62). London: Routledge and Kegan Paul.

Hughes, M., Ribbins, P., & Thomas, H. (1985). *Managing education: The system and the institution.* London: Holt, Rinehart & Winston.

Hunt, O., Tourish, D., & Hargie O. D. W. (2000). The communication experiences of education managers: Identifying strengths, weaknesses and critical incidents. *The International Journal of Educational Management, 14*(3), 120–129.

Ivancevich, J. M., & Matterson, M. T. (1993). *Organisational behaviour and management.* Boston: Richard D. Irwin.

Jackson, D. (1997). *Dynamic organizations: The challenge of change.* London: Macmillan.

Jay, A. (1976). How to run a meeting. *Harvard Business Review, 54*(2), 43–57.

Jebb, F. (1999). Getting to the meet of the matter. *Management Today*, February, 76–77.

Jeheil, P. (1999). Information aggregation and communications in organizations. *Management Science, 45*(5), 659–669.

Johnson, J. (1996). Time to rebuild human resources. *Business Quarterly, 61*(2), 46–52.

Kalleberg, A. L., & Moody J. W. (1994). Human resource management and organizational performance. *American Behavioral Scientist, 37*(7), 948–963.

Kanter, R. M. (1984). *The change masters: Innovation and entrepreneurship in the American corporation.* New York: Simon and Schuster.

Karpin, D. (1995). *Enterprising nation: Renewing Australia's managers to meet the challenges of the Asia-Pacific century* (Karpin Report). Canberra: AGPS.

Katz, D., & Kahn, R. L. (1966). *The social psychology of organizations.* New York: John Wiley and Sons.

———. (1978). *The social psychology of organizations* (2nd ed.). New York: Wiley.

Katz, R. L. (1974). Role of an effective administrator. *Harvard Business Review, 52*, 94–103.

Kaufman, R. (1995). Mapping school success (Rev. ed.). Thousand Oaks, California: Corwin Press, Inc.

Kay, G. (1995). Effective meetings through electronic brainstorming. *Journal of Management Development, 14*(6), 4–25.

Kelly, P. K. (1994). *Team decision-making techniques.* Irvine: Richard Chang Associates, Inc.

Kemp-Longmore, C. (2000). Conflict resolution in the workplace. *The Black Collegian, 30*(2), 131–134.

Kimbrough, R. B., & Burkett, C. W. (1990). *The principalship: Concepts and practices.* Englewood Cliffs: NJ: Prentice Hall.

Klecker, B. J., & Loadman, W. E. (1998). Defining and measuring the dimensions of teacher empowerment in restructuring public schools. *Education, 118*(3), 358–371.

Kreitner, R., & Kinicki, A. (2001). *Organizational behavior* (5th ed.). Boston: Irwin/ McGraw-Hill.

Kroeber, A. L., & Kluckhohn, C. (1952). *Culture: A critical review of concepts and definitions.* New York: Vintage Books.

Lam, J. Y. L. (1989). Patterns and constraints of external environment of teaching: A regional comparison. *Educational Research Quarterly, 13*(1), 11–21.

Langdon, A., & Marshall, P. (1998). *Organisational behaviour.* South Melbourne: Addison Wesley Longman Australia Pty Ltd.

Law, R., & Wong, M. (1997). Evaluating the effectiveness of interviews as a selection method. *Australian Journal of Hospitality Management, 4*(1), 27–34.

Lee, V. E., & Smith, J. B. (1996). Collective responsibility for learning and its effects on gains in achievement for early secondary school students. *American Journal of Education, 104*(2), 103–147.

Legge, K. (1992). Human resources management: A critical analysis. In J. Storey (Ed.), *New perspectives on human resource management* (pp. 19–40). New York: Routledge.

Leithwood, K., Begley, P. T., & Cousins, J. B. (1992). *Developing expert leadership for future schools.* London: Falmer Press.

Lekein, A. (1974). *How to get control of your time and your life.* New York: Signet.

Lewin, K. (1943). Defining the field at a given time. *Psychological Review, 50*(2), 292–310.

———. (1951). *Field theory in social science.* New York: Harper and Row.

Likert, R. (1961). *New patterns of management.* New York: McGraw Hill.

———. (1967). *The human organization: Its management and values.* New York: McGraw-Hill.

———, & Likert, J. G. (1976). *New ways of managing conflict.* New York: McGraw Hill.

Lindblom, C. E. (1968). *The policy making process.* Englewood Cliffs: Prentice Hall.

———, & Cohen, D. K. (1979). *Usable knowledge: Social science and social problem solving.* New Haven, CT: Yale University Press.

Lindelow, J., & Scott, J. (1989). Managing conflict. In S. C. Smith & P. K. Piele (Eds), *School leadership: Handbook for excellence* (3rd ed.). Eugene, OR: ERIC Clearinghouse on Educational Management, University of Oregon.

Liontos, L. B., & Lashway, L. (1997). Shared decision-making. In S. C. Smith & P. K. Piele (Eds.), *School leadership: Handbook for excellence* (3rd ed.) (pp. 226–250). Oregon: ERIC Clearinghouse on Educational Management.

Lippitt, G. L. (1983). Can conflict resolution be win-win? *School Administrator, 40*(3), 20–22.

Litwin, G. H., & Stringer, R. A., Jr. (1968). *Motivation and organizational climate.* Cambridge: MA: Harvard University Press.

Louis, K. S., & Marks, H. M. (1998). Does professional community affect the classroom? Teachers' work and student experiences in restructuring schools. *American Journal of Education, 106*(4), 532–552.

Louis, K., & Miles, M. B. (1991). Managing reform: Lessons from urban high schools. *School Effectiveness and Improvement, 2*(1), 75–91.

Louis, M. R. (1985). Perspectives on organizational culture. In P. J. Frost, L. F. Moore, M. R. Louis, C. C. Lundberg & J. Matin (Eds.), *Organizational culture* (pp. 27–29). Newbury Park: Sage Publications.

———. (1986). Putting executive action in context: An alternative view of power. In S. Srivasta, et al. (Eds.), *Executive power: How executives influence people and organizations* (pp. 111–131). San Francisco: Jossey-Bass.

Lussier, R. N. (1993). *Human relations in organisations: A skill building approach* (2nd ed.). Homewood: Richard D. Erwin, Inc.

Machiavelli, N. (1938). *The prince.* New York: P.F. Collier.

Maeroff, G. I. (1988). A blue print for empowering teacher. *Phi Delta Kappan, 69* (7), 472–477.

Maidment, R., & Bullock, W. (1985). *Meetings: Accomplishing more with better and fewer.* Reston, Virginia: National Association of Secondary School Principals.

March, J. G., & Simon, H. (1938). *Organizations* (2nd ed.). Cambridge: Blackwell.

Martin, D. D., & Shell, R. L. (1998). *Management of professionals insights for maximizing cooperation.* New York: Marcel Dekker.

Maslow, A. H. (1970). *Motivation and personality* (2nd ed.). New York: Harper and Row.

Maude, B. (1975). *Managing meetings.* London: Business Books Limited.

Maurer, R. E. (1991). *Managing conflicts: Tactics for school administrators.* Boston: Allyn and Bacon.

Mayo, G. E. (1933). *The human problems of an industrial civilization.* Boston, MA: Harvard Business School, Division of Research.

McCamy, J. L. (1947). An analysis of the process of decision-making. *Public Administration Review, 7*(1), 40–49.

McGregor, D. (1960). *The human side of the enterprise.* New York: McGraw Hill.

McLain, D. L., & Hackman, K. (1999). Trust, risk, and decision-making in organizational change. *Public Administration Quarterly, 23*(2), 152–156.

Metcalf, H. C., & Urwick, L. F. (Eds.). (1941). *Dynamic administration: The collected papers of Mary Parker Follett.* New York: Harper & Row.

Meyer, M. W. (1977). *Theory of organizational structure.* Indianapolis: Bobbs-Merril.

Micklethwait, J., & Wooldridge, A. (1996). *The witch doctors: Making sense of the management gurus.* New York: Times Books.

Millerson, G. (1964). *The qualifying associations: A study in professionalization.* London: Routledge and Kegan Paul.

Mintzberg, H. (1973). *The nature of managerial work.* Englewood Cliffs: Prentice Hall.

———. (1983). *Power in and around organizations.* Englewood Cliffs: Prentice Hall.

———. (1993). *Structure in fives: Designing effective organizations.* Englewood Cliffs: Prentice-Hall, Inc.

———, Raisinghani, D., & Theoret, A. (1976). The structure of "unstructured" decision process. *Administrative Science Quarterly, 21*(2), 246–275.

Mishra, J., & Morrissey, M. A. (1990). Trust in employee/employer relationships: A survey of West Michigan managers. *Public Personnel Management, 29,* 443–486.

Moffett, C. A. (2000). Sustaining change: The answers are blowing in the wind. *Educational Leadership, 57*(7), 35–38.

Moore, H. E., & Walters, N. B. (1955). *Personnel administration in education.* New York: Harper and Brothers.

Moore, W. E. (1970). *The professions: Roles and rules.* New York: Russel Sage.

Morgan, G. (1997). *Images of organization* (new edition). Thousand Oaks: Sage Publications Ltd.

Morley, C. L. (1994). *How to get the most out of meetings.* Alexandria: Association for Supervision and Curriculum Development.

Moroz, R., & Waught, R. F. (2000). Teacher receptivity to system-wide educational change. *Journal of Educational Administration, 38*(2), 159–178.

Mukhi, S. K., Hampton, D., & Barnwell, N. (1988). *Australian management.* Sydney: McGraw-Hill.

Mullen, C. A., & Kochan, F. K. (2000). Creating a collaborative leadership network: An organic view of change. *International Journal of Leadership in Education, 3*(3), 183–200.

Mullins, L. J. (1999). *Management and organisational behaviour* (5th ed.). London: Pitman.

Murningham, J. K. (1982). Game theory and the structure of decision-making groups. In R. A. Guzzo (Ed.), *Improving group decision-making in organizations* (pp. 73–93). New York: Academic Press, Inc.

Nankervis, A. R., Compton, R. L., & McCarthy, T. E. (1999). *Strategic human resource management* (3rd ed.). Melbourne: Nelson.

Nash, N., & Culbertson, J. (1977). *Linking processes in educational improvement: Concepts and applications.* Columbus: University Council for Educational Administration.

National Audit Office. (1997). Linking strategic planning with the budgetary process. In M. Preedy, R. Glatter, & R. Levacic (Eds.), *Educational management: Strategy, quality and resources* (pp. 194–204). Buckingham: Open University Press.

National Commission on Excellence in Education. (1983). *A nation at risk.* Washington DC: Government Printing Office.

New South Wales (NSW) Department of Education and Training (DET). (2000). *Annual report — 2000.* Sydney: DET.

Newell, C. (1978). *Human behavior in educational administration.* Englewood Cliffs, New Jersey: Prentice-Hall, Inc.

Newman, W. H. (1951). *Administrative action.* Englewood Cliffs: Prentice Hall.

Nutt, P. C. (1984). Types of organizational decision processes. *Administrative Science Quarterly,* September, 414–450.

O'Dempsey, K. (1982). Time analysis of activities, work patterns and roles of high school principals in Cyprus. In W. S. Simpkins, A. R. Thomas & E. B. Thomas (Eds.), *Principal and task: An Australian perspective* (pp. 58–65). Armidale: NSW, University of New England.

Oregon School Study Council. (1974). *Bulletin,* April Issue.

Orton, J. D., & Weick, K. E. (1990). Loosely coupled systems: A reconceptualization. *Academy of Management Review, 15*(2), 203–223.

Oswald, L. J. (1997). Quality work teams. In S. C. Smith & P. K. Piele (Eds.), *School leadership: Handbook for excellence* (3rd ed.) (pp. 204–225). Oregon: ERIC Clearinghouse on Educational Management.

Ouchi, W. (1981). *Theory Z: How American business can meet the Japanese challenge.* Reading, MA: Addison-Wesley.

Owens, R. G. (2001). *Organizational behavior in education: Instructional leadership and school reform* (7th ed.). Boston: Allyn and Bacon.

———, & Steinhorf, C. R. (1976). *Administering change in schools.* Englewood Cliffs: Prentice Hall.

Pang, N. S. K. (1992). *School climate: A discipline view.* A paper presented at the 7th Regional Conference of the Commonwealth Council for Education Administration, Hong Kong, August 17–21, 1992. [ERIC Document Reproduction Service No. ED 354 589].

———. (1995). The development of the school values inventory. In R. Cotter & S. J. Marshall (Eds.), *Research and practice in educational administration,* the ACEA pathways series No. 6 (pp. 160–186). Hawthorn, Victoria: Australian Council for Education Administration.

————. (1996). School values and teachers' feelings: A LISREL model. *Journal of Educational Administration, 34*(2), 64–83.

————. (1998a). The binding forces that hold school organizations together. *Journal of Educational Administration, 36*(4), 314–333.

————. (1998b). Managerial practices in Hong Kong primary schools. *Journal of Basic Education, 8*(1), 21–42.

————. (1998c). Organizational values and cultures of secondary schools in Hong Kong. *Canadian and International Education, 27*(2), 59–84.

————. (1998d). Should quality school education be a kaizen (improvement) or an innovation? *International Journal of Educational Reform, 7*(1), 2–12.

————. (1998e). *Organizational values and cultures of excellent schools in Hong Kong.* Paper presented in the Annual Conference of the American Educational Research Association, San Diego, California, 1998.04.13–17, 26 pages. [ERIC Document Reproduction Service No. ED 429 866]

————. (1999a). Students' perceptions of quality of school life in Hong Kong primary schools. *Educational Research Journal, 14*(1), 49–71.

————. (1999b). Students' quality of school life in Band 5 schools. *Asian Journal of Counselling, 6*(1), 79–106.

————. (1999c). The plain truth is out there. In A. Holbrook & S. Johnston (Eds.), *Supervision of postgraduate research in education* (pp. 157–161). Victoria: Australia Association for Research in Education.

————. (1999d). *Review and prospect of school management reform in Hong Kong* (Educational Policy Series, Occasional Paper No. 22). Hong Kong: The Faculty of Education of the Chinese University of Hong Kong and the Hong Kong Institute of Educational Research.

————. (2000). In search of excellent schools: The case of Hong Kong. In D. Clive, and A. Walker, (Eds.), *Future school administration: Western and Asian perspectives* (pp. 269–290). Hong Kong: The Chinese University Press and Hong Kong Institute of Educational Research.

————. (2001a). *What we know and how we know it: A preliminary study of managerial practices of high school in Shanghai.* Paper presented at the Annual Conference of the American Educational Research Association, Seattle, WA, April, 10–14, 2001, 15 pages. [ERIC Document Reproduction Service No. EA 031073]

————. (2001b). The impacts and challenges of restructuring the governance system in aided schools. *Educational Research Journal, 16*(1), 157–173.

————. (2002). Towards school management reform: Organizational values of government schools in Hong Kong. In J. K. H. Mok & D. K. K. Chan (Eds.), *Globalization and education: The quest for quality education in Hong Kong* (pp. 171–193). Hong Kong: Hong Kong University Press.

Pang, N. S. K. & Cheung, M. (in press). Learning capacity of primary schools in Hong Kong. In J. C. K. Lee, L. N. K. Lo & A. Walker (Eds.). *Partnership and change: Towards school development.* Hong Kong: The Hong Kong Institute of Educational Research and The Chinese University Press.

Pang, N. S. K. & Lam, J. Y. L. (2000). *How can school tackle the challenges arisen from the reform proposals in the new millennium?* (Educational policy series, occasional paper No. 35). Hong Kong: The Faculty of Education of the Chinese University of Hong Kong and Hong Kong Institute of Educational Research.

Pang, N. S. K. & Yeung, W. C. (2001). Pleasurable learning in a project-based interdisciplinary curriculum. *Educational Research Journal, 16*(1), 99–130.

Parkin, J. (1994). *Public management: Technocracy, democracy and organisational reform.* Aldershot: Avebury.

Parks, B. (1998). Got a conflict with a colleague? Here's how to resolve it now! *Instructor, 107*(7), 74–75.

Parsons, T. (1960). *Structure and process in modern societies.* New York: Free Press.

———. (1967). *Sociological theory and modern society.* New York: Free Press.

Pashiardis, G. (2000). School climate in elementary and secondary schools: Views of Cypriot principals and teachers. *The International Journal of Educational Management, 14*(5), 224–237.

Peters, T. J. & Waterman, R. H. (1982). *In search of excellence.* New York: Harper & Row.

Peters, T. J., & Austin, N. (1985). *A passion for excellence: The leadership difference.* USA: Random House.

Peterson, K. D., & Deal, T. E. (1998). How leaders influence the culture of schools. *Educational Leadership, 56*(1), 28–30.

Pettigrew, A. M. (1979). On studying organizational cultures. *Administrative Science Quarterly, 24,* 570–581.

Porter, L. W., & Roberts, K. H. (1976). Communication in organizations. In M. D. Dunnette (Ed.), *Handbook of industrial and organizational psychology* (pp. 1553–1590). Chicago: Rand McNally.

Pugh, D. S., Hickson, D. J., Hinnings, C. R., & Turner, C. (1968). Dimensions of organization structure. *Administrative Science Quarterly, 13*(2), 65–105.

Purkey, S. C., & Smith, M. S. (1985). School reform: The district policy implications of the effective schools literature. *Elementary School Journal, 85*(3), 353–389.

Rebore, R. W. (1998). *Personnel administration in education: A management approach* (5ᵗʰ ed.). Boston: Allyn and Bacon.

Reddin, W. J. (1970). *Managerial effectiveness.* New York: McGraw-Hill.

Redfield, C. E. (1958). *Communication in management: The theory and practice of administrative communication.* Chicago: The University of Chicago Press.

Reichers, A. E., & Schneider, B. (1990). Climate and culture: An evolution of constructs. In B. Schneider (Ed.), *Organizational climate and culture* (pp. 5–39). San Francisco: Jossey-Bass Inc.

Reissman, L. (1959). *Class in American society*. New York: Free Press.

Rice, E. M., & Schneider, G. T. (1994). A decade of teacher empowerment: An empirical analysis of teacher involvement in decision-making, 1980–1991. *Journal of Educational Administration, 32*(1), 43–58.

Richer, H., & Stopper, W. G. (1999). Hiring to build change capacity: The human resource role. *Human Resource Planning, 22*(2), 8–10.

Robbins, S. P. (1974). *Managing organizational conflict: A non-traditional approach*. Englewood Cliffs, New Jersey: Prentice Hall.

———. (1976). *The administrative process*. Englewood Cliffs: Prentice Hall.

Robey, D. (1991). *Designing organizations* (3rd ed.). Homewood, Ill.: Irwin.

Roethlisberger, F. G. & Dickson, W. J. (1939). *Management and the worker*. Cambridge, MA: Harvard University Press.

Sathe, V. (1983). Implications of corporate culture: A manager's guide to action. *Organizational Dynamics, 12*(1), 5–23.

Savery, L. K., Soutar, G. N., & Dyson, J. D. (1992). Ideal decision-making styles indicated by deputy principals. *Journal of Educational Administration, 30*(2), 18–25.

Schein, E. H. (1992). *Organizational culture and leadership: A dynamic view* (2nd ed.). San Francisco: Jossey-Bass Inc.

Schelling, T. C. (1980). *The strategy of conflict*. Cambridge: Harvard University Press.

Schmidt, W. H., & Tannebaum, R. (1972). Management of difference. In W. W. Burke & H. A. Hornstein (Eds.), *Social technology of organization development* (pp. 127–140). La Jolla: California University Associates.

Schmuck, R. A., & Miles, M. B. (1971). *Organization development in schools*. New York: Mayfield Publishing Company.

Schmuck, R. A., & Runkel, P. (1994). *The second handbook on organizational development in schools and colleges* (4th ed.). Prospect Heights: Waveland Press.

Scott, C. R., Shaw, S. P., Timmerman, C. E., Frank, V., & Quinn, L. (1999). Using communication audits to teach organizational communication to students and employees. *Business Communication Quarterly, 62*(4), 53–70.

Scott, W. R. (1981). *Organizations: Rational, natural, and open system*. Englewood Cliffs, NJ: Prentice-Hall.

Sergiovanni, T. J. (1984). Leadership and excellence in schooling. *Educational Leadership, 41*(5), 4–14.

———. (1992). *Moral leadership: Getting to the heart of school improvement*. San Francisco: Jossey-Bass Publishers.

Sergiovanni, T. J., & Carver, F. D. (1980). *The new school executive: A theory of administration*. New York: Harper & Row.

Sergiovanni, T. J., & Corbally, J. E. (1984). *Leadership and organization culture: New perspectives on administrative theory and practice.* Urban and Chicago: Illinois Press.

Sergiovanni, T. J., & Staratt, R. J. (1988). *Supervision: Human perspectives* (4th ed.). New York: McGraw Hill.

Sergiovanni, T. J., Burlingame, M., Coombs, F. S., & Thurston, P. W. (1999). *Educational governance and administration.* Boston: Allyn and Bacon.

Sheanh, G. (1996). *Helping kids deal with conflict.* Canada: Peguis Publishers.

Simon, H. A. (1957). *Administrative behavior.* New York: Macmillan.

Simpkins, W. S. (1982). The principal: Leadership stress, performance and credibility. In W. S. Simpkins, A. R. Thomas & E. B. Thomas (Eds.), *Principal and task: An Australian perspective* (pp. 103–112). Armidale: University of New England.

Smircich, L. (1983). Concepts of culture and organizational analysis. *Administrative Science Quarterly, 28,* 339–358.

Smith, S. C., & Piele, P. K. (1997). *School leadership: Handbook for excellence* (3rd ed.). Eugene, OR: ERIC Clearinghouse on Educational Management, University of Oregon.

Starratt, R. J. (1996). *Transforming educational administration.* New York: McGraw Hill.

Stogdill, R. M. (1974). *Handbook of leadership: A survey of theory and research.* New York: Free Press.

Su, Z., Gamage, D. T. & Mininberg, E. (2001). *Profile characteristics of school leaders in Australia and the United States.* A paper presented at the World Congress of Comparative Education Societies Conference held in Seoul, South Korea, in July, pp. 1–29.

Sullivan, T. J. (1999). Leading people in a chaotic world. *Journal of Educational Administration, 37*(5), 408–423.

Sungaila, H. M. (1982). The principal experience: What the position can do to the woman in charge. In W. S. Simpkins, A. R. Thomas & E. B. Thomas (Eds.), *Principal and task: An Australian perspective* (pp. 95–102). Armidale: NSW, University of New England.

Sweeny, J. (1980). Training education change agents: The effects of the internship. *Educational Technology, 20*(6), 42–47.

Tagiuri, R., & Litwin, G. (Eds.). (1968). *Organization climate: Explorations of a concept.* Boston: Division of Research, Harvard Business School.

Tannenbaum, R. T., & Schmidt, W. H. (1958). How to choose a leadership pattern. *Harvard Business Review, 36*(2), 95–101.

Tapsell, S. (1999). Ten business resolutions for 2000. *New Zealand Management, 46*(11), 98–99.

Taylor, F. W. (1911). *Principles of scientific management.* New York: Harper and Row.

Tead, O. (1951). *Art of administration*. New York: McGraw Hill.

Telford, H. (1996). *Transforming schools through collaborative leadership*. London: The Falmer Press.

Teller, E. (1995). Change: Overcoming resistance. In C. Charney (Ed.), *The instant manager: Practical ideas on the 100 most important tasks facing managers today* (p. 33). London: Kogan Page.

Timmons, J. A. (1999). *New venture creation: Entrepreneurship for the 21ˢᵗ century* (5ᵗʰ ed.). Chicago: Irwin.

Tom Peters Group, The. (1986). *A world turned upside down*. Palo Alto: Excel.

Torrington, D., & Hall L. (1991). *Personnel management: A new approach*. New York: Prentice Hall.

Tschannen-Moran, M., Uline, C., Hoy, W., & Mackley, T. (2000). Creating smarter schools through collaboration. *Journal of Educational Administration, 38*(3), 247–271.

Turney, C. (1992). Conceptualizing the management process. In C. Turney, N. Hatton, K. Laws, K. Sinclair & D. Smith (Eds.), *The school manager* (pp. 92–108). North Sydney: Allen & Unwin Pty Ltd.

Ubben, G. C., Hughes, L. W., & Norris, C. J. (2001). *The principal: Creative leadership for effective schools* (4ᵗʰ ed.). Boston: Allyn and Bacon.

Urwick, L. (1952). *Notes on the theory of organization*. American Management Association.

Vecchio, R. P., & Norris, W. R. (1996). Predicting employee turnover from performance, satisfaction and leader-member exchange. *Journal of Business and Psychology, 11*(1), 113–125.

Vecchio, R. P., Hearn, G., & Southey, G. (1992). *Organisational behaviour: Life at work in Australia*. Sydney: Harcourt Brace Jonavich, Publishers.

———. (1996). *Organisational behaviour* (2ⁿᵈ ed.). Sydney: Harcourt Brace Co.

Vickery, J. (1990). Output driven development model. *Educational Leadership, 47*(7), 64–70.

Wageman, R. (1997). Critical success factors for creating superb self-managing teams. *Organisational Dynamics, 26*(1), 49–61.

Walker A., & Dimmock C. (2000). Mapping the way ahead: Leading educational leadership into the globalised world. *School Leadership and Management, 20* (2), 227–233.

Waugh, R. F. (2000). Towards a model of teacher receptivity to planned system-wide educational change in a centrally controlled system. *Journal of Educational Administration, 38*(4), 350–367.

Webber, C., & Robertson, J. (1998). Boundary breaking: An emergent model for leadership development. *Education Policy Analysis Archives, 6*(21), 1–21.

Weber, M. (1947). *The theory of social and economic organizations* (T. Parsons & A. M. Henderson, Trans., Eds. with an introduction by T. Parsons.). New York: Free Press. (Original work published in 1925).

Weick, K. E. (1976). Educational organizations as loosely coupled systems. *Administrative Science Quarterly, 21,* 1–19.

———. (1979). Cognitive processes in organizations. *Research in Organizational Behavior, 1,* 41–74.

Weindling, D. (1997). Strategic planning in schools: Some practical techniques. In M. Preedy, R. Glatter, R. & R. Levacic (Eds.), *Educational management: Stragety, quality and resources* (pp. 218–233). Buckingham: Open University Press.

Welch, M. (1998). Collaboration: Staying on the Bandwagon. *Journal of Teacher Education, 49*(1), 26–35.

Wertheim, E., Love, A., Littlefield, L., & Peck, C. (1992). *I win: You win.* Melbourne: Penguin Books.

Westoby, A. (Ed.). (1988). *Culture and power in educational organizations.* Buckingham: The Open University Press.

Whitehead, J. L. (1984). Improving meeting productivity. *Professional Communication in the Modern World: Proceedings of the Southeast Convention of the American Business Communication Association, Hammond, Louisiana,* April 5–7.

Williams, H. (1963). *Ceylon: The pearl in the east.* London, Robert Hale Ltd.

Willis, Q. F. (1982). Uncertainties as a fact of life (and work) for the school principal. In W. S. Simpkins, A. R. Thomas & E. B. Thomas (Eds.), *Principal and task: An Australian perspective* (pp. 66–72). Armidale: University of New England.

Willower, D. J., Eidell, T. L., & Hoy, W. K. (1973). *The school and pupil control ideology* (2nd ed.). University Park, PA: University of Pennsylvannia.

Wilson, W. (1887). The study of administration. *Political Science Quarterly, 2*(2), 197–222.

Wolcott, H. F. (1973). *The man in the principal's office: An ethnography.* Prospect Height, Ill.: Waveland Press.

Wood, J., Wallace, J. & Zeffance, R. M. (2001). *Organisational Behaviour: A Global Perspective,* Brisbane, John Wiley & Sons.

Wood, J., Wallace, J., Zeffane R., Kennedy, D. J., Schermerhorn, J. R., Hunt, J. G., & Osborn, R. N. (1998). *Organisational behaviour: An Asia Pacific perspective.* Singapore: John Wiley and Sons.

Wrege, C. D. & Stotka, A. M. (1978). Cooke creates a classic: The story behind F. W. Taylor's principles of scientific management. *Academy of Management Review, 3,* 736–749.

Wynn, R., & Guditus, C. W. (1984). *Team management: Leadership by consensus.* Columbus: Charles E. Merrill Publishing Co.

Yukl, G. (2002). *Leadership in organizations* (5th ed.). Upper Saddler River: Prentice Hall.

Index

本社其他相關題材的書籍

Special Needs Education: Children with Exceptionalities
Kim Fong Poon-McBrayer and Ming-Gon John Lian (2002)

《家庭學校與社區協作：從理念研究到實踐》
何瑞珠著 (2002)

《課程、教學與學校改革：新世紀的教育發展》
李子健編著 (2002)

《有效的中文科教學法》
周漢光著 (2000)

《尋找課程與教學的知識基礎：
香港中小學中文科課程與教學研究》
黃顯華編著 (2000, 2002)

《課堂管理技巧》
David Fontana著 (2000)

Future School Administration: Western and Asian Perspectives
Edited by Clive Dimmock and Alan Walker (2000)

《閱讀與寫作教學》
周漢光編 (1998)

Helping Students with Learning Difficulties
Edited by David W. Chan (1998)

《課程：範式、取向和設計》(第二版)
李子建、黃顯華著 (1996, 2002)